SCHOOL OF ACES

SCHOOL OF ACES

The RAF Training School that Won the Battle of Britain

Alastair Goodrum

AMBERLEY

Half title page: Hurricane N2359 saw combat with 17 Squadron during the Battle of Britain in 1940. It was sent to 6 Operational Training Unit (OTU) Sutton Bridge and was involved in a mishap on 11 June 1941.

Title page: Central Gunnery School (CGS) Air gunner pupils at an open-air training session using models to try out various defensive options against a fighter attack. (Courtesy of Long Sutton Civic Society)

First published 2019

Amberley Publishing
The Hill, Stroud
Gloucestershire, GL5 4EP

www.amberley-books.com

British Library Cataloguing in Publication Data.
A catalogue record for this book is available from the British Library.

ISBN 978 1 4456 8617 2 (hardback)
ISBN 978 1 4456 8618 9 (ebook)

Typesetting and Origination by Amberley Publishing.
Printed in the UK.

Contents

Acknowledgements

During my years of research, I have had the pleasure of meeting and/ or corresponding with many individuals and members of organisations across the globe. Some, sadly, are no longer with us, but I wish to thank them all and without wishing to diminish any single contribution, the following deserve particular mention:

Douglas Broom, Air Cdre Alan Deere, Jack Flint, Jens Ipsen, Bill Law, Air Cdre Harold Maguire, Peter Montgomery, Olive Moule, Albert Norton, Mahinder Pujji, Eric Raybould, Gp Capt Desmond Scott, Norman Warren, Bill Whitty, Gp Capt Allan Wright for detailed accounts of their time at RAF Sutton Bridge.

John Barwell, Tom Dolezal (Free Czechoslovak Air Force Association), Norman Franks, Peter H. T. Green, Don Hannah, Tony Hancock, Wendy Jeffery, Tor Idar Larsen (Norwegian Spitfire Foundation), Larry McCallister, Tim McCann (4th FG Association), Air Cdre Graham Pitchfork, Jagan Pillarisetti and Seetal Patel (Bharat Rakshak.com: Indian aircrew website), Mikkel Plannthin (Danish WW2 Pilots), Winston G. Ramsey, Wilhelm Ratuszynski (Polish Sqns Remembered), Nigel Rumble, Peter Saunders, John Sigmund, Ray Sturtivant, Kelvin T. Youngs (Aircrew Remembered).

Martyn Chorlton for his valuable advice and help with contacts.

Simon Parry of Flight Leader/WW2images for his generous help with photographs.

Ian Reed, Director of Allied Air Forces Memorial & Yorkshire Air Museum.

Museum of the Order of the Liberation, Paris web site for information about Free French pilots at Sutton Bridge.

Lt Col James A. Gray, Eddie Miluck, Humphrey Wynn, Tony Broadhurst, Russell Ives, Mark F. Benstein and the US Eagle Squadron Association for information about American volunteers in the RAF.

Dave Stubley, Ian Blackamore and the Lincolnshire Aircraft Recovery Group (LARG). Bill Welbourne and the Fenland & West Norfolk Aircraft Preservation Society. (FAWNAPS). Jeff Carless, East Anglian Aircraft Research Group. Jim Clarey, 453 BG Museum.

Phil Bonner and Dave Harrigan MBE of Aviation Heritage Lincolnshire.

Museum of Danish Resistance

Graham Platt of Bomber County Aviation Resource.

Air Britain Historians

Jeremy Ransome (editor) and Denise Vickers of *Lincolnshire Free Press* and *Spalding Guardian* newspapers.

Editors and staff of *Stamford Mercury; Lynn News & Advertiser; Wisbech Advertiser; The Times of India.*

Lincolnshire and Cambridgeshire County Library Services for access to archive material.

MOD Air Historical Branch; National Archives and RAF Museum Library. Relating to Crown copyright material, this book contains public sector information licensed under the Open Government Licence v 3.0 (www.nationalarchives.gov.uk/doc/open-government-licence.version/3/).

Connor Stait and the team at Amberley Publishing.

1

Silver Wings

When First World War fighter ace Squadron Leader Raymond Collishaw – victor of at least sixty aerial combats – thrilled the villagers of Sutton Bridge with a breathtaking display of aerobatics in his silver Gloster Gamecock fighter, it heralded the start of a twenty-year association of the aerodrome with the cream of RAF pilots.

'Sutton Bridge? Where's that, mate?'

RAF Sutton Bridge is sometimes perceived as a minor, unglamorous air force station in a quiet backwater of England. While the latter point might be conceded, to persist with the former view is to completely ignore – and seriously undervalue – the true situation. From the story of its flying operations – even from just the sheer variety of aeroplanes, whose evocative names themselves conjure up and chart the changing fortunes of the RAF – over those twenty years will be seen evidence of a vital role played by this station in peace and war. In particular, the story that follows emphasises and brings to life the airmen who passed through its portals as they honed those skills that were their stock in trade: air gunnery and fighter tactics. From stories of their wild, daring and courageous exploits it is easy to see how and why these pilots became the men who gave the RAF the dash, camaraderie and professionalism for which it is so widely renowned. Sadly, some were destined never to leave, as casualty lists and the lines of military headstones in the local parish churchyard testify. Further evidence of the intense activity over its air weapons range in The Wash still turns up in the sand in the form of spent cartridge cases of various calibres, the sparse detritus left over from the millions of rounds fired off by generations of pilots and air-gunners. It is considered no exaggeration to make the claim that the evolution of and activity at RAF Sutton Bridge and its associated firing range on Holbeach Marsh was important in preparing personnel of both RAF Fighter and Bomber Command for the entire air war. Furthermore, as we shall see later, it played a vital role in that most crucial of all air battles of the Second World War, The Battle of Britain (B of B), during which no fewer than 389 of its pupils and staff are numbered among that illustrious band of men known for ever as 'The Few'.

How and why, then, did this RAF airfield at Sutton Bridge spring up and what went on there?

At the end of the First World War in 1918 the legacy of peace, as far as the Royal Air Force was concerned, was a massive cutback in the quantity of active squadrons and a woefully limited financial budget. From 188 front-line squadrons active at the end of hostilities, Major-General (Air Marshal) Sir Hugh Montague Trenchard, (later Marshal of the Royal Air Force (MRAF) Viscount Trenchard GCB OM GCVO DSO) to whom, as Chief of the Air Staff, fell the task of trimming and re-shaping the post-war junior service within the constraints allowed, had by the end of 1919 just twenty-five squadrons at home and overseas with which to begin his task. His personal vision, however, was to achieve long-term quality in men, machines, training and organisation – in spite of intense politicking by the Army and Navy to strangle at birth the RAF as an independent service.

In 1923 it was reported by the national press and repeated in provincial newspapers that Trenchard, now advanced to the rank of Air Chief Marshal (ACM) in the new RAF rank system, envisaged an establishment of fifty-two squadrons for home defence. At the time of the press reports, however, only eighteen actually existed. In that same year, clear evidence of the enormity of the political in-fighting with which Trenchard had to contend emerged into the light of day, again through the medium of the press. Under a heading: 'The Costly Air Force – Admiralty control or Air Board', the following report appeared in the *Wisbech Advertiser* dated 25 July 1923, culled no doubt from the national newspapers:

> The agitation by the Admiralty for control of their own branch of the Royal Air Force has assumed almost the air of a political crisis. The rumour that the Board will resign if their claims are not allowed is not taken seriously. The Committee of Imperial Defence is understood to have reported to the Cabinet in favour of a separate Air Force. A statement on the subject by the Prime Minister is expected shortly. A manifesto, supporting the claims of the Admiralty, was signed by fifty Conservative MPs.

By 1925 Trenchard, enthusiastically – if not always productively – supported by Winston Churchill from his position as Secretary of State for War and Air, had consolidated this cadre of the RAF, having fought off the Army and Navy predators and survived. The success story of Trenchard's policies and the performance of the RAF during that crucial gestation period is a matter of historical record and will not be elaborated upon here. Now, though, he could plan expansion, albeit still constrained by a miserly budget. In this new phase, emphasis was placed on the control of English airspace by the RAF with a new structure collectively known as Air Defence of Great Britain (ADGB). Trenchard was also keen to encourage the use of the RAF as a cavalry of the air in the policing of outposts of the vast British Empire. It is also not proposed to examine this complex organisation here but simply to note that ADGB came into existence on 1 January 1925, with Air Marshal (AM) Sir John Salmond as its Air Officer Commander-in-chief (AOC-in-C), with four sub-divisions: Fighting Area, Bombing Formations, Special Reserve and Auxiliary Air Force. Since fighter defence was regarded at this time as mainly metropolitan in nature, Fighting Area – covering London and the south-east of England – might be regarded as a precursor to what became known later as 11 Group, Fighter Command.

In 1925 additional fighter and bomber squadrons were slowly being activated, in the case of the former, equipped with a variety of types such as Gloster Grebe, Gloster Gamecock, Hawker Woodcock and Armstrong Whitworth Siskin. It was very important for their pilots to be brought to the highest state of proficiency and this, of course, included attention to air gunnery. An integral part of Trenchard's master plan, therefore, made provision to establish a small number of permanent live firing and bombing ranges to keep his aircrew efficient in the skills so fundamental to their roles. Indeed, this objective would, by the end of the decade, be enshrined within the pages of the *RAF Flying Training Manual (AP 928)*, in that part relating to Applied Flying (Part II). This document summed it up rather nicely:

> The utmost skill in flying is of no avail unless pilots and gunners attain complete efficiency in the use of their weapons and sights and they receive continual practice in firing and aiming while in flight, at stationary and moving targets.

Much of an inter-war RAF pilot's time in the air, however, was used to practise formation-flying and aerobatics, with firing guns being regarded as something to be tossed in once a year. The effect of Trenchard's miserly budget was particularly evident in the context of armament. For example, practice with live munitions was severely limited due to Treasury mandarins not being keen to spend public money on things that went bang for no apparent benefit! It was also, of course, quite tricky to find somewhere safe to carry out this activity. Thus, live air gunnery usually only occurred during a squadron's two weeks of annual detachment to an armament practice camp – and in those days, for a fighter pilot, that meant Sutton Bridge.

In its wisdom, the Air Ministry also pursued policies based on bombers being the main RAF, and potential-enemy, weapon of choice and that fighters were there to engage enemy bombers. Hence the notion that formations and formation-keeping discipline was considered to be the best way of bringing large numbers of guns to bear upon the expected formations of enemy bombers – rather than against enemy fighters. Thus it followed that air gunnery techniques such as short, sharp bursts from all angles at nimble targets and the science of deflection shooting – skills that were painfully learned by the aces in the heat of combat in the First World War – were sadly neglected during training, until the Operational Training Unit (OTU), Central Gunnery School (CGS) and, not least, the live air-firing range on Holbeach Marsh brought these issues to the fore. To reiterate then: pretty aerial evolutions are all very well but if the effect of firing at a moving, aggressive target is not experienced, a fighter pilot or an air gunner will have a serious handicap.

It would be some years before squadron official diaries (known as Form 540, or Operational Record Book or ORB) made reference to individual gunnery performances but, taken at random, 19 Squadron's overall average pilot score while attending camp at Sutton Bridge from 9 to 27 July 1928, for example, was a dismal 22 per cent. This rose to 39 per cent in 1929, when they were at camp from 17 June to 5 July, with top scorer Flight Lieutenant (Flt Lt) Edward Reginald Openshaw achieving 68 per cent. It is significant that Openshaw had been a Royal Flying Corps (RFC) pilot during the First World War before, in 1930, becoming Officer Commanding (OC) 111 Squadron and later Wing Commander (Wg Cdr), AFC**. In 1930, when 19 Squadron was at camp between 20 June and 4 July, Sergeant (Sgt) Ralph Cleland scored 83 per cent and 15 June to 3 July 1931 saw Flt Lt Edward Collis de Virac Lart (later Wg Cdr, DSO) score 82 per cent, so things did seem to be improving somewhat.

Notes about gunnery scores lapsed for a time until in 1935, with justifiable pride, 19 Squadron recorded Flt Lt Harry Broadhurst as winner of the Brooke-Popham Trophy for Air Firing (*see* below), competed for, as usual, at Holbeach range during September. Broadhurst repeated his success in 1936, with a record score of 89 per cent. He went on to earn, in addition to high rank, acclaim in the RAF as an exceptional aerial marksman whose prowess was proven in combat during the Second World War (13 destroyed, 7 probables, 10 damaged). He had a stellar career in the post-war RAF, retiring in 1959 as Commander, Allied Forces Central Europe with the rank of Air Chief Marshal (ACM) and a knighthood. It is interesting to note that the runner-up to Broadhurst, Sgt Stringer of 54 Squadron, was a long way behind, only managing to score 53 per cent. Strange to relate, the Brooke-Popham Trophy competition is never mentioned again in the pages of Sutton Bridge station ORB. In respect of the 1937 competition, it has been suggested that 'Harry Broadhurst won the trophy three years hand-running' but that seems a little unlikely since he was posted to the Middle East in late 1936 and did not return to the UK until late 1937, when he was posted to an administrative job at 2 Group Headquarters (HQ).

As for 1938, in 19 Squadron's ORB there is evidence of the competition for air firing being run that year because its pages state that 'Plt Off Andrew Ian Robinson won the Air Firing Cup for highest aggregate score.' Having shown his marksmanship ability, Robinson was detached to Sutton Bridge during February 1939 to undertake an Air Firing Instructor course. Posted to 222 Squadron at the outbreak of war, he saw action over Dunkirk and during the Battle of Britain, being credited with 3 enemy aircraft destroyed and 2 probables.

The final resting place of the Brooke-Popham Trophy for Air Firing has never been tracked down and the trophy may well reside in 19 Squadron's silverware collection locked away in a warehouse at some obscure RAF storage site. It has since emerged, according to Squadron Leader (Sqn Ldr) Payne, OC 32 Squadron – whose account is supported by the then Pilot Officer (Plt Off) Peter Brothers, later Air Commodore (Air Cdre), CBE DSO DFC* (* = one bar to the award), one of Sqn Ldr Payne's squadron companions – that Sgt Albert Edward Rumble (later Sqn Ldr AFC), surpassed Broadhurst's 1936 so-called record score with his own score on 19 May 1938 during his squadron's annual firing camp at Sutton Bridge – although that date is well before the usual end-of-season period when the actual competition was normally held. The winner of the Brooke-Popham Trophy for 1937 is unknown – and aerial shooting at the end of 1939 was for real!

Sites for these potentially dangerous – not least from a general public viewpoint – live weapons activities were duly investigated, with a prerequisite being to select locations that, while accessible by road and rail, would minimise danger and disturbance to both public and military personnel and property. The Wash out-marsh adjacent to the villages of Gedney Dawsmere and Gedney Drove End, generally known as Holbeach marsh, was one site to meet the criteria. Thus during 1925 Air Ministry inspectors visited the district and, despite objections from the East Elloe Rural District Council (RDC), prior to June 1926 steps were taken to hand over the necessary area of the marsh on the seaward side of the flood bank from the jurisdiction of the Agricultural & Fisheries Ministry to the Air Ministry for use as a gunnery and bombing range.

During 1925 the Air Ministry had given serious consideration to re-activating the former First World War aerodrome of Tydd St Mary, then prime farmland owned by Mr George Thompson, but logistical difficulties – not least an inadequate water supply and fierce opposition from East Elloe RDC – ruled this out in favour of starting anew on the far side of the River Nene, where the infrastructure was considered to be better. Indeed, in November 1925, Cllr T. W. Banks was reported as saying: 'Tell them [the Air Ministry] the water supply is poisonous. We don't want them at Tydd, we had enough of them in the war!'

As a result, some parcels of land in the Wingland area, east of the River Nene and adjacent to Chalk Lane, were acquired for the construction of an aerodrome to service the range. These comprised 90 acres of land from Mr Hugh Watson, by non-renewal of his lease for Chalk House Farm; 20 acres of then derelict arable land purchased from Messrs Baxter & Barnes; and 7 acres of land purchased from Mr Button, all of which would be combined to form a service base and a grass-surface airfield to support activities over the range. One cottage off Chalk Lane, occupied by Mr Seaman, was to be taken over as it fell within the designated area and during April 1926 the land was formally appropriated. Heavy steam engines were brought in to uproot hedgerows, rollers firmed the silt soil and grass was sown in the process of combining all the parcels of land into a single airfield. Locals sagely shook their heads about the suitability of silt soil for this purpose, although the truth might have been regret for the loss of good farmland. However, history proved their doubts unfounded. Construction of roads and buildings was undertaken by Messrs Thomson & Son of Peterborough. Four canvas hangars were delivered to site in late August, to be erected by RAF personnel, and an aeroplane landed on 16 August to carry out some trial runs over the range.

Down at the range, six targets were erected side by side, comprising canvas target squares secured to robust wooden frames, which sloped in a way that angled the target skywards; they were mounted on concrete bases. A light, narrow-gauge railway, to help with servicing the targets, was built out from the sea bank for about 1½ miles along the bank of the Fleet Haven before turning to run parallel with the sea bank for another ½ mile. This was submerged when the tide raced in but, when revealed, a truck loaded with wood and various repair materials could be propelled along it, safely and easily bridging the mud and creeks, to get out to the targets. There is no record of when this light railway ceased to operate but the ravages of salt water and the treacherous nature of the mud flats would not have endowed it with a long life. Back in the 1990s one might glimpse a fragment of rail or a rotting metal sleeper poking out of the mud, but in the 21st century there is no sign of the old railway. Now a hardcore road snakes out from the foreshore to the targets but even that needs constant repair.

This, then, is the background for the presence of these two facilities – an aerodrome at Sutton Bridge and a weapons range on Holbeach Marsh – at the western end of The Wash in South Lincolnshire. Two other similar airfield/range establishments were created at about the same time as Sutton Bridge/Holbeach. At first, all three were known simply as Armament Practice Camps – sometimes referred to as Summer Armament Practice Camps – with no formal unit number allocated to them. However, on 1 January 1932 this situation changed when they were each given a more permanent-sounding status by acquiring a number and being designated as:

1. Armament Training Camp (1 ATC) located at Catfoss on the north bank of the Humber in Yorkshire, with its range at Skipsea; used primarily by night bombers.
2. ATC located at North Coates Fitties on the Lincolnshire coast, south of Cleethorpes, with its range at Donna Nook; this dealt with day bombing practice.
3. ATC located at Sutton Bridge, which handled fighter squadrons.

On 1 December 1937 all three establishments were transferred to the administrative control of 25 (Armament Training) Group – within RAF Training Command – and re-designated as Armament Training

Stations (ATS). Subsequently their emergence as permanent RAF Stations (e.g. RAF Sutton Bridge) reflected the huge strides each had taken in conjunction with the development of the RAF itself.

Thus a mere six years after the closure of Royal Naval Air Service (RNAS) station Freiston – a First World War airfield, with an adjacent air weapons range located just across The Wash near Boston – Sutton Bridge (Armament) Practice Camp came into being on 1 September 1926. RAF staff arrived on 2 September and the Air Ministry officially accepted total possession of Sutton Bridge camp on 15 September 1926. All was set for the arrival of the first squadrons. The station ORB was opened with the entry: '1 September 1926. Unit personnel mobilised at Bircham Newton and proceeded in convoy to Sutton Bridge the following day.' The establishment was three officers and thirty airmen but the personnel was 'attached only'. Flt Lt Andrew Ronald Mackenzie became its first commandant, supported by Flying Officer (Fg Off) E. R. H. Coombes as adjutant and Fg Off J. O. Priestley as Medical Officer (MO). On detachment from RAF Bircham Newton, Mackenzie was ordered to establish a base camp and landing ground on the land acquired by the Air Ministry to the east of the horizontal-swing bridge known as Cross Keys Bridge. His team was also responsible for setting up, operating and maintaining ground targets on a range for machine gun firing and bomb dropping by aeroplanes. The location of this range was at the edge of the salt marshes between the villages of Gedney Dawsmere and Gedney Drove End, about 5 miles north of the Sutton Bridge camp – and less than 4 miles, as the seagull flies, from the old RNAS Freiston range. It seems reasonable to conclude that the First World War decision to locate a range at the desolate western end of The Wash (i.e. RNAS Freiston) was also a factor in making a similar decision for Trenchard's new post-war RAF. That the new range was created such a short distance away from the old one seems to confirm that the remoteness of the tidal marsh area worked satisfactorily, but also that there was a need for a larger facility that could be further expanded if necessary – and the Dawsmere marsh 'frontage' offered this prospect. Road access was better than at Freiston and when Sutton Bridge camp came into use, its adjacent railway station – and to some extent its small port – offered significant advantages for the movement of men and materials.

Accommodation on the airfield for both men and machines was pretty basic, being canvas Bell tents and marquees for the former and Bessonneau wooden-framed canvas-type hangars for the latter. Officers were fortunate to be billeted in private houses in the village, for autumn in the fens can be right cold and damp. Aircraftman (later Flt Lt) Jack Flint, arriving at the camp in 1929 found living conditions, even a few years after it had opened, still somewhat primitive. 'Drinking water,' he recalled, 'was not piped on to the camp yet, as it was on the opposite side of the river from the village. Twice daily a water tanker journeyed back and forth to King's Lynn to bring in supplies. Electricity was generated on the camp and the generator was shut down prompt at 9.30 each evening.'

Mobilised at RAF Bircham Newton and manned by personnel from that station, the embryo unit proceeded in convoy on 2 September 1926 to its new abode to begin the task of target building. By 27 September all was ready and the first 'customers' fired over the area known as Holbeach Marsh. And so it was that a long line of evocative aeroplane names – Grebe, Siskin, Flycatcher, Woodcock, Bulldog, Fury, Hart and so on – began an association with The Wash marshes and air firing. Ninety years on, this association, though much modified over time, remains active in the twenty-first century with Typhoon and F-15 jets emulating their ancestors – just faster and with more precision.

Flying continued for just over a month in that first year, with each squadron spending one week at Sutton Bridge. By 31 October the weather was pretty grim and firing was halted for the 'season' but during that time 19, 23, 29, 43 and 111 (Fighter) Squadrons had passed through the camp – not necessarily in that order.

This brings us back to Sunday 10 October 1926, the day that the 'ace Canadian pilot' wowed the villagers. During the previous day or two, rumours ran rife in the village that an airman would be putting on a show. A *Spalding Guardian* reporter witnessed the exhibition.

At 2.45 pm an aeroplane went up and after making a good height, it made a sudden dive towards the ground with its engine roaring at full speed. The pilot held this dive until near the ground, then pulled up into a loop followed by spiral dives and sideways rolls. After half an hour of this flying the pilot swerved towards the ground but pulled up again, just missing telegraph wires and trees. Then the pilot flew north before dropping down to fly along the river only a few feet above the water, swooping up to skim the turret on top of the [Cross Keys] bridge. Pulling round in a tight turn he dived at the crowd on the river bank, who ducked in anticipation. After more daring feats and putting the wind up the crowd, the pilot landed and taxied straight inside a hangar, whereupon the crowd drifted away. It has been learned that the pilot was a Canadian known in the RAF as the 'Canadian ace' who was awarded several medals for his service in the Great War.

Research shows this could only have been the great Sqn Ldr Raymond Collishaw DSO* OBE (Mil) DSC DFC (later Air Vice Marshal (AVM) CB OBE (Civ)), OC 23 Squadron, which brought its Gloster Gamecocks from RAF Halton to Sutton Bridge in October of that year. Would those villagers ever realise what perfection they had just witnessed – and who among us would not have wished they had been on that river bank to see it?

As an experiment, 19, 29, and 111 Squadrons worked their spells at the range by flying from their home station, Duxford, landing at Sutton Bridge every day, then returning home in the evening. This was inefficient due to the time consumed in flying back and forth and these three squadrons failed to fully complete their firing programme. Operating from a base other than Sutton Bridge was thus proving most unsatisfactory, a situation which undoubtedly contributed to the subsequent development of the airfield facilities as time wore on.

An excellent example of a pilot's range-flying programme for that first 1926 season has been discovered in the early pages of the logbook of a junior pilot in 19 Squadron named Philip Reginald Barwell. His informal childhood name within the family was 'Dickie' (sometimes written as Dickey) and this name stuck with him when he joined the RAF. We shall hear more of Dickie later in this story when he returned as Station Commander of RAF Sutton Bridge during the Second World War.

Plt Off Barwell flew to and fro between Duxford and Sutton Bridge between 21 October and 27 October 1926 to perform local exercises and to fire on the range. His log book for that week shows he flew twelve sorties to fire at ground targets for which his total flying time was 7 hours 45 minutes and he made these sorties in Gloster Grebes J7396, J7568, J7577, J7592. The Grebe was equipped with two .303-inch calibre Vickers machine guns, synchronised to fire through the propeller arc and its total ammunition capacity was a maximum of 1,200 rounds (600 per gun). It is not known if the aircraft were loaded with ammunition to their full capacity for these sorties but in order to assess the scores accurately, the quantity loaded would certainly have been carefully counted. There is some anecdotal evidence from a couple of press reports that the guns were loaded with just 100 rounds each for these practice sorties – and this would certainly promote economy by the pilot and keep HM Treasury happy too. Further critical evaluation of the range operating procedure itself suggested that it, too, was unsatisfactory. Initially the system adopted was for a formation of six aeroplanes to approach the range in line astern. Working a left-hand circuit during firing passes at the ground targets, as they finished each aeroplane broke to starboard and left the formation. This procedure was found to be neither safe nor efficient and was discontinued when the camp closed for that year.

It was 1 April 1927 when Sutton Bridge Armament Practice Camp re-opened again, this time with Sqn Ldr Anthony Rex Arnold DSC DFC posted in as commandant, together with three officers and 49 airmen. Usually known as 'Rex', Arnold joined the Royal Naval Air Service in 1916 and went on to become an ace with five aerial victories to his name while flying Sopwith Triplanes with 8 (Naval) Squadron. He commanded 79 Squadron during the First World War; saw service with the Fleet Air Arm in the 1930s; became Senior Air Staff Officer (SASO) in 24 (Training) Group before finally retiring from the RAF as a Group Captain at the end of the Second World War.

Air firing began on the 19th of that month just in time for an inspection visit by Air Marshal (AM) Sir John Salmond, recently appointed as the first Air Officer Commanding (AOC) of the newly independent RAF command, known as Air Defence of Great Britain (ADGB), which administered all the operational fighter and bomber elements of the RAF on home soil. In 1930 John Salmond took over as Chief of the Air Staff (CAS) from Hugh Trenchard until 1933, when his brother Geoffrey Salmond succeeded him. Sadly, Geoffrey died within a month of taking command and John stood in for a few more months until that post was filled by ACM Edward Ellington.

Not unsurprisingly, the arrival of the Royal Air Force on their doorstep made quite an impression on the small rural community on the other side of the river, but the RAF was anxious to show that it was keen to integrate with the locals. This was enthusiastically brought to the attention of the public when on 7 May 1927 the *Spalding Guardian* newspaper carried the following article:

The advent of the airmen to Sutton Bridge has changed the life of the village and the very frequent stunts performed are very interesting. Tuesday evening was an exception to the rule, for the airmen gave a special display, held a comic football match and finished with a grand dance at the Oddfellows Hall. A number of airmen turned up at the impromptu football ground which had been gaily decorated. The goalposts were adorned with flags and the picturesque and humorous costumes of the players added greatly to the delight of the spectators.

The aerial display was given by three of the smaller planes, which performed a number of daring feats. Hardly had the planes ascended than the crowds began to gather and at one time there must have been almost a thousand people on the [river] banks.

As I assembled with the crowd to watch this display, I was thrilled by a daring exhibition of looping. The planes, three of them, had just risen into the air as graceful as three birds, their bright fuselage glistening like silver in the brilliant sun. Round they flew, the tips of their wings appearing almost to touch as they circled the aerodrome, flying in strict formation, even as if they were connected one to the other by an invisible cord.

Gracefully they swooped downwards – 'they're coming down!' someone shouted – but they were not. The wheels almost touched the earth, but the engines roared again and up they went, far into the sky. They swooped again, not so low this time, before gliding upwards to complete the stirring loop. Even in this, the planes worked as one, maintaining perfect formation.

This little programme was repeated two or three times and then the centre plane broke away – darting forward, as if it was a runaway and wished to escape capture. Then commenced a game of follow-your-leader, for the others gave chase and round they went, time after time, never disappearing from view. Then the foremost plane swooped and looped, the others following and taking just the same line of circle. Then they came closer together – this time the foremost plane rose gracefully for the loop and ere it had reached the bottom of the loop, the others had commenced. For a moment they appeared to hang as if suspended; one, its nose downward; one, upside down on top of the loop and the third, nose upwards. Truly a most magnificent spectacle. Cheers rang out from the crowd. This manoeuvre was repeated again and the programme continued for about an hour. Then the leader swooped down, sending up a cloud of dust as he landed on the soft dry dust, followed by his companions.

It is not stated from which squadron these aeroplanes were and the station's RAF Form 540 only records at the end of the year a list in ascending squadron number order. From that day though, the village of Sutton Bridge was won over to the RAF cause.

Working practices were again carefully examined to try to improve range operating efficiency. In June, accommodation for the range working party was erected on ground adjoining the range itself, just to the landward side of the sea bank. Subsequently this became a permanent arrangement – in use, but modernised, even to this day – to obviate the need to travel to and from Sutton Bridge when firing was in progress. The precise nature of the accommodation is not recorded but it could not have been a popular posting in view of the uninviting, wind-swept countryside out there at the edge of The Wash.

At the close of firing operations in 1926, a brief résumé of byelaws and range procedure had been published in local newspapers principally, it seems, as a warning to the public to keep well away when firing recommenced. A plan of the range was also printed, showing the position of targets and the line of fire. The public was advised that there were nine warning flags and danger notices. On the seaward side, markers were erected to warn ships and boats of the danger area limits. Six canvas firing targets would be permanent features on the seaward side of the marsh bank. Air-to-ground gunnery was planned to take place between 1 April and 31 October, between 7.00 am and 6.00 pm on weekdays and 7.00 am to 12.00 noon on Saturdays. Thirty minutes before firing was scheduled to begin, range staff would raise red flags, post sentries and bar public access to that part of the marsh. Aircraft, flying singly or in flights, would fire .303 ammunition from a height of 500 feet (e.g. from a two-seater carrying a gunner) or by diving onto targets from 800 feet down to about 100 feet. Bomb dropping would be with practice smoke or alternatively with light to medium weight HE bombs.

It was not until 2 July 1927 that the local population first gained a peep behind the scenes on the actual airfield itself. The veil of official secrecy was lifted to allow a visit by a special correspondent and a photographer from the *Spalding Guardian* whose report provides further enlightening details of life at the station:

Abutting upon the southern bank of the Nene, the camp, with Bell tents arranged in orderly rows, covers eighty acres [sic], of which seventy acres are devoted to the landing ground itself. A solitary aeroplane, indulging in a clear case of 'loop-itus', flew overhead as we began our tour, while others were being readied for the firing range. Bombs, painted white and of light calibre, could be seen being fitted to racks beneath their wings. Airmen were scurrying about loading belts of cartridges into

21

machine guns. Our presence on the airfield coincided with the arrival of three flights of Bristol Fighters, from Andover and Old Sarum, about to begin their fourteen-day visit to the range facility. Together with [Hawker] Woodcocks of 17 Squadron from Upavon, the Bristol Fighters brought the total of aeroplanes at the camp to twenty-one, well within the capacity of the four spacious hangars.

According to the station's Form 540, these arrivals seem to confirm the entries referring to 13 (Army Co-operation or AC) Squadron, at that time based at Andover, and to 16 (AC) Squadron, from Old Sarum. The third flight might refer to the arrival of a detachment from 4 (AC) Squadron, which operated Bristol F2B Fighters (affectionately known as Brisfit) at Farnborough and which is also recorded as using Sutton Bridge that summer. Since there were no aeroplanes on the station's own establishment at that time, it can be reasonably assumed that 17 Squadron might bring a full squadron complement of twelve Woodcocks, suggesting that the other three flights observed represented a flight of three aeroplanes from each Army Co-op Squadron. Again, no individual dates for each squadron's attendance at Sutton Bridge are listed in the Form 540 but it seems likely that the reporter's visit took place during June for his report to be published on 2 July. He continued:

> Our attention was drawn to a firing butt, for static testing of the alignment of aeroplane gun-sights. Another butt, containing innumerable sand-bags, was in the course of construction. Under the guidance of Sqn Ldr Leacroft we were then conveyed to Gedney Drove End, to the firing range itself.

Sqn Ldr John Leacroft MC* was Officer Commanding 17 Squadron, whose permanent base at that time was RAF Hawkinge. He was an outstanding pilot with considerable operational experience, having claimed twenty-two aerial victories while flying SPAD VII and Sopwith Dolphin fighters with 19 Squadron in France during the First World War. The press report continued:

> Here we took up position on the sea bank behind the machine gun targets. Soon aeroplanes began swooping down, spattering the targets liberally with bullets. After each firing exercise is complete, the target is repaired by range staff.

Bombing practice was also demonstrated but since that target was well out on the marsh, only occasional clouds of white smoke could be seen. The machine gun targets are easily served by a light railway but repairs to the distant bombing target is a far more troublesome matter it consisting of a raft in a large white circle, submerged at high tide. To reach the target a repair squad is compelled to go out by boat from King's Lynn dock.

Public access is barred by stringent laws, sentries and warning flags, with dire penalties for those who dare to wander onto the range. In general, however, our visit was most hospitable. The health of the troops seems reasonably good, while the landing ground has not fulfilled the forebodings of numerous local farmers, who were of the opinion that the ground would be too soft for the aeroplanes.

Observing that only two minor mishaps had occurred during its first two years of operation, the Special Correspondent was perhaps tempting fate. The first of these two occurred on 19 October 1926 as the result of a pilot raising the tail of his aircraft too high during take-off. The propeller was smashed when it struck the ground, causing the aeroplane to end up ignominiously on its nose. It was not long before that same newspaper was reporting the first of what was to become a sad litany of accidents.

The Gloster Gamecock – really a development of Gloster's Grebe – was a relatively sleek and agile design. Early problems, known as 'wing flutter' were resolved, but its liveliness also brought with it a reputation as a handful in a spin and when landing. Nevertheless, it was considered a popular aeroplane by its pilots, even though records suggest its other qualities contributed to an attrition rate of 25 per cent – and only 90 were built! The worst year for accidents was 1927 when no less than 18 Gamecocks were lost in crashes.

Aerodynamic flutter is a complex technical issue but, in very simple terms, it is a potentially destructive vibration, sometimes caused by the combined effects of changes in pressure distribution of the flow of air over aerofoil surfaces – e.g. wings and control surfaces – as their angle of attack to the airflow alters. It is a result of a flaw in the design and construction that may manifest itself during relatively rare flying situations peculiar to the given aeroplane. Elastic forces set up by the distortion feed on themselves and in the worst cases it may cause a loss of control and/or disintegration of the wing. Remedies can be found, for example, by adding an external strut, or struts, to strengthen a wing structure, which is what happened in the case of the Gamecock.

On Wednesday 20 July 1927 two serious crashes occurred at the range. The first, at around 11.30 am, involved Gloster Grebe II, J7580, from 19 Squadron based at Duxford, which was on its summer camp from 9 July to 23 July. On this fateful morning the Grebe was flown out to the firing range by Fg Off William Arthur Andrews. After making a firing pass at one of the ground targets, the aeroplane was seen to circle in the general direction of Gedney Drove End. It was during this time that the pilot appeared to lose control of his aeroplane at low altitude and it entered a dive at high speed on the range side of the sea bank. The Grebe crashed into about 3 feet of water – the tide was coming in – sending up a huge fountain of spray as it went in at a shallow angle. Luckily for Andrews, the water cushioned his impact and undoubtedly saved the airman's life. In the process of turning over, as the aeroplane's nose dug in, his seat harness snapped, catapulting him 60 yards through the air. Lady Luck was with him though and his parachute partially opened – whether by accident or design he could not remember – but in streaming out behind him it slowed his headlong flight. He was quickly rescued from the rising tide by range staff who found him soaked to the skin, bruised, shaking like a leaf – but alive. It is this incident that gives Plt Off Andrews the dubious honour of being involved in the first aero accident at the Holbeach Marsh range.

A year later – still flying fighters – Andrews, who joined the RAF on a short-service commission in September 1925, was posted to 41 Squadron at RAF Northolt where, aged twenty-two, unfortunately he appears to have put up another 'black'. On 4 April 1929 he found himself in Wimbledon magistrates court where he was convicted on two charges; one of being drunk at the wheel of a motor vehicle and another of driving in a dangerous manner at West Side, Wimbledon Common, on Wednesday 3 April 1929. He had made quite a hash of things. A police constable told the court that, at 11 pm on the night of the 3rd, he tried to stop Andrews in New Malden but failed when the car slid 50 yards along a grass embankment then disappeared at high speed across Kingston by-pass narrowly missing two other cars. At Copse Hill another police officer tried to stop Andrews' car but had to leap out of the way to avoid being knocked down. The car finally came to a grinding halt when it turned towards Crooked Billet but ran onto a grass verge and dropped into a deep gully. When told he would be arrested, a constable said Andrews replied: 'I've been on the loose. I have had fifteen, or maybe seventeen whiskies with a friend.' He was arrested and at 12.15 am, a police surgeon found him suffering from the effects of alcohol and deemed him in no fit state to drive a vehicle. Later, in court, Andrews said he had been in a Kingston restaurant with a friend for a couple of hours during which time he had consumed six or seven whiskey and sodas. He claimed a flabby tyre was responsible for his car's erratic movement; he denied being drunk and considered his speed of 35 mph was quite reasonable as he was in complete control! He was fined a total of £20 and his driving licence was suspended for twelve months. As well as being reported by *The Times*, the case was widely aired in provincial newspapers as far afield, for example, as Dundee and York – all of which may well have contributed to his fall from grace in his squadron. Indeed, Fg Off Andrews' service career came to an end when, as reported in the *London Gazette*, he resigned his RAF short-service commission with effect from 31 May 1929. It has been suggested that he subsequently became a civilian flying instructor at Hanworth Park airfield near London, before emigrating to the Sudan in 1937 where he flew commercially with Air Commerce Ltd.

The second incident on 20 July has acquired the unfortunate statistic of being the first fatal accident to occur at either Sutton Bridge or its range. Fg Off Richard Griffith Pace of 32 Squadron, Kenley, became this first fatality when he was killed while flying Gloster Gamecock J7907. It was just after 3.30pm that Fg Off Pace flew off to the range in company with a second aircraft from his squadron, flown by Plt Off Grosvenor Selk. According to later testimony by Flt Lt John Denholm, range officer, and Aircraftman Douglas Littleton of the range staff, Fg Off Pace made several firing passes at No.1 ground target. These were correctly carried out and upon completion of each one, the pilot turned away seawards. Plt Off Selk was also firing correctly at No.4 target. Pace's aeroplane had just climbed away seaward to 700 feet when its engine seemed to falter and it lost height. The engine seemed to open up again and the aeroplane visibly surged forward, but it still carried on at the same angle of dive as before. It dived into the mud-flats in a cloud of smoke. So hard was the impact that its force shattered the machine completely, broke the pilot's seat straps and pitched him through the air. Pace's parachute is believed to have been ripped from its pack as the canopy was seen to billow and collapse beside the wreckage. Picking their way across the sand and mud-flats as fast as they could, range staff found the pilot unconscious about 15 yards from the wreck. He was stretchered to a point where the medical officer (MO), having been summoned instantly from Sutton Bridge, could reach the rescue party. Fg Off Pace died a few minutes after the doctor had completed his examination. The body was conveyed to King's Lynn hospital where the coroner's inquest took place. Fg Off Richard Pace was aged twenty-two and from Leyton, Essex, and had joined the RAF on a short-service commission in March 1926.

Ninety Gloster Gamecock Mk Is were built and issued to five squadrons including 32 Squadron but Fg Off Pace's Gamecock, J7907, was originally issued to 43 Squadron. During 1927, or possibly late in 1926, J7907 crashed while being flown by Sgt Lionel Richard Stanford Freestone (commissioned in 1929 and Air Commodore OBE, 1950) during an over-enthusiastic demonstration of dive-bombing at his airfield. In an effort to achieve absolute spot-on delivery of his bombs, Sgt Freestone adopted an ever-steeper dive trajectory until, on his final attempt, he dived vertically on the target with dire results. He actually went over the vertical and the aeroplane, fortunately, hit the ground inverted but at a fairly shallow angle. It rolled end-over-end and came to a crumpled halt. Sgt Freestone was a very lucky man. It is said that rescuers watched him emerge from his shattered cockpit, dust himself off and cycle back to dispersal on a borrowed bike! It appears that Gamecock J7907 was re-built and issued to 32 Squadron – perhaps knowing its history, 43 Squadron would not touch it with a barge-pole! The official reason for the final demise of J7907 is not known but perhaps it is likely that Pace's aeroplane was not re-built in an entirely satisfactorily manner.

Business returned to normal after the mishaps of July and almost inevitably, to add incentive and appeal to the natural instincts of the fighter pilot, it was not long before a gunnery competition was introduced. At the end of September, when the firing season was complete, the best shots from each of the Fighting Area squadrons passing through Sutton Bridge returned to the station to compete for what became known as the Brooke-Popham Air Firing Trophy, donated in 1927 by and named after, the AOC-in-C Air Defence of Great Britain, Air Chief Marshal (ACM) Sir Henry Robert Moore Brooke-Popham GCVO KCB CMG DSO AFC, and awarded for the overall top score. In that inaugural year it was won by Flt Lt Harold Charles Calvey from 23 Squadron. It will be seen from time to time that in these early inter-war years many of the pilots mentioned in various aspects of this narrative had combat experience during the First World War, which surely made live firing in peacetime quite a bit easier for these 'old hands'. Flt Lt Calvey was one such pilot, having served as a Second Lieutenant (2/Lt) in the RFC, flying FE2b fighters with 11 Squadron. He had been in several air combats with the enemy and had at least one victory to his name, an Albatros Scout driven down on 25 March 1917. We shall hear more of Calvey a little later.

Even from the limited records kept, it is clear that the armament camp was well into its stride, with men and aircraft from 1, 3, 4, 13, 16, 17, 19, 23, 25, 29, 32, 41, 43, 56 and 111 Squadrons all completing a two-week stay at Sutton Bridge that year. From this list of fifteen squadrons it can be seen that silver, gaudily painted fighters from all frontline fighter units must have kept the air above south Lincolnshire fairly buzzing with noise for seven months of the year – so, in the twenty-first century: what's new? With the onset of winter, the tents, marquees and Bessonneau hangars were taken down and transported away; all staff returned to Bircham Newton and tranquillity returned to Sutton Bridge.

Spring 1928 brought the arrival of the usual convoy of vehicles of all shapes bringing tents, hangars and equipment, this time under the leadership of Sqn Ldr William Sowrey DFC AFC (later Air Commodore, CBE) with three officers and fifty-two airmen. Sutton Bridge Practice Camp re-opened on 28 March, with air firing beginning on 16 April and continuing unabated until the end of September. By the close of operations, the same units as recorded in the previous year, with the further addition of 2 (AC) Squadron, had passed through the camp. October brought the end of 'season' Brooke-Popham competition to find the best overall shot and was won this year by Fg Off Chester Thompson from 43 Squadron who, like many of his contemporaries, had had the benefit of combat experience.

Sqn Ldr William Sowrey was one of an RAF dynasty from which he and two brothers saw service with the RFC/RAF during the First World War – and far beyond. On 9 January 1916 William transferred from the Royal Berkshire Regiment to the RFC for pilot training. Posted to 60 Squadron, he became a flight commander with that squadron before taking command of 50 Squadron. Between 1918 and 1927 he was OC of a succession of squadrons including Nos.50, 152, 6, 30, 84 and 2, before being posted to Sutton Bridge in 1928. The Armament Officer on Sqn Ldr Sowrey's staff that year was Flt Lt John Denholm. He, too, had served in the RFC in the First World War after transferring from the Argyll & Sutherland Highlander regiment. He was appointed Temporary Lieutenant in February 1917 as an Observer flying officer.

Born in 1899 Chester William McKinley Thompson, winner of the 1928 Brooke-Popham Trophy, was an American by birth but in the First World War served as a Lieutenant with 22 Squadron RFC, which

he joined in the Spring of 1918. He was shot down while flying Bristol
F2b Fighter E2517 near Cambrai on 29 September 1918, was made a
POW and demobilised at the war's end. During the intervening months
Chester Thompson was credited with twelve aerial victories – shared
of course with his observer/gunner – to become one of twenty-seven
pilot and observer aces in the squadron. In 1923 Thompson reapplied
to join the RAF and was granted a short-service commission, serving
until 1937 when he went on to the RAF Reserve. Mobilised for the
Second World War, he rose to the rank of Squadron Leader but on
16 September 1940, while serving with 19 Operational Training Unit
(OTU) at RAF Kinloss, he undertook a solo flight to RAF Manby in
a Miles Magister, ran into bad weather and died when his aeroplane
crashed near Dalwhinnie.

At Sutton Bridge, 1928 did not pass without mishap – which, sadly,
would be the pattern for the years that followed. Fg Off Geoffrey
Bradbury of 41 Squadron was fatally injured at the range on 8 May.
Bradbury was considered a proficient pilot, who had been in the RAF
for just more than three years of a five-year short-service commission.
By the time of the accident, though, he had accumulated only 171 solo
flying hours.

Midday sunshine warmed the airfield when Fg Off Bradbury, in
company with another aircraft, flew Armstrong Whitworth (AW)
Siskin IIIA, J8402, down to the range. He made several firing passes
at No.4 target, pulling up into right-hand circuits after each dive. His
method of approach appeared to follow a flat glide, with the engine
throttled back, continuing to glide as he put the nose down towards
the target. By keeping the approach speed down, could this have been
his wheeze of achieving a longer, better-aimed and thus higher-scoring,
firing pass?

It was from one of these slow dives that Bradbury failed to pull out.
At first it seemed his aeroplane would recover but the undercarriage
hit one of the many creeks that criss-cross the marsh and it was torn
away. J8402 staggered, disintegrating in an explosion that ripped
the engine from the fuselage. Pinned beneath the wreckage, Fg Off
Bradbury lay unconscious for nearly an hour before rescuers reached
him through the maze of muddy creeks. He was rushed to King's Lynn
hospital where, after fighting bravely, he succumbed to his injuries
twelve days later.

Asked for an opinion at the inquest, Flt Lt Denholm, the Range
Control Officer, considered Fg Off Bradbury ought to have lined up
on the targets with the engine power on and then only throttle back

during the firing dive itself. Due to the gliding approach Bradbury adopted, the aeroplane appeared to lose even more speed and may have either stalled or the engine failed to respond quickly enough when the throttle was eventually re-opened. It would appear that this accident owed more to pilot error than a structural issue.

The AW Siskin III was the UK's first 'all-metal' – actually a fabric-covered aluminium alloy structure – fighter and it first entered RAF service with 41 Squadron in May 1924. Sixty-four examples of the Mk III were built with a 325 hp Jaguar III engine. This engine was subsequently developed into the supercharged Jaguar IV of 420–450 hp which, with minor structural modifications, produced the Siskin IIIA of which 348 examples were built. The Mk IIIA was first delivered to 111 Squadron in September 1926 with 41 Squadron being re-equipped in March 1927 along with, eventually, a further nine squadrons before it was withdrawn from service by the end of 1932. It was well-liked and considered an excellent aerobatic machine and became a familiar sight at Sutton Bridge for several years.

In May, to provide a run-about aeroplane for the camp, Avro 504N, H2434, was allocated to Sutton Bridge on the 25th; it did not, however, last very long. Flt Lt Harold Calvey of 23 Squadron, who it will be remembered was the winner of the first Best Shot competition, was killed on 1 July in H2434 while returning to Sutton Bridge from a trip to RAF Kenley. With him when he crashed at Clifton, near Henlow, was Flight Sergeant (Flt Sgt) William Charles Holker, who also lost his life in the accident.

Tragedy continued to punctuate operations at the camp, rearing its head again the following month.

2

On Target

Flt Lt Lance Browning MC DFC, another veteran of the First World War, now a flight commander with 3 Squadron, took off in Hawker Woodcock, J7974, from Sutton Bridge airfield on the morning of 2 August 1928, bound for the firing range.

Emerging from the ashes of the old Sopwith Aeroplane Company, a victim of the immediate and deep post-First World War decline in British aircraft production, Hawker Engineering Company's first offering, the Woodcock, was its attempt to meet a government specification for a single-seat night fighter but it was not a shining advert for the company – although Hawker learned and improved with great success thereafter. The Woodcock, a contemporary of those Gloster products, Grebe and Gamecock and Armstrong Whitworth's Siskin, was not without its share of teething problems, which also seemed to dog its short, unimpressive service life. Displaying a tendency to wing 'flutter' at high speed and a reputation for weakness in the main spar, it was considered unsuitable for aerobatics, and spinning was definitely discouraged. In the event, sixty-two were built for the RAF and only two squadrons were allotted this fighter, the first being 3 Squadron at Upavon, relinquishing its aging Sopwith Snipes for the Woodcock in May 1925. Another year elapsed before 17 Squadron then took delivery of its allocation. In service for three years, by 1928 3 Squadron was the only Woodcock unit remaining, as 17 Squadron had converted to the Gloster Gamecock. Having acquired a poor reputation during its service life, what happened at Holbeach range on 2 August seemed to seal the type's service fate. From the inquest evidence it appears quite clear that the cause of the accident was failure of the main spar and shortly after, on 21 August 1928, the

Air Ministry grounded all Woodcocks. By September, 3 Squadron was re-equipped with the Gloster Gamecock.

This incident was recalled at the King's Lynn coroner's inquest, which was reported by the *Spalding Guardian* as follows:

> The story of an airman's crash while engaged in firing practice at Holbeach Marsh was told to the Lynn Borough coroner, Dr M. Chadwick, at an inquiry at West Norfolk & Lynn hospital on Friday evening [10 August] into the death of Flt Lt Lancelot [Lance] Harold Browning [MC, DFC].
>
> An eyewitness told how he saw the officer recovering from a dive at one of the targets and how, when he was about to ascend, a wing of the machine folded back and dropped off, leaving the aeroplane to roll, a helpless cripple and then crash.
>
> The first witness, Sqn Ldr Johnson, OC 3 Squadron, said he was stationed at Upavon but temporarily on duty at Sutton Bridge. He gave evidence of identification and said he was at the aerodrome at 10.35am on Thursday [2 August] when Browning took off alone to proceed to the range for firing practice.

Sqn Ldr Eric Digby Johnson AFC transferred to the RFC from the East Surrey Regiment in 1915 and, after flying training, was posted to 21 Squadron in which he was promoted to Captain, becoming a flight commander and remaining with the squadron until the end of the First World War. Johnson continued flying with 2 Air Issue Section, earning an AFC dated 8 February 1919 for his work as a test pilot. Later in 1919 he was offered a short-service commission (SSC) in the rank of Flt Lt and after a number of postings became OC 3 Squadron on 15 September 1927. He saw service in staff posts during the Second World War and rose to the rank of Air Commodore.

The newspaper report continued:

> Describing the accident, Fg Off Empson, Practice Camp adjutant and acting as range officer that day, said he saw the machine, a Woodcock, diving at No.2 target. After firing, the pilot flattened out and was about to climb when the witness heard a crackling noise. He said: 'I looked around and saw the starboard wing had folded back. Within a second or two it had broken off and came into several pieces while falling. The machine rolled once or twice to the right and continued its course for about one hundred yards. She struck the ground while upside down then

turned over. I called the medical orderly with his equipment and the range party. We ran to the wreckage and after removing a piece of fabric, saw the deceased lying on his right side. He died within a few seconds of our arrival. I gave instructions for him to be placed on a stretcher and conveyed to the sea bank, where there is a hut and the MO then took charge.'

Corporal (Cpl) Bryan, fitter, and Leading Aircraftman (LAC) Short, rigger, said they carried out their usual inspection of the machine at 8.00 am and found everything as it should be and entered this fact in the log books.

Fg Off O'Brian, medical officer, said the unfortunate airman was dead when he arrived. He described the man's terrible injuries and said there was scarcely a whole limb in the body.

Civilian eyewitness Mr S. Elmes of Gedney Drove End, was working in a field close to the range. 'I saw something fall from the machine and it was the wing torn away. The machine turned over and over several times in the air and fell with a terrific crash.' Another witness, Mr Durrance, foreman for Mr W. R. Caudwell, said the machine was rendered a complete wreck and seemed to strike the ground with terrific force behind the first shooting range.

The coroner recorded a verdict of accidental death.

From information provided by the eminent aviation author Norman Franks, we have a brief insight into this unfortunate airman's short life. Lance Browning was born in Bournemouth in 1897 and went to school in Banstead, Surrey, then Wellington College. On the outbreak of the First World War, he joined the Army, being gazetted as a second Lieutenant in the Royal Field Artillery in July 1915. In May 1916, he volunteered for secondment to the RFC as an air observer and after training was posted to 30 Squadron in Mesopotamia in the Middle East. There, he flew on operations as an observer until August 1917 when he requested to train as a pilot. That training was completed in Egypt then he flew more operations as a pilot with 30 Squadron, flying aeroplanes such as the Royal Aircraft Factory RE8 and BE2; Martinsyde G102 Elephant and Bristol Scout. During his tour he was awarded a Military Cross (MC). The citation read:

For conspicuous gallantry and daring while carrying out independent bombing behind enemy lines. He was attacked by a fast enemy scout machine which, by skilful piloting and accurate shooting he drove down to its aerodrome. No sooner had the enemy aeroplane landed than Lt Browning dropped a bomb, completely obliterating the enemy pilot who had begun to run away and damaged his machine. He then continued bombing and while doing so was attacked by two more enemy scouts, both of which he drove off, he showed fine skill and courage throughout.

Promoted to Captain, Browning was posted to 111 Squadron – also in Egypt – in September 1918. At the war's end he returned to England, remaining in the RAF and in 1919 again flew out to Mesopotamia, seeing service in the Kurdistan campaign flying RE8s from Samara and Baghdad. These efforts won him a DFC, awarded in July 1920. Posted back to England again, by 1928 he was a flight commander with 3 Squadron and at the age of twenty-eight, he died in the accident mentioned above on 2 August 1928. It was a sad end to a distinguished flying career.

With 1928 only seven months old, Flt Lt Browning's became the fifty-second serious accident sustained by the RAF that year. By comparison, the total at the beginning of the post-First World War era was fifty-seven in 1921, of which twenty-two were fatal. A total of fifty-five serious accidents were recorded in 1927.

The rapidly escalating demands of Trenchard's air force development scheme clearly had its human price since, by 1931, the accident total for that year reached ninety-seven, of which forty were fatal. On the positive side, however, although quantity was increasing, the rate at which flying accidents occurred was, fortunately, decreasing as the following table shows.

Date	1921	1931	+/-%
Military flying hours	50,000	340,000	+600%
Serious accidents	57	97	+70%
Fatalities	22	40	+80%
Rate of serious accidents	1 in 900 hrs	1 in 3,500 hrs	-300%
Rate of fatal accidents	1 in 2,200 hrs	1 in 8,600 hrs	-300%

So, another busy and eventful year drew to a close. Sixteen fighter squadrons – virtually the entire fighter squadron strength of the RAF – had passed through the camp, whose sterling work was rewarded by a visit from Marshal of the Royal Air Force, Sir Hugh Trenchard himself, on 27 September 1928.

Winter was still much in evidence when, on 19 February, an advance party of two corporals and seven airmen unlocked the camp gates to begin the 1929 season. After a spell of sick leave, the former RFC pilot Sqn Ldr Cyril Bertram Cooke (later Air Marshal Sir Cyril, KCB CBE), who had extensive operational flying experience in the Middle East during the First World War, assumed command with an establishment split as follows.

- Three officers and forty-five other ranks at the main camp.
- Two officers, twelve other ranks at the range.
- One civilian warden at the range.

While Sqn Ldr Cooke was on sick leave, Sqn Ldr Alexander McRitchie Moffatt – another First World War veteran flyer – took temporary command of the station from 4 to 19 April until Cooke assumed command for the rest of the season. It is indicative of the advancing status of RAF Sutton Bridge's role that the commandant's rank was shortly to be upgraded to that of Wing Commander.

Down at the range, the quantity of ground targets remained at the six of previous years but a second bombing circle was constructed. Such was the pressure on the range facilities that practice bombing was even permitted over the airfield itself. That year also saw the introduction of a station flight, formally recorded in the Form 540 in April 1929, a further indicator of the developing nature of aerial gunnery training in line with Trenchard's quest for quality.

Station flight was perhaps rather a grandiose title at this stage since its sole aeroplane appears to have been a venerable Bristol F2b Fighter Mk IV. The identity of this Brisfit, adapted to carry RAE sleeve target towing gear is not recorded but H1634, of 1918 vintage modified to J-series standard, is believed to have arrived at Sutton Bridge in July of the previous year. Although not recorded by the camp diarist of 1928 as being on the establishment, this may simply reflect the generally sparse nature of the diary entries for that year. 1929's diarist was clearly of different calibre, which is reflected by the – relatively – more comprehensive entries that include, at the start of business, the comment about a Bristol Fighter. It is worthy of note, too, that from that example and from a multitude of similar sources examined in the course of this project, the usefulness of unit diaries to the researcher is directly in proportion to the time, effort and personal interest each diarist was prepared to put into that task all those years ago. Each squadron attending Sutton Bridge in 1929 was allowed to put two of its pilots through air-to-air firing practice at a towed sleeve target and at the close of the year this procedure was deemed to have been a great success.

Bristol F2b Fighter H1634 appears to have left Sutton Bridge at some point, possibly at the close of the 1929 season, as this serial turns up on the establishment of 5 FTS at Sealand in 1930. Scrutiny of other Bristol Fighter serial records indicates this type was still in use at the camp for sleeve target towing until at least the end of 1931. For example, D7835, F4741 and F4845 are noted as allocated to Sutton Bridge in early 1931. First customers and taking up the whole of April 1929, were the Army Co-operation (AC) squadrons, 4, 13 and 26, bringing with them a mixture of Bristol F2b Fighters and the new Armstrong Whitworth Atlas. May saw them give way to a steady stream of fighter boys, which seems to confirm the order of events of previous years. In the first week of May, 29 and 43 Squadrons arrived, followed by 41 and 17 at the end of that month.

It appears the management was always striving to become more organised, with the objective of maximising the amount of actual gunnery time at the range for all pilots. A room was established at the camp as a focal point for pilots, where they could meet for briefings and information exchange. Regular weather charts were displayed there – a wise move in view of the fickle nature of The Wash weather – so that interruptions to the programme could be planned around it. Range plans and firing procedures were also displayed, so that pilots could manage their firing time effectively. All small changes in their own right but collectively, professionalism and efficiency were becoming the order of the day. Meanwhile, down at the range, pilots were able to assess and correct their gunnery more quickly now that a new system of ground-to-air 'position of burst' signals was introduced. Gunnery at the range was also helped by the setting up of a wind indicator and large red bulls-eye aiming marks were painted in the centre of the air-to-ground targets – as they still are to this day. Then it was down to the real business with the arrival of 41 Squadron on 27 May, followed by 17 Squadron on 29 May and 19 Squadron on 17 June.

At least it could not be said that the top brass was not taking an interest in the expenditure of all this hot lead, for there was yet another VIP visit in June when the AOC ADGB, AVM Sir Edward Ellington KCB CMG CBE (later MRAF, GCB) and the AOC Fighting Area, AVM Francis Scarlett CB DSO, kept the camp on its toes. An outcome of their inspection was a conference at 23 Group HQ to hammer out even more ideas for speeding up air firing procedures. Flt Lt Crawford, the camp armament officer, came up with a design for a new type of target frame. Made of steel, he believed it would be resilient to the ravages of machine gun bullets, thus taking less time to repair. In the event, his steel-framed target, when tested, proved to be 'very bad'. No reason is recorded but in view of the modern practice of still using stout, wooden telegraph poles to support the air-to-ground targets – being attacked with anything from heavy machine-gun rounds up to 20 mm to 30 mm cannon shells – it is reasonable to surmise the reason might be the danger from ricochets. That is a very real danger now but even in those early days with lower air speeds and bullet velocity, close spatial factors would produce relatively similar dangers.

Halcyon summer days saw a steady flow of fighters through camp, with 1 and 25 Squadrons arriving on 15 July, then 23 and 111 Squadrons flying in on 7 August. 23 Squadron's stay was marred that summer by the tragic death of Fg Off Charles Henry Jones.

Fg Off Jones was a diminutive Scotsman who joined the RAF in 1924 and by March 1927 was a fighter pilot with 23 Squadron based at RAF Kenley. Alongside his pal Fg Off Harry Alexander Purvis, the pair made quite a name for themselves by winning the RAF Fighter Aerobatics Competition, held at Northolt on 16 May 1929.

What would be a fateful summer for both men began when they reported to RAF Northolt as the representatives of 23 Squadron in the annual RAF fighter squadron aerobatic competition. The winners would perform at the tenth RAF Display at Hendon on 13 July that year and it was an honour to be selected to represent your squadron, let alone the whole of the RAF fighter fraternity. Squadrons and pilots taking part were:

Squadron Number	Team Members	Aeroplane Flown
1	Fg Offs T. B. Byrne and P. F. Laxton	Siskin IIIA
3	Fg Offs E. S. Finch and J. E. Jorgensen	Gamecock
17	Fg Off P. M. Watt and Sgt Burch	Siskin IIIA
19	Fg Off J. W. Bayes and Sgt Parsons	Siskin IIIA

23	Fg Offs C. H. Jones and H. A. Purvis	Gamecock
25	Fg Off J. A. Ford and Sgt Bicknell	Grebe
29	Fg Off J. Clarke and Sgt Morton	Siskin IIIA
32	Flt Lt J. N. Boothman and Fg Off W. Charnock	Siskin IIIA
41	Flt Lt F. K. Damant and Fg Off T. J. Arbuthnot	Siskin IIIA
43	Fg Off L. W. Howard and Plt Off H. H. Leech	Siskin IIIA
56	Fg Offs L. R. Stokes and R. K. Hamblin	Siskin IIIA
111	Fg Off J. W. Gillan and Plt Off F. Whittle	Siskin IIIA

The Treble-One pilots are a pair who went on to great things in later years. John Woodburn Gillan is a name that will always be associated with the Hawker Hurricane and he will appear in a later chapter, while Frank Whittle became a household name and was immortalised as the inventor of the jet engine.

The competition required each pair of pilots to carry out a 10-minute programme divided into 7 minutes of set evolutions identical for all pairings, followed immediately by 3 minutes of voluntary evolutions that must include an inverted sequence. The 7-minute set routine was as follows and the components could be flown in any order.

1. Loop by No.1 aeroplane flying towards the judges and a simultaneous loop by No.2 aeroplane at an angle of 60° from No.1's track.
2. No.1 into a zoom followed by a flick loop, flying away from the judges and the same by No.2 on a directly opposite track to the previous evolution.
3. A slow roll by No.1 while flying parallel to the judges and a slow roll by No.2 flying at right angles to No.1's track and away from the judges.
4. An upward roll flown in the same direction as the slow roll.
5. Stall turn after a zoom in the same direction as the loop.

6. Half-roll off top of loop in same direction as the zoom, followed by the flick loop.
7. Half-roll followed by a loop in the same direction as the slow roll.

Points, totalling 100, were awarded: 10 for the quality and accuracy of each of the 7-set evolutions and 30 for the voluntary section. Deductions would be made if evolutions were flown so that the judges could not see them comfortably while sitting as pseudo-spectators at the Hendon Pageant. The aeroplanes were to be equipped as for completely standard squadron use.

According to *Flight* magazine, the performance of the winning pair, Fg Offs Jones and Purvis from 23 Squadron, was outstanding with a smoothness, precision and symmetry which were almost perfect. The reporter recalled seeing this same pair – together with Flt Lt Calvey of whom we heard earlier – giving a good show in vile weather at Hooton Aerodrome air meeting on 24 September 1927.

Despite the event being populated by the best aerobatic pilots in the RAF, the day was marred by an accident to one of the competing pilots: Fg Off John Walden Bayes. He crashed after coming out of a very low roll and was killed. After a pause, the competition continued 'in accordance with RAF traditions'.'

Jones and Purvis's big day at the RAF Hendon Pageant came on 13 July 1929. They were event No.2 in the afternoon programme. Taking off together in their Gloster Gamecocks they did several simultaneous stunts, then separated. Flying to opposite ends of the aerodrome, they turned and dived towards each other, meeting, passing and zooming upwards to complete a loop, a roll, and the rest, perfectly synchronised. This was repeated over and over, with the two aircraft always seeming to meet at the same spot; each a reflection of the other. They were a huge success and a credit to the squadron and the RAF. After all the excitement of the Pageant of course it was back to routine squadron life and in August, 23 Squadron was detached to RAF Sutton Bridge for its two weeks' annual gunnery practice. Commanding the unit at this time was Sqn Ldr Arthur Gordon Jones-Williams OBE, MC*, a First World War ace with eleven aerial victories but a pilot most famous for his non-stop distance record attempt from Cranwell to Bangalore in April 1929 in the Fairey Long-range Monoplane.

In the midday sun of 14 August 1929, Sutton Bridge camp seemed eerily quiet, with little outward sign that a tragedy had just occurred. A flag outside the adjutant's hut fluttered sadly at half-mast. Clutching a sheaf of papers and attended by three grim-faced officers, an Air Ministry crash investigator hurried purposefully past hangars where mechanics worked quietly upon their aeroplanes. Nearby, a cluster of pilots discussed gunnery scores just received from the ammunition store. Crossing the camp perimeter, the little group moved on into an adjoining arable field. Here lay a twisted heap of charred metal, the object of their attention, an ugly scar among a broad expanse of green carrot tops. It was all that remained of J7914, the single-seat Gloster Gamecock fighter in which Fg Off Jones had taken off at 9.20 that morning.

In addition to being among the best aerobatic pilots in the RAF, he and Fg Off Purvis, were both considered 'crack shots' who had been briefed to fly to the firing range on the desolate marshes at Gedney Drove End. Both aeroplanes were loaded with 200 rounds of ammunition with which to fire at ground targets.

Purvis took off first. Then his friend opened the throttle of J7914 and followed in his wake. Jones had climbed just 40 feet in the air when he banked his machine steeply. Sgt James Hickling, a pilot with 111 Squadron, also at the camp, witnessed what happened next.

At 09.20 I was standing on the 'drome, not more than 200 yards from the crash, when the Gamecock took off. It rose quite normally but soon after crossing the airfield boundary, turned steeply to the right and the nose dropped. In an instant the aeroplane dived into the ground with its engine full on and burst into flames.

Later, when asked by the Coroner for an opinion as to the cause of the accident, Sgt Hickling replied, 'I should say it was through turning too soon after leaving the ground. He should not have tried to turn at all at that height.' Another eyewitness referred to the aeroplane being in 'a sixty-degree turn', before the crash. Exploding ammunition, intense heat and flames prevented would-be rescuers from approaching the stricken pilot but it was soon clear to all that he was beyond help.

Stunned by what he had seen, Fg Off Purvis circled the scene twice before landing to have his worst fears confirmed. It was now that discipline and camaraderie prevailed. Purvis was ordered to carry on with his gunnery practice but first, as a mark of respect, he and other pilots of 23 Squadron flew over the crash site. Then, alone, Fg Off Purvis flew off to the range, fired his 200 rounds and came away to find he had made the highest score of any pilot in 23 or 111, since both squadrons arrived at the camp. The newspaper reporter chatted to some of the other pilots, remarking that they did not seem very upset. One replied:

'Some people would say Purvis must be a callous sort of bloke but I should say he was a man, behaving as a man would. What is the good of wearing your heart on your sleeve? A man has his feelings but he does not show them to the world. That is what I call real nerve.' Another agreed: 'What's the good of being upset,' he said, 'it's fate. If you were born to die flying, you won't get hung; and if you were born to be hung, you won't die flying. That's all there is to it! I saw old Jones pulled out of that kite and I didn't like it, but there you are.

Much discussion ensued at the inquest, held in sombre mood in the pilots briefing room. The verdict of accidental death was inevitable and thus did the official curtain fall on the all-too-short life of Fg Off Charles Jones.

And what do we know about Fg Off Purvis? Born in 1905 Harry Alexander Purvis, a former Cranwell cadet, was posted from RAF fighters to train RN pilots for the Fleet Air Arm. In 1932 he was posted again to the Torpedo Development Flight at Gosport, then, in 1936, to the Royal Aircraft Establishment at Farnborough to undertake test flying duties. In the Second World War he commanded a Hudson squadron at RAF Leuchars and after evaluating American aircraft over in the USA, he returned to take command of the Performance Testing Squadron at Aeroplane & Armament Experimental Establishment (A&AEE) Boscombe Down until the end of the war. Retiring from the RAF after the war, he became a civilian test pilot at Boscombe Down, working on many of the famous airliners of the 1940s and '50s. He died in 1967 having been awarded the DFC and AFC*.

There was a lull in the Sutton Bridge programme when the next two squadrons, 56 and 32, which had arrived on 26 August, flew out on 5 September. This was to allow permanent staff officers an opportunity to attend the Schneider Trophy Competition, held over the Solent on 6th and 7th. No doubt they much enjoyed their well-earned break, rejoicing in a second successive win for Great Britain.

The gunnery year drew to a close with the arrival of 3 Squadron on 16 September with nine of its new mounts, the Bristol Bulldog, a beautiful sight that would grace the sky around The Wash for many years to come. 3 Squadron stayed until 25 September when competitors began to assemble at Sutton Bridge for the annual Brooke-Popham Air Firing Trophy competition, which took place on the 26th and 27th. After two days of intensive competition, Fg Off Paul Gardner Thomson of 56 Squadron was declared the winner with a score of 88 per cent. All that remained now was for the events of the year to be analysed so that the lessons learned could be incorporated into next year's programme. It was considered that the trial use of airborne sleeve-targets by two pilots from each squadron had been a success and would be expanded upon. Confirmation of the success of the camp and range facility was evident from the visit in October 1929 of Sqn Ldr P. Huskinson, an Air Ministry staff officer, to select suitable adjacent fields for the expansion of the aerodrome. In addition to the camp facilities it was also considered vital to enlarge the range too.

Underpinning these expansion plans were reasons of simple logistics. New aeroplane types, such as the Bulldog and soon the Hawker Fury, would be entering service and fighter squadrons were anxious to reach proficiency as quickly as possible. Even more units, for example, Fleet Air Arm Fighter Flights and coastal defence squadrons such as the Fairey IIIs of 35 Squadron at Bircham Newton, were bidding for time on the range. Coupled with this pressure was the constraint placed upon the time available for operations by the weather – bear in mind aeroplanes in those days did not have all-weather capability and The Wash has a reputation for its unpredictable mists.

In consequence, more targets were needed to allow more aeroplanes to use the range simultaneously. There was a need to disperse the targets over a larger area of the marsh to avoid increasing the danger to pilots. From the experiments with sleeve targets in 1928 and 1929, it seemed that air-to-ground targets would increasingly be supplemented by air-to-air, towed targets and this will be seen to be the case in subsequent years. All in all, 1929 can be considered a watershed in the life of Sutton Bridge camp and the Holbeach range in terms of expansion. As the 1930s unrolled and dark clouds of war loomed, this camp would play a vital role in training fighter pilots and air gunners in their science. The soundness of Trenchard's system, the methods evolved at the range and the beneficial effects of regular practice would be seen in the quality of pilots who had to bear the initial brunt of air fighting in France and Britain in 1940. The quality of men and aeroplanes is usually undoubted but can the same be said of aeroplane armament?

Among the local villagers there has always been a tale of 'the man who flew under the bridge' and during the research for this book, the truth of this piece of folklore emerged.

One of twins serving in the RAF, Flight Lieutenant Richard Atcherley – known throughout the service as 'Batchy' – was already revered by many of his contemporaries as an outstanding aerobatic pilot. His name arose as a likely candidate for the dubious honour of flying beneath the bridge, during conversations the author had with former Aircraftman Jack Flint, stationed at Sutton Bridge camp during the period in question, and until his death, one of the best-known former residents in the village, having retired there from the RAF in 1945. Jack, while admitting he did not witness the incident personally, was most emphatic in his claim:

> Richard Atcherley of 23 Squadron flew under the Bridge in 1930. Batchy was returning from the gunnery range at Holbeach Marsh and later claimed he wanted to pull up [he would have to be flying well below the bank top!!] but had got too close to do so. He was not court-martialled but I remember hearing that he was hauled before the station commander and given a right rocket for it.

Richard Atcherley certainly appears to have all the right credentials for pulling off such a stunt. Winner of many aerobatic competitions; a member of the 1929 RAF Schneider Trophy team – and holder of the fastest lap time (although disqualified) – he constantly pulled at the reins of authority. In his autobiography, no less a person than the C-in-C Fighter Command, Air Marshal Sholto Douglas spoke thus of Richard Atcherley:

> I was well aware that one of my responsibilities ... was to keep a tight rein on the natural exuberance of my fighter pilots. Of all of them, the most colourful were the Atcherley brothers. These twins were exceptionally fine pilots and had become well known during the 1930s for their astonishing feats in aerobatics; but their force of character, or the ways in which they expressed it, was always getting them into scrapes which on several occasions resulted in first-rate rows and losses of seniority. Dick Atcherley [Batchy] was perhaps the slightly better pilot of the two ... eventually both reached Air rank. After the war David disappeared on a jet fighter flight over the Mediterranean. Richard went on to become Air Marshal with a knighthood before retiring as C-in-C Flying Training Command.

Such was Atcherley's reputation that even the local newspaper, the *Spalding Guardian*, was moved to report on 12 July 1930:

> Sutton Bridge Local Notes; RAF; Flt Lt Atcherley, winner of the King's Cup in 1929 and also a member of the Schneider Trophy Team last year, is now at Sutton Bridge with the 23rd Squadron. It is likely that aero-acrobatics will be frequent at Sutton Bridge until the end of the month.

The official diary of 23 Squadron records that Richard Atcherley rejoined the squadron on 9 December 1929, and went with the squadron to Sutton Bridge for summer practice camp in July 1930.

Returning now to our original theme of flying under the bridge; versions of this tale abound among Sutton Bridge residents who were children back in the 1930s. No official evidence – probably for the sake of 'maintaining good order and discipline' – of the escapade has yet come to light but there are several Sutton Bridge residents, with whom the author has corresponded, who claim to have witnessed it while playing as children on the river bank near the bridge. Daredevil exploits are the stuff by which reputations are made and perpetuated. As to whether the feat could be done at all depends, of course, on whether certain measurements would allow it in the first place. The Gloster Gamecock aeroplane operated by 23 Squadron in Atcherley's day had a wingspan of 30 feet and a height from tyre-tread to propeller-tip of 12 feet. With a space beneath the main bridge span at low tide estimated as 50 feet wide and 20 feet vertically, the probability of success by any candidate who held his nerve has to be pretty high – but it was certainly not for the faint-hearted! Bravado is all very well, but what about opportunity? Fenland rivers, particularly the Nene, are noted for their high, steeply banked outfalls, which at low tide create ruler-straight, deep, wide canyons. How tempting it must have been for a budding fighter tyro to dice as low as he dare, skimming the turgid water until that bridge and the close presence of 'officialdom' forced him to pull up and over.

The naturalist Peter Scott, a man gifted with an artist's eye for detail, provides an eyewitness account of an incident in 1936, which by its nature offers an interesting perspective on the issue of temptation. For a number of years during the 1930s, Peter lived in the East Lighthouse, one of a pair of mock-lighthouse dwellings set opposite each other atop the Nene banks, 3 miles down-river from the aerodrome.

Acting Plt Off John William Henry Radice, a distant relative of the present-day Labour peer, Baron (Giles) Radice, was 22 years of age and had been a member of 111 Squadron for just two months. Since joining the RAF he had accumulated 148 flying hours. On 5 May 1936 Plt Off Radice was detailed by his squadron commander, Sqn Ldr G. Vivian Howard DFC, to fly a weather test over Holbeach range. Just before noon that day he took off from Sutton Bridge in Bristol Bulldog K1683 but failed to return to the airfield. What happened to him is the subject of two differing stories – an official and an unofficial version. The official version runs thus:

> This pilot was returning from a weather test flight to ascertain the height of clouds over Holbeach range. It is thought he may have stalled in cloud at about 300 feet, leaving the cloud in a dive. The neutral colour of the river may also have caused him to think he was still in cloud. He failed to level out before hitting the water with great force. The aeroplane sank and was not recovered until next day, with the pilot still strapped inside. The only eyewitness was Mr Peter Scott, the naturalist, who was outside his lighthouse-home by the river at the time.

Fifty years later and just a few years before his death, that gentleman, now Sir Peter Scott, sent the author his recollections of that day. 'I remember this accident very clearly indeed,' he wrote.

> There was a target bombing range lying just to the west of the mouth of the River Nene. Aircraft coming back from practice bombing or machine-gunning would frequently drop down over the river in between the straight banks at low tide and fly back up to RAF Sutton Bridge below the level of the banks on each side. This was a fairly common practice and on the day in question I happened to be standing outside my lighthouse door, looking down-river and saw this aircraft low over the water. I glanced down for a moment and when I looked up again the aircraft was not there. We took a boat down to the spot and hoped that the pilot might be found alive but a floating object seen earlier turned out to be one of the wheels, which had been torn off and was bobbing in the waves. I do not recall any particularly low cloud on that day and for a significant period before the accident the aircraft was flying at wave-top height. The pilot must have gone just a little bit too low, hit a big wave and that was the end.

Although memory can play tricks, particularly after many years have elapsed, this eyewitness would undoubtedly be considered reliable. Sir Peter's version differs significantly in two ways. First, in the way he refers to the aeroplane flying at wave-top height 'for a significant period'. The second way is how he refers to aircraft 'frequently dropping down over the river in between the straight banks at low tide and flying back up [river] to Sutton Bridge'.

Does Peter Scott's statement lend weight to that legend relating to flying beneath the Bridge? If such an eyewitness as this, with his reputation for a keen eye and attention to detail, living for several years in a house perched on the riverbank itself saw the practice of flying between those high banks as a regular occurrence – then might not one intrepid pilot, braver or more foolhardy than the rest, take the next step? Well, whichever is the accurate version, Acting Plt Off Radice's aeroplane sank into the mud where the Lutton Leam outfall joins the main river at Guy's Head, a few hundred yards from the two dwellings. Twenty hours elapsed before a diver working from a tugboat was able to release and raise the wreckage, allowing the body to be recovered.

So, are the 'under the bridge' stories just a line-shoot, or did someone really pit his skill and nerve against that tempting structure? Finally, after much probing, in 1992 an eyewitness to this hair-raising event, still living in the village, was tracked down. Brought up in Custom House Street close by the river, Mrs Muriel Morley looked back with enthusiasm to the day in 1930 when, aged 15, she remembered clearly watching an aeroplane fly under the bridge.

[I was] standing with my friends on the west bank, at the top of Lime Street, I saw this aeroplane go by below our level. To my astonishment it went right under the bridge, tilting sideways a bit as it passed under. I thought he must have been a crazy man and everyone said afterwards that he was a real daredevil pilot.

Muriel went on further to say that her friend Dorothy Peace (née Oldham) and two other friends all watched in amazement as the aeroplane flew under the bridge.

Cyril Atkinson, another Sutton Bridge resident, said he, too, remembered seeing the incident as a young lad and he was on the opposite side of the bridge to Muriel.

I was delivering newspapers and was standing on the bank top on the west side of the bridge. Across the river, a small ship was moored at Travis & Arnold's wharf and timber was being unloaded from it. One of the ship's mooring ropes ran low across the river to a metal post on the opposite bank to keep it stable. I saw a Gamecock come under the bridge and it only just missed hitting that mooring rope!

Of course, it will never be admitted officially that Richard Atcherley performed this feat but it seems indisputable that it was actually done. 23 Squadron, with Richard Atcherley in attendance, was indeed at Sutton Bridge between 8 July and 20 July 1930. Is it not curious then to discover that on 8 October – within three months of the alleged offence – Flt Lt Atcherley, the foremost single-seat fighter pilot of his day, an aerobatic wizard and a pilot to whom speed and daring were the very spice of life, was posted to 14 Squadron in Amman in the stifling heat of the Trans-Jordanian desert, to fly the two-seat Fairey IIIF reconnaissance bomber? The incident at Sutton Bridge may have been hushed up but was this a punishment posting to put a brake on this young hot-head?

Turning back to more routine matters, the arrival of the new decade found the majority of permanent staff reassembled at Sutton Bridge on 10 March 1930, under the command of Wg Cdr Dermott Lang Allen AFC. Wg Cdr Allen's flying career went back to the very early days of the RFC; borne out by his flying certificate being No.31 and he had been among the first pilots to fly and fight in the air over France in 1914/15. His AFC was awarded for the key role he played in establishing a very effective flying training scheme in Canada during the First World War.

The remainder of March was spent preparing both the camp and the range for the coming training season. Most onerous of these tasks was that of putting canvas onto the four Bessonneau hangar frames, left bare over the previous winter months. Much grumbling was inevitable as all airmen were obliged to work on Saturday afternoons and Sundays to complete the work in time for the 1 April opening date.

Two Army Co-operation squadrons, 4 and 13, were first to use the camp facilities. Between 1 April and 31 October, they were again followed by most of the squadrons from Fighting Area. Representative of these was 23 Squadron whose CO, Sqn Ldr Henry Winslow Woollett DSO MC*, a First World War RFC veteran with thirty-five air victories to his name, brought the squadron from Kenley in July. For the second year running, it would return to Kenley with fewer aeroplanes than it took to Sutton Bridge.

Line of approach to the ground targets was from the landward side of the sea bank and those aeroplanes waiting their turn to fire manoeuvred in the vicinity of the range between the village and the sea bank.

Although aeroplanes wheeling above land-workers' heads had become an everyday occurrence, the planes still provided a welcome diversion from toiling among the thousands of acres bordering Holbeach range. Hoeing sugar beet was a tedious job at the best of times but on 16 July the sight and sound of Fg Off Peter Bagwell Rogers' silver Gamecock, J7894, caught the eye as it fell into a left-hand spin, flashing in the sunlight, twisting in its death throes. Its brief plunge from 400 feet ended abruptly in George Caudwell's beet field where, in the words of young Arthur Edgley from Lutton: 'It looked just like an enormous heap of crumpled silver paper.' Rescuers uncovered Rogers to find him dead but with his seat straps unfastened, leading them to believe he had tried in vain to bale out.

The accident occurred soon after 5.00 pm as Rogers was circling while the targets were patched. It was during this interval that the aeroplane seemed to fall into a spin and crash in plain view of an RAF officer driving along the road and two or three civilians nearby.

Mr G. F. Pearl described to a reporter what he saw:

> I was cycling from my home in Dawsmere Bank to my work in a seed field after having my tea. As near as I can say, it was about 5.20 pm on Tuesday afternoon and I was coming to the corner of the field where the aeroplane crashed. When I first saw the machine, it was over Caudwell's field on the other side of the road. It came towards the hedge and I thought it was going to hit it. It was just above me and I was so startled that I jumped off my bike. It was practically as low as the hedge. Then it shot up over the road just above me and nose-dived into the beet field. There was a tremendous crash which seemed to shake the ground and a cloud of smoke went up and pieces of aeroplane were scattered about. I dashed across the field just as an airman appeared from a motor car. The pilot lay at the back of one of the wings and was terribly injured. I stayed at the machine at the request of the airman from the car, while he went for assistance. An ambulance from the range arrived in a few minutes.

Flt Lt Victor Croombe from 23 Squadron gave evidence of identification at the inquest held later, on Sutton Bridge camp. In addition, he explained that he was driving the car mentioned above, from the range back to the camp when he saw a Gamecock in a spin. It did about two or three turns to the left in a spin and hit the ground. He went to the crash to see what could be done but although he found the pilot on the ground, there was no sign of a pulse and he presumed the man was dead. The site was about half a mile from the range. The pilot had undone his seat harness but it would have been difficult to exit the aircraft due to the force of the spin and in any case, he was too low for the parachute to fully deploy. There was no clear evidence of a reason for the spin and subsequent crash; the coroner also said there appeared to be no negligence on the part of anyone and the jury returned a verdict of accidental death. This was the only major accident at the camp that year.

During the final week of the 1930 season, from 5 to 12 October, representative pilots from the fighter squadrons competed for the annual Air Firing Trophy, won that year by Sgt Ralph Cleland, who, since we last heard of him above, had been posted from 19 to 29 Squadron. Sgt Cleland's ability was duly rewarded when he was offered a permanent commission as a pilot officer with effect from 29 May 1931, while also remaining with 29 Squadron. He held many flying and staff posts, rising to the rank of Group Captain (Gp Capt), CBE, but sadly died of natural causes in 1948 while still serving in the RAF.

The competition heralded the closure of the camp and the permanent staff set about the job of removing canvas from the hangars yet again. Sutton Bridge then took on a desolate air as staff drifted back to their units and the camp was left in the care of Station Warden, Mr Pettit and another civilian assistant, Mr Barnshaw, who settled down for their long winter vigil.

According to the RAF Flying Training Manual, referred to earlier, among the qualities required of pilots and air gunners was: 'a considerable amount of practice in developing their judgement of distance in the air, so that they can manoeuvre close to the enemy without risk of collision.' Misjudging one's attack approach was indeed a very real hazard now that air-to-air targets featured strongly in the range training programme. Bristol Bulldogs were not a great deal faster than the fighters they replaced (+ 20 mph above Gamecocks and Siskins) but they were substantially heavier aeroplanes (+25% loaded). Because of this, extra care was needed when cavorting around at low level as they were not as responsive as their lighter predecessors. From time to time, therefore, during their earlier years, a few came to grief on The Wash range.

On 20 September 1932, for example, during the annual Brooke-Popham competition, Fg Off Bernard Nelson Matson, representing

19 Squadron, misjudged the approach speed of a target-towing Westland Wapiti and flew into the drogue. The latter was, of necessity, quite a sturdy affair and did substantial damage to the upper starboard wing of Bulldog K2160 forcing Matson to make a very hasty, but successful, landing on Durham's Farm close to the range. Matson remained in the RAF into the Second World War, rising to the rank of Group Captain. Sadly, while on active service in India, he succumbed to polio at the age of 35 and is buried in Delhi war cemetery.

29 Squadron was halfway through its annual air-firing practice when, on 6 June 1933, a similar mishap befell a South African-born pilot, Flt Sgt Jacobus Gustaaf Strauss. Diving from 2,000 feet towards a towed drogue, he 'over-cooked it' and in his efforts to swerve out of danger, hit the towing cable with the lower starboard wing. His Bulldog immediately fell into an uncontrollable spin but keeping a level head, Strauss baled out with just sufficient height to deploy his parachute safely. Landing heavily, he hurt his right foot but considered this a small price to pay for his life – bearing in mind his Bulldog lay completely wrecked just a short distance from where he came down. Strauss flew Mosquito night fighters with 29, 256 and 151 Squadrons during the Second World War and was killed in action with the latter on a bomber support operation on 11 February 1945. His Mosquito was badly damaged during a successful engagement with an Me 410 over Germany; his navigator baled out safely but Jacobus Strauss went down with the aircraft.

It was perhaps inevitable that the odds – or is it luck – would change against some unfortunate pilot. Flt Sgt Frank Baker, newly posted to 41 Squadron just a month earlier, was flying the first detail to Holbeach range at 8.15 am on 18 May 1934. The target drogue was being towed at 1,500 feet when he dived on it. Misjudging his dive sent Bulldog K2194 crashing into the steel-framed neck, severing the drogue completely from the towing cable. This time there was no escape from the resultant spin for Flt Sgt Baker and he perished in a plume of spray 4 miles offshore. A fast-rising tide hampered rescuers who had to wait 6 hours for the water to recede sufficiently for Baker's body to be recovered.

It is strange to relate that, apart from these three Bulldog incidents, there is no evidence of any further mishaps at Holbeach range involving collision with towed targets during the remainder of the decade. Maybe the difficulty simply arose as a transient situation marked by the arrival of this significantly heavier fighter coinciding with the introduction of the new practice of manoeuvring with towed targets.

Of all the many aeroplane types to use Holbeach range between the wars, the Bristol Bulldog features most frequently in accidents. This is no reflection on its record as a frontline aeroplane, however, as most of the incidents seem to fall into the category of pilot error rather than through some fundamental flaw in the design. In addition to the three accidents involving collision with towed targets mentioned earlier, Flt Lt H. A. Simmonds of Treble-One Squadron bent K2209 when he landed at Sutton Bridge on 10 January 1936. In common with many grass airfields, Sutton Bridge in wet weather could become a quagmire for the unwary pilot. On this occasion it might have been wiser to have sent out more than just one airman to guide a wingtip as Simmonds taxied in. One wheel sank into a soft patch while the aircraft was moving quite quickly and over it went in a somersault as the nose dug in. Flt Lt Simmonds clambered out unscathed but his aeroplane was severely damaged.

Treble-One returned to Sutton Bridge for annual firing practice in May 1936 and left, no doubt, more subdued than when it arrived. The squadron returned to Northolt with three Bulldogs and one pilot fewer than when it set out.

First to go, on 5 May, was K1683 in the fatal accident near the mouth of the River Nene that was described earlier. Just one day later, 6 May, K2208 of 111 Squadron was next to go. Plt Off Geoffrey Gardner Cornwall choked the engine after take-off, forcing him to make a hurried return to earth. On his way to the range it seems he opened the throttle a bit too quickly while climbing away from the airfield and the engine spluttered to a halt. To his credit Plt Off Cornwall got the nose down swiftly and landed straight ahead in a ploughed field. The aeroplane, however, ran headlong into a hedge, turned over and came to rest, completely wrecked by the side of the M&GN Railway line a few hundred yards beyond the airfield perimeter. On this occasion Plt Off Cornwall escaped injury but, just over a year later, his luck ran out, for he was killed in an accident, near Beaconsfield, South Bucks, Buckinghamshire, on 16 July 1937 while flying a Gloster Gauntlet.

A great deal of effort, over many decades, has been put into raising awareness, in the Air Force in particular, of the dangers of 'foreign object damage' (FOD). This is not a modern phenomenon by any means, since a little carelessness on the ground at any time may become lethal in the air. Such was the verdict of an enquiry into the loss of another 111 Squadron Bulldog, K1672, only a week later. On 14 May 1936, 20-year-old Acting Plt Off Mervyn Seymour Bocquet not only joined the ranks of the Caterpillar Club that day but could also count himself fortunate to be alive to do so. A small (19 mm long) badge in the form of a gold caterpillar was presented to RAF personnel who had baled out successfully using an Irvin parachute, made by the Irvin Air Chute Co. It was an unofficial award worn on civilian clothing.

Over the range on a firing exercise, the controls of K1672 jammed at an altitude of 1,500 feet. The aeroplane became uncontrollable and began to lose precious height rapidly. Plt Off Bocquet kept his head though and baled out with sufficient height remaining to land safely on the foreshore, watching his Bulldog hurtle into the sea nearby. Interviewed by a *Lincolnshire Free Press* reporter at the range hut, the slim fair-haired pilot said: 'All I can say is that I was damned glad to get out of it when the controls jammed.' Nearby his parachute was spread out to dry on a patch of grass; he had landed on the wet mud left by a receding tide. Later he helped the range staff to fold it up before returning to Sutton Bridge. Subsequent enquiry into the accident considered the controls probably locked due to a loose machine-gun cleaning-plug rolling about and fouling the base of the control column. Bocquet continued to fly with 111 Squadron and made the transition to modern fighters when the squadron was re-equipped with the Hawker Hurricane in January 1938. Sadly, however, Fg Off Bocquet's luck finally ran out when he died as the Hurricane he was flying, L1556, crashed 1 mile west of his base at RAF Northolt on 1 February 1938.

Thus ended one of the most eventful and costly two-week practice camps for any single squadron since Sutton Bridge opened. On the other hand, by the end of 1936, the prospect of war loomed larger with each new year. Not only would the pace of activity at the camp and the range move into top gear but the volume of mishaps that increased activity brought with it, would increase substantially up to the beginning of the Second World War.

Returning to the year 1931, 5 March saw the by now familiar sight of an advance party arriving at Sutton Bridge, followed on the 10th by the main body of staff, that year drawn from 2 Flying Training School (2 FTS), RAF Digby. Only the bare minimum of effort seems to have been spent that year by the station's official diarist. Hiding behind an illegible signature, his record of events occupies a mere sixteen lines of scrawling text on a single page of the Form 540. It appears that Wg Cdr Kenneth Caron Buss OBE (later AVM) was posted in as officer commanding for that season but even this event did not warrant a note from the diarist!

The demise of one of 4 (AC) Squadron's Armstrong Whitworth Atlases, J9540, which crashed on landing at the airfield on 9 April was considered sufficiently noteworthy. Flt Lt Davies, pilot, was unhurt although his unnamed passenger received slight injuries. More aerial tow-target gear was installed in the station flight Brisfits during April under the watchful eye of a certain Mr Ashworth from the Royal Aircraft Establishment (RAE). Fierce storms hit the district towards the end of April, causing damage to a hangar, requiring a week-long repair by MOD 'Works and Bricks' Department. Hangarage at this time was still of the 'portable' canvas-covered Bessonneau variety but later, in 1933, the first rigid hangar, an Hinaidi design, was erected by the Air Ministry's contractor En-Tout-Cas Company Limited of Syston near Leicester. This structure still exists at the time of writing and is believed to be the only surviving example of its type in Lincolnshire and possibly the UK.

Among the litany of accidents to equipment and personnel, an unusual item stands out, recorded thus:

> 30 April 1931. A horse, property of Mr H. C. Wright, wounded
> by shot from a Lewis gun near the range.

Over the next three months not a single entry described events at the station and, apart from a Bulldog of 54 Squadron force-landing at the range on 1 August 1931, seems to have been accident-free.

It has been noted elsewhere that 25 Squadron visited Sutton Bridge from 25 May to 12 June and that their representatives in the Brooke-Popham competition in September, Flt Lt Charles Ronald Hancock DFC (OBE 1941) and Fg Off Harry St George Burke, tied for 4th and 7th places respectively. Hancock had won his DFC flying operations on the north-west frontier of India in 1930. He rose to the rank of Wg Cdr as OC RAF Ballyhalbert, Northern Ireland, but died on a training flight in Spitfire AD457 which he had borrowed from 303 (Polish) Squadron and crashed on 29 December 1943.

Whilst 25 Squadron seemed pleased to record the competition event in their own ORB, beyond noting that the competitors arrived on 28 September and left on 30 September, the parsimonious Sutton Bridge diarist deigned not to record the eventual winner. Closing officially on 26 October, the clearing-up party departed on the 30th and the camp was again left silent and deserted.

Sutton Bridge station flight, the permanent (at least while the camp was open) flying unit employed to tow aerial targets over The Wash range, expanded rapidly from the venerable Bristol F2B Fighter of the 1929 to 1931 period. As mentioned earlier, that lone Brisfit of 1929 appears to have been augmented later, since at least three were in use by 1931.

The precise aircraft establishment for 3 Armament Training Camp, as it was known from 1932, is obscure but, following the Bristol Fighters, the principal towing types in use during the 1930s were Westland's Wapiti and Wallace, Fairey's IIIF and Gordon, with the Hawker Henley arriving just prior to the war. Judging by the amount of flying these tugs were required to perform, it is not surprising to find mishaps occasionally occurring in their ranks, in addition to those among the visiting units. In 1932, for example, Fairey IIIF, J9144, crashed at the range on 11 July, injuring the pilot. The next day a replacement Wapiti was flown up from Eastchurch but that, too, failed to reach its destination intact. Nearing The Wash, its pilot, Sgt Nunnerby, became lost in low cloud and mist. Spotting what he thought was a suitable grass field he decided to land to establish his whereabouts. Unfortunately, the 'grass' turned out to be a field of barley, the stems of which clogged the propeller and undercarriage to such an extent that the Wapiti turned somersault. Both Nunnerby and his observer, Corporal Dobson, pinned beneath the wreckage, were injured by the impact and ended up in King's Lynn hospital.

3

Black Clouds

In contrast to 1931, 1932's Form 540 positively exudes activity and in particular a resurgence of interest from the brass-hats, the latter being evidenced by a procession of VIPs visiting the camp that year. Flt Lt Connelly brought in the advance party on 3 March, which soon had the transportable wireless station set up in time for the arrival of the main party, whose staff was drawn from a variety of units. Station Commander, the newly promoted Wg Cdr William Sowrey, arrived a day later, bringing 3 ATC under the control of the Air Armament School (AAS) with its HQ located at RAF Eastchurch.

Under the watchful eye of Fg Off Hooper, the range party began their own task of erecting targets out on Holbeach Marsh and 16 March saw two Fairey IIIFs fly in to Sutton Bridge, bringing Fg Off's Hales and Hyland to assist with range duties.

The procession of VIPs included three visits by Sqn Ldr Ivens from Eastchurch, Sqn Ldr MacKenzie from HQ Fighting Area, Air Commodore Henry Le Marchant Brock CB DSO, AOC 22 Group; Brigadier Archibald Wavell (later Field Marshal, Earl Wavell) and several visits each by Air Marshal Sir John Higgins KCB KBE DSO AFC, Air Member for Supply & Research; Major General Jackson; Air Commodores Bowen, Masterson and Gossage; Gp Capt Tedder; a group of Danish air officers... And so the list went on. The Station Warrant Officer must have had a field day for hardly a month seemed to pass without VIP visits of some sort, a pattern that continued for many years. It had taken a long time – ten years – but these visits were a visible sign of the changing mood among the service higher echelons in general. War was coming and Sutton Bridge was a vital cog in the machinery of war.

As far as the real business of the camp was concerned, first to fly in on 26 March was Sqn Ldr Sturley Philip Simpson MC with the brand-new Hawker Audaxes of 4 (AC) Squadron; they remained until 29 April. The next to arrive were the shiny new Hawker Furies of 1 Squadron and the Bulldogs of 3 Squadron

Deliberations by the top brass seemed to bring about a short experiment to lengthen the range's opening hours. Peacetime working hours of the RAF were traditionally Monday to Friday plus Saturday mornings but on two weekends, 7/8 May and 14/15th, the range was kept open from 7.00 am to 6.00 pm on both Saturday and Sunday. There is no sign of longer hours occurring again that year and setting a precedent for present-day objectors, it may be due to the local population, and fishermen in particular, voicing disapproval. On several occasions the diary notes visits by senior officers and meetings with Boston fishermen, local community representatives, as well as wildlife and countryside protection groups.

The departure of 1 and 3 Squadrons was on 21 May, this pair being replaced by Bulldogs of 19 and Siskins of 29 Squadrons. During their first week, 29 Squadron had a spot of bother with its gun synchronising gear. Reports of bullets hitting propellers filtered back to the Air Ministry, two of whose inspectors hurried north to investigate the cause. No explanation was recorded in the station diary and although the reason for the trouble remains a mystery, both squadrons departed on 11 June at the end of their allotted time. In his biography, Douglas Bader recalled a narrow escape when he, too, shot off part of his propeller over Holbeach range during summer camp with 23 Squadron in 1931. A couple of days later, 23 Squadron (minus its 'A' Flight which is believed to have been detached for duty at the Hendon Pageant) and 56 Squadron flew in to Sutton Bridge. The latter is actually written in the diary as '54', the error coming to light through closer examination of an unusual incident noted on 16 June.

As mentioned earlier, the River Nene flows close to the airfield, the camp entrance perimeter, for example, being separated from it only by the huge bank surmounted by a tarmac road. Ruler-straight for mile after mile, the banks at this point have broad, gently sloping grassy tops that suddenly drop away to an extremely deep-cut channel. It was on this day that a pilot from 56 Squadron, Sgt Leslie Stephen Holman, became a local hero by helping to save a child from drowning in that fast-flowing tide. Reported by the *Spalding Guardian*, the story went as follows:

Little Owen Burton [age 11] fell into the river while playing on the airfield-side bank, near the swing bridge. Shouts for help brought railway porter Mr J. R. Harper running from the nearby station. Although in poor health and practically exhausted by his run from the station, Harper plunged into the river and brought the boy to the surface. A strong current was running though and had not Sgt Holman also dived fully clothed into the river and gone to Mr Harper's aid, in all probability both he and the boy would have perished. Good fortune prevailed, however, and the boy was brought out unconscious but alive.

There was a happy sequel to this incident when, on 27 August 1932, *The Times* announced that the Royal Humane Society had awarded its Testimonial on Vellum to both Sgt Holman and Mr Harper (of Lime Street, Sutton Bridge) for the act of saving Owen Burton from drowning. Sgt Holman eventually reached the rank of Wing Commander with an AFC.

56 Squadron left Sutton Bridge for its base at North Weald on 1 July followed the next day by 25. With its sleek Fury Is, 25 Squadron had the camp to itself until replaced by 17 Squadron on 16 July, which itself was joined shortly after by 'A' Flight of 23 Squadron on 23 July. Then came 41, 111, 32 and 54 Squadrons in turn throughout the summer, the last-mentioned leaving Sutton Bridge on 9 September. Of these units, only 25 Squadron suffered one minor landing accident, that incident occurring on 11 July.

Extending the Holbeach Marsh range boundaries brought the opening for business of No.2 air firing range on 25 July 1932. This additional facility also heralded the arrival of Fleet Air Arm (FAA) aircraft to use the range simultaneously with the RAF. First to arrive were 402 and 407 Flights FAA (both Fairey Flycatcher), using the camp at the same time as 43 Squadron RAF. What a feast of fighters to be seen over The Wash in those days!

On 21 September 1932, while 402 flew north to join HMS *Courageous* at Invergordon, 407 Flight left for RAF Netheravon. These two were replaced by 404 Flight coming in from Netheravon, and 401 Flight direct from HMS *Furious*.

Tragedy struck in the afternoon of 26 September.

One of 401 Flight's Fairey Flycatcher aeroplanes, N9929, loaded with four 20 lb Cooper bombs swooped repeatedly over the bombing targets. A key factor in this accident – and other similar incidents – was that the four 20 lb Cooper bombs were loaded onto what were known as 'comb' carriers attached to the bottom of the fuselage, just behind the undercarriage supports. The undercarriage wheels themselves were joined by an axle. The angle of the dive during which a bomb was released also played a significant part in the incident.

Three times Lt Henry Maitland King RN released a single bomb at the white circle floating below. He was seen to circle twice more but without releasing the remaining bomb. As the silver biplane dived for a third time there was a flash followed a second later by the dull, flat report of an explosion. Engulfed by flames the stricken Flycatcher fell vertically onto the wild marshland below, burying itself in the oozing mud. Running and stumbling 500 yards across the mudflats, the NCO in charge of the range reached the wreckage only to be held at bay by intense flames. It took 20 minutes for the blaze to subside, too late to be of any help to the poor pilot. Returning a verdict of accidental death, the Coroner's jury brought this sad episode to a close in sombre mood at an inquest held in Sutton Bridge camp education hut next evening. In the best tradition of the service, Lt King's body, escorted by his friend Lt Garnett RN, was conveyed by rail to his home in Llanfairfechan for burial.

The art of dive-bombing at this time was mainly pursued by the RAF-controlled Fleet Air Arm – although the Army Co-operation squadrons also indulged from time to time – and it was the Fairey Flycatcher that was most suited to this role. Initially, practice attacks against static targets with four small bombs were usually carried out by pulling up the nose of the Flycatcher and stalling the aircraft at about 2,500 feet altitude near the target. The aircraft then dropped vertically and the pilot lined up on his aiming point and released one bomb at a time. This procedure, however, was found not particularly accurate and brought with it an occasional problem when the bomb struck the undercarriage on its way down! Dive-bombing procedure was therefore modified to a profile of a very steep dive from 2,000 feet, lining up the aiming point then at 150 feet, pulling sharply out of the dive and releasing one, or more, bomb(s). Despite this change, which was found to be more accurate, there were still incidents when a bomb hit the aircraft undercarriage.

It appears that the official Air Ministry Court of Inquiry's view of Lt King's incident at Holbeach range was that the mid-air explosion that wrecked King's Flycatcher was due to the detonation of the last bomb as it hit the undercarriage structure, due to the steepness of Lt King's angle of dive affecting its trajectory after release. As a result of the Sutton Bridge accident, at the end of 1932 the RAF put a temporary halt on dive-bombing training until a safer procedure and better bomb-mounting equipment could be found. As far as the Flycatcher was concerned, it was all about the unsatisfactory position of the bomb racks under the centre-section of the lower wing and the bomb trajectory clearances produced by certain angles of dive. It was not long, however, before bomb racks were positioned further outboard, beneath the middle sections of the Flycatcher's lower wings. New regulations were introduced that made use of shallower diving angles – but Lt Henry King's death was the sad watershed for these changes. The Flycatcher would not remain long in service after this incident as units of the FAA began to be re-equipped with the Hawker Nimrod, a naval version of the land-based Hawker Fury.

With the air firing season drawing to a close, 3 October saw an experimental demonstration of a 'flag' towed target, arranged by the station flight for the benefit of Gp Capts Tedder (OC AAS Eastchurch), Bradley and Baldwin with Mr Howarth, a civilian from the Royal Aircraft Establishment Farnborough, in attendance. 401 and 404 Flights returned to their bases that week and 25 Squadron flew in to complete its period of practice, having been interrupted in July by its participation in the RAF Pageant at Hendon. When it departed on 12 October this signalled the arrival of pilots for the two-day annual Brooke-Popham Trophy competition, won that year by Sgt Jack Williams of 3 Squadron. Promoted to Flt Sgt, Williams was awarded an AFM in January 1938 and as a Warrant Officer he was awarded an AFC in 1942 while serving at the Central Flying School. As usual, the competition drew the 1932 season to a close. Post season conferences, reviewing events at the range, were held at AAS HQ Eastchurch at the end of the month and the camp officially closed down with the departure of Wg Cdr William Sowrey on 14 November. On 3 March 1933 he was back at Sutton Bridge in command for a new firing season.

It is difficult to quantify the amount of .303 ammunition fired annually during the biplane era of the inter-war period at the Holbeach range but it could easily have been half a million rounds.

If, for example, fifteen squadrons attended during the year; each bringing twelve aeroplanes, these 180 pilots could have fired 200 rounds per sortie, thus they would consume 36,000 rounds. It is not unreasonable to assume each pilot might complete ten sorties during his two-week camp. If this were the case, then that alone would produce an overall expenditure of nearly 400,000 rounds for a season. Allowing for the annual firing competition and a margin of error it is reasonable to suggest that well over half-a-million rounds would need to be stocked at the camp, all of which – at least according to ORB entries for 1933 – was brought in by railway to the village station. Bearing in mind the range also catered for bombing, villagers might have been quite alarmed had they been aware of the scale of explosive ordnance moving through their back yard. The annual ordnance quota usually arrived with the main party, which in 1933 occurred on 3 March. The officers' and airmen's messes were opened up, telephones laid on to camp and range and the wireless station set up again as 3 ATC blossomed into life like a new plant in the fenland springtime. Three Fairey Gordon target towing aircraft were flown in from AAS Eastchurch to form the station flight under the command of Flt Lt Clark and notices circulating in the district and in local newspapers announced the imminent opening of the range.

In the months from 27 March 1933, 2 (AC) Squadron led a procession of 32, 54, 29, 41, 56, 17 (after the Hendon Pageant) and 111 Squadrons; 800 Flight FAA (HMS *Courageous*), 801 (HMS *Furious*) followed by 3, 25, 1, 43, and 19 Squadrons. On 11 September the camp even managed to squeeze in a four-day visit by four Bulldogs from the Air Armament School (AAS) for air firing practice (these were probably K1638, K1648, K1669 and K1670).

As an example of the RAF's Fleet Air Arm participation at Sutton Bridge, it is known from the log book of Flt Lt John Alexander Thomson Ryde that 801 Squadron (OC: Sqn Ldr Charles E. W. Foster) disembarked from HMS *Furious* on 20 July 1933 for a week at the airfield. 801 Squadron was only formed in April that year by raising 401 (Fleet Fighter) Flight to squadron status and Flt Lt Ryde was attached to the squadron for a just less than a year from his experimental-flying post at RAE Farnborough, to which he subsequently returned. Ryde flew Hawker Nimrod K2827 on a 90-minute trip from HMS *Furious* to Sutton Bridge Armament Practice camp on 30 July 1933. He stayed there until 28 July when he flew his Nimrod to RAF Netheravon, where the squadron remained until 7 September before re-embarking aboard *Furious*. While at Sutton Bridge Flt Lt Ryde made one 20-minute sortie to fire at the ground targets then, over the next five days, he made a total of thirteen sorties of between 20 and 60 minutes duration each to fire at towed targets. In his final couple of days, he logged three practice bombing sorties of 25 minutes each, then it was off to Netheravon having completed all his armament practice in K2827. 111 squadron flew in to Sutton Bridge on 10 July for its two-week summer camp, together with 800 Squadron FAA which stayed until 19 July. 801 arrived the next day. When 801 left so, too, did 111 Squadron, to be replaced by 3 and 25 Squadrons for their two-week stay – and so on throughout that summer.

Activity at Sutton Bridge was now subject to almost continuous direct interest by the top brass, led by the Under-Secretary of State for Air, Sir Philip Sassoon, who made two visits and the AOC-in-C ADGB, Air Marshal Sir Robert Brooke-Popham who made no less than five visits to the camp during the year. One of these was to personally present his Air Marksman trophy to Fg Off Edward Mortlock (Teddy) Donaldson of 3 Squadron. Donaldson was destined to achieve prominence as a Second World War fighter pilot, and hold a post-war air-speed record (615.78mph in a Gloster Meteor in 1946) before retiring as an Air Commodore CB CBE DSO AFC*, after which he became the much-respected air correspondent of the *Daily Telegraph* until 1979.

Station flight aircraft flew back to AAS Eastchurch on 30 October but, unusually, there was an air of indecision about closure of the camp for the winter. Posting of all airmen was placed in abeyance on 3 November then, just a week later, was reinstated for all except a small group detailed to keep the camp open during winter.

Having completed its allotted two weeks on 7 October, the Hawker Demons of 23 Squadron were held back to undertake a significant experiment involving air-firing at night, using tracer ammunition fired at illuminated targets. To help accomplish this exciting new task, a detachment of soldiers arrived on 9 October with two lorries – on each of which was mounted a large searchlight. Positioned on the sea bank at each end of the range, these searchlights sought out and illuminated towed drogues, holding them in their beams while the two-seaters let fly with tracer rounds. Night trials continued under the watchful eye of Gp Capt Tedder from HQ AAS until 18 October when, at last, 23 Squadron departed and made way for the annual Brooke-Popham air-firing competition.

There is no record of the success or otherwise of the 1933 night-firing trial but from the reappearance of 23 Squadron in a similar role for a week in October 1934, it is reasonable to assume it would be only a short time before practical operating problems were ironed out and more squadrons would fire over the range at night. Not least of these difficulties (apart from the obvious one of actually piloting an aeroplane in the dark) was the co-ordination needed to bring the target tug into close proximity to its attacker over the desolate Holbeach Marsh. No mean feat even with the aid of searchlights! By the time the 1935 season got under way, it was clear that night firing was to remain an established feature of training at Sutton Bridge. Extending the range programme in this way brought with it problems of manning and organisation, matters which were delegated to Wg Cdr Hugh Vivian Champion De Crespigny MC DFC from HQ Fighting Area, who arrived in March to sort out more formal administration, accommodation and personnel arrangements.

Returning now to 1934, aerial towing duties were taken over by Fairey Gordon aircraft, a few examples of which were involved in accidents at the airfield and range from time to time. Equipped with external drogue storage boxes, these Gordons had cable reels installed inside and beneath their long cockpit. Boxes containing targets were attached to the fuselage sides. Drogues were coloured white and resembled an oval wind-sock in shape, with the dimensions of a fighter fuselage. Flags consisted of a flat length of canvas about 5 feet wide and 8 feet long, with the leading (short) edge fixed to a pole with 'teardrop' lead weights; it could be towed in the vertical or horizontal plane. Flag targets were often used for anti-aircraft gunnery practice. Another target variation was a cone, generally coloured red; shorter than a drogue and with netting on it, allowing more 'aerobatic' movements to be made during towing and was often used for the naval squadrons. Targets were streamed out attached to a thin steel cable, winched out to a distance of about 1,000 feet behind the Gordon, flying at heights varying between 1,500 and 2,000 feet.

Towing aircraft cautiously prescribed a large circle over the range, in order to avoid being in a direct line of fire. Attacking pilots were briefed to begin their practice upon a hand signal from the winch operator in the towing aircraft. Up to three targets were carried and on completion of each attacking section's session against a target, that target was released to drop down onto a grass field near the range admin site for marking. Ammunition for each individual attacker was smeared with a distinctive colour paint prior to take-off. This colour would later show clearly round each shot-hole, thus enabling the performance of a particular pilot or gunner to be identified.

The training routine began with each pilot or air-gunner firing at the wooden-framed canvas ground targets. When considered proficient, they graduated to air-to-air firing and it was scores in this latter stage which counted towards a course assessment. Marking for low-level bombing practice involved range staff taking bearings on the flash and smoke from explosions, from several observation towers. These bomb-plots were telephoned to the main range control tower where the fall of bombs was quickly co-ordinated. Each pilot's results were then telephoned to the airfield for discussion when he landed. This aspect of a pilot's training drew acutely upon his perception of distance, height, angles, speed and in-flight attitude. Such factors were often influenced by the poor weather conditions for which The Wash area is notorious and at the prevailing operating heights there was little margin for error, as has been demonstrated in this narrative so far.

Former LAC J. L. Goward was, from 1937, an airframe rigger at RAF Sutton Bridge. Fifty years on he recalled: 'It was the custom for the engine fitter or rigger ground crew of a particular aeroplane to double-up as drogue operator on towing trips. There was no "air crew brevet" for us winch operators and pay for that extra duty was the princely sum of one shilling (5p) per day as flight pay.' Confirming implementation of the experiments mentioned in 1933, he went on: 'Towing duty could occur at night as well as daytime, particularly as the war drew closer. Illuminated by searchlights at each landward end of the range, targets were held in the beams while aircraft made several firing passes.'

Fairey Gordons were in evidence at Sutton Bridge by mid-1934 and as LAC Goward observed: 'We enjoyed many hours of day and night flying, interspersed with hairy experiences which made that shilling-a-day flight pay well-earned indeed.' One such incident alarmed those on the ground just as much as those in the air.

Engaged in target towing on 3 July 1934, a Gordon suffered engine failure. Losing height rapidly its pilot pointed the nose inland, seeking a flat field near the range. It appeared to the villagers of Gedney Drove End though that he might drop into their school playground but the pilot (who may have had similar misgivings), lifting the nose a fraction more, reached the safety of Mr Slater's grass field next door, clipping a hedge with the starboard wingtip as he slid the big biplane in. Mechanics from Sutton Bridge could not restart the engine so the aeroplane was dismantled and carted ignominiously back to camp. A whole year passed by before another Gordon mishap which, in view of their high workload, is a very creditable record. Perhaps it was the reporting of this sort of occurrence to HQ that resulted in a proposal to acquire a field adjacent to the range as the site of a new emergency landing ground. Whatever the cause, it warranted a visit by AM Brooke-Popham and Wg Cdr De Crespigny to the camp in May 1934 in connection with the project, which subsequently came to fruition, contributing much to the future safety of pilots in trouble over the range.

Returning from leave on 13 December 1933 all airmen were greeted by the news that the ground firing range was to be ready for action by 29 January 1934. It must have been a cold, uncharitable job out there on the marsh in the depth of winter but the seeds of war were being sown and the expanding Air Force needed more live firing capacity. Firing therefore began much earlier than had been the practice in previous years – and on the date stipulated!

Five squadrons sent small detachments at two- or three-day intervals, flying into Sutton Bridge then returning to base daily. This was a departure from the usual practice but the camp accommodation facilities and majority of staff were not yet in place for a full-scale programme under winter conditions, so there was nowhere for aircrew to bed down nor have their aeroplanes serviced. The officers' mess remained closed until March when the main party staff arrived from Eastchurch. Until then, 19 (Duxford), 29 (North Weald), 41 (Northolt), 54 and 111 (Hornchurch) Squadrons operated from their bases during the month of February.

From time to time new aircraft appeared over the range, as time permitted. For the first time mighty Handley Page Hinaidi bombers from 503 Squadron at Waddington trundled across the range to give their gunners a bit of practice, returning intermittently in ones and twos. Similarly, Wapitis of 600 Squadron from Hendon popped up on other days while 207 Squadron, just down the road at Bircham Newton, despatched a single Wallace for gun tests every now and again. Good use seems to have been made of the extra month of toil.

Arriving on 8 March 1934, Wg Cdr Frederick Sowrey DSO MC DFC (later Gp Capt), a relative of William the earlier CO and famous for shooting down Zeppelin L32 in 1916 – and a dozen other air victories – took command and with the officers' mess open and main staff operational, two days later declared the range fully open. By that time station flight aeroplanes, under the command of Flt Lt Vivian Quentry Blackden, had also arrived.

Over the previous winter a new training syllabus had been prepared and it was decreed that Camp Armament officers drawn from all three Armament Camps would test it at first hand. For this purpose, Bulldog aircraft were sent to Sutton Bridge from AAS HQ Flight, Eastchurch. Between 9 and 16 March these new operating procedures were tried out over Holbeach range, under the watchful eye of Air Commodore Lawrence Arthur Pattinson DSO MC DFC, Commandant of AAS and many of his subordinates. Evidently it all worked well since AAS staff and Camp Armament Officers dispersed to their bases and the firing programme got under way on 23 March with 13 (AC) Squadron being first to arrive. 3 ATC armament officer at this time was Flt Lt Charles Beamish, destined to return to Sutton Bridge as station commander when the resident unit between 1942 and 1944 was Central Gunnery School.

23 Squadron followed on and, interspersed by VIP visits, the now familiar procession of fighter squadrons graced the broad fenland sky. Brightly decorated Bulldogs abounded when, in May, 41 and 54 Squadrons flew in, the former losing Sgt Frank Baker in K2914 in an accident referred to earlier. June brought 32 and 56 Squadrons, and 3 Squadron in July, the latter accompanied by 800 Flight FAA. Navy blue was much in evidence on the ground when Rear Admiral Sir Alexander Ramsey, C-in-C Aircraft Carriers paid a visit to watch some of his charges practising. It was noted in the diary that Wg Cdr Frederick Sowrey was promoted to Group Captain on 1 July but he remained in situ until the camp closed in November.

Annual air exercises interrupted 19 and 25 Squadrons' attachment during mid-July 1934 but both returned to complete their practice at the month end. While these two were absent, 'B' Flight Bulldogs from AAS HQ brought a batch of potential Squadron Armament Officers under training to sample the joys of air firing at first hand for a week. August saw 43 Squadron Furies sharing Wash airspace with aircraft of 802 Flight FAA, followed by Furies from 1 Squadron and Bulldogs of Treble-One in September. The programme was brought to a close by 17 and 29 Squadrons, both of which departed on 9 October. Ten days later Air Marshal Brooke-Popham, accompanied by a veritable posse of brass-hats, graced the annual air-firing competition, won for the second time by Fg Off Teddy Donaldson of 3 Squadron.

Autumn brought a repetition of the night flying trials of the previous year when 23 Squadron, no doubt to the dismay of the local villagers, flew between 6.00 pm and 2.00 am firing off loads of tracer for a couple of weeks. No attempt was made that year to keep the camp open through the winter so perhaps the logistical problems involved were deemed not worth the effort. Whatever the reason, on 21 November shortly after the station flight left for Eastchurch, the camp gates were padlocked for the winter.

Early starts to the firing season were now an established pattern. In mid-January 1935 this meant target repairs were set in hand out on the bleak marsh, mains water turned on to the camp and tested early in February, and even the drains were subjected to inspection by the Command medical office. By the time telephone service was connected towards the end of February, all was ready for the fifteen-strong advance party.

Command was assumed that year by the veteran First World War two-seater pilot Sqn Ldr Charles Ley King MC DFC (later Air Commodore, AFC) who declared the range open on 4 March, coinciding with the arrival of 41 and 111 Squadrons. Thereafter, 2, 3 and 25 Squadrons; 800 FAA (HMS *Courageous*), 802 FAA (HMS *Eagle*), 56, 54, 65, 29, 600, 32, 17, 1 and 23 Squadrons all followed during that summer, with 19 Squadron the last to arrive in mid-September.

Mishaps still occurred from time to time as, for example, when 600 Squadron wrote off Hawker Hart K2985 on 18 August in a landing accident and Canadian Fg Off James Robert MacLachlan of 19 Squadron 'put up a black' by taxying his shiny new Gloster Gauntlet, K4083, into K4095, his CO's personal mount. James MacLachlan, another typical product of the mid-1930s RAF, redeemed himself later, not least as CO of 46 Squadron during the majority of the Battle of Britain, retiring in the 1950s as a Group Captain. He died in 1989.

1935 was, of course, the year of King George V's Silver Jubilee for which the RAF staged a flypast. Sutton Bridge played host to nine Hawker Harts from 15 Squadron for a day on 2 July, as part of the practice for this royal event.

Playing host was also regarded as a necessary part of maintaining good relations between the camp and the local community. It was in this context that a motley group of clergy and gentry, representing the Society for the Protection of Rural England, accompanied by two senior RAF officers, visited Holbeach range to observe the effect of air firing on local bird life. Taking place on 11 July, it could not have been a particularly thorough examination as later the same day the two RAF officers also managed to find time to visit the schoolmaster at Gedney Drove End to investigate a complaint of annoyance caused by aircraft as they proceeded to and from the range. The school visit seems to have been a more productive session since station standing orders were amended to try to alleviate the problem.

Fairey Gordon aircraft still equipped the station flight. Fg Off W. C. Williams, an Australian in the RAF on a short-service commission, was getting the hang of life as a tug pilot by the time he was briefed to tow targets over the range on 3 July 1935. Lifting the nose of K1766 off Sutton Bridge's grassy acres, the engine suddenly spluttered to a halt. Dropping like a brick from 30 feet into a wheat field, the Gordon turned somersault as the tall crop acted as a vicious brake on the undercarriage but Williams emerged unhurt from beneath the wreckage. At the start of the Second World War he was a flight commander with 112 Squadron, flying the Gloster Gladiator in the North African desert campaign.

On the subject of VIP visits, 1935 events at the camp are quite well documented and while not an exceptional year, nevertheless no less than fifty-four separate visits by senior officers were recorded between the opening on 5 March and closure on 21 November. Sqn Ldr King's tenure as OC was short-lived when, in August, he was promoted to Wing Commander and posted away, leaving the damp fens for sunnier climes of HQ RAF Iraq. Wg Cdr Harry Augustus Smith MC took his place as OC, this popular man remaining in command for a number of years until posted in November 1938 to command 9 Squadron at Stradishall where sadly, just a few months later, he met with a tragic death in an air crash.

19 Squadron arrived at Sutton Bridge for its annual practice on 9 September 1935 and returned to Duxford on the 20th. During this time, it fell to 19 to conduct night firing trials in conjunction with the searchlights. A name already notable in the RAF as a marksman par excellence, and soon to become even more prominent, Flt Lt Harry Broadhurst, established a record score during the night trials. Furthermore, when in 1935 the Brooke-Popham trophy competition was cancelled (for reasons not stated), Broadhurst was adjudged the winner of the Trophy based on his performance from the annual squadron training programme results, in which 19 Squadron also emerged in first place.

Annual leave for Sutton Bridge ground staff in 1935 began in October of that year. Another innovation, winter firing practice, began on a reduced scale with what was called No.1 Short Armament Training Course, which began on 1 November. Detachments of fighter aeroplanes from 4, 13, 16 (AC) and 18 followed by 57 (Bomber), Squadrons arrived at Sutton Bridge, staying until 21 November. Further small numbers flew in from 2, 4, 13, 16, 26 (AC), again swelled by bombers from 15 and 18 Squadrons, collectively forming No.2 Short Armament Course, which finished on 16 December.

The bombers noted above were Hawker Hart two-seat light bombers. At the end of these two short courses, 3 Armament Training School, Sutton Bridge, rapidly went to sleep for its regular winter hibernation. When it re-awoke in the spring of 1936 life at the camp would never quite be the same again. The country was heading inexorably towards war. From 1936, Sutton Bridge, while continuing to do what it did best, would gradually cast off its summer camp image and take on the role of finishing school in the run up to war.

In July 1936 the RAF was re-organised into four new Commands: Bomber, Fighter, Coastal and Training. From 1 March that year, Sutton Bridge ceased to be known as a Summer Armament Training Camp and was given the status of a permanent RAF Station – RAF Sutton Bridge – while remaining under the control of Air Armament School (Eastchurch). The main function of the station was as the home of 3 Armament Training School in whose revised identity still resided the now well-established live firing role. With the advent of the new Command structure that July, RAF Sutton Bridge was transferred, for all technical and equipment matters, to direct control of the newly created HQ Training Command. In matters of personnel, discipline and training, it was controlled by HQ Armament Group whose AOC was Air Commodore Lawrence Arthur Pattinson DSO MC DFC.

At this point in its life, the Sutton Bridge Station's '540' becomes decidedly sparse again, recording only Air Commodore Alfred Guy Roland Garrod OBE MC DFC taking over from Air Cdre Pattinson in February 1937, the latter being promoted to AVM as AOC 23 Training Group. Wg Cdr Frank Ormond Soden DFC*, a First World War ace credited with twenty-seven victories, took over command of Sutton Bridge from Wg Cdr Smith in February 1938. It is recorded elsewhere that, at long last, the station acquired the first of its married quarters, housing some of the permanent staff of 3 Armament Training School.

Now occupied by civilian families, these houses can still be seen in Chalk Lane.

Despite the paucity of the station's Form 540 entries, newspaper reports and the diaries of other squadrons show it was business as usual for at least another three years. As noted in the previous chapter, 1936 saw no less than four Bulldogs lost at Holbeach range; all from 'Treble-One' Squadron. Setting the scene for the remaining years running up to the war it is possible through the medium of accident reports, both official and those carried by the local newspapers, for some of the gaps in the station's '540' to be filled.

In his excellent book *Fighter Command* (London: Dent, 1980) author Chaz Bowyer summarises the sea-change in RAF organisation after 1936. Hugh Dowding was appointed AOC Fighter Command that year and Bowyer states:

> Equally important to Dowding were his reserves in both men and machines. In 1935 five fresh Flying Training Schools (FTS) were opened (Nos.7 to 11). In addition, nine Armament Training Camps were to be opened as soon as suitable sites could be agreed and purchased by the Air Ministry.

In addition to the three ATCs already mentioned in this narrative, a further six would indeed open in the UK between January 1937 and June 1939, then yet more during the Second World War.

Whereas in past years, virtually only front-line fighter squadrons came to Sutton Bridge, 1936 saw the regular use of the range and airfield by FTS pupils, too. June of that year saw pupils of No.1 course from 7 FTS RAF Peterborough (Westwood) arrive at Sutton Bridge while in August 1936, for example, three pilots from 6 FTS suffered accidents while attached for air firing. Clearly it had become policy to include air firing practice into the final stages of the flying training programme, rather than leave it until a pilot was posted to a squadron. Many other old lessons were going to have to be re-learned, too.

Back in 1935 it had been deemed essential to have a landing ground immediately adjacent to Holbeach range, for emergencies; easing movement of range staff to and from Sutton Bridge and aircraft or drogue servicing. A grass field was therefore purchased that year adjacent to the range accommodation site on Durham's Road near the sea bank at Gedney Dawesmere. Acting Plt Off Geoffrey Burr Andrews from 6 FTS at RAF Sealand had mixed feelings for that small strip of grass when, on 18 August 1936, the engine of his Fury K3738 failed. Attempting a forced landing, he undershot his approach, stalled while trying to hop over a fence, crashed and overturned. By now the sleek Fury was somewhat dated and being gradually relegated to training duties. 6 FTS also operated Hawker Hart Trainers at this time but two of these, K5842 and K6428, were reduced to matchwood at Sutton Bridge rather suddenly on 21 August.

Acting Plt Off Norman Maxwell Boffee, in one of three Harts making a formation landing, drifted into his leader's slipstream. The lower wing of K5842 dipped and hit the ground while the upper wing caught K6428 alongside, locking them together and causing both to crash to the ground. Despite this shaky start Boffee went on to have a distinguished flying career as a bomber pilot during the Second World War. He flew Wellingtons with 214 and 75 Squadron, winning a DFC for an operation to Munich in 1940.

Units of the Royal Auxiliary Air Force (RAuxAF) augmented regular squadrons but only three RAuxAF fighter squadrons, 600, 601 and 604, existed in 1936, operating the Hawker Demon. Two-seat biplane fighters were much in vogue in the late 1930s but fortunately for their crews, were very soon rendered obsolete. Budding Battle of Britain pilot Fg Off Stanley Skinner of 604 Squadron took Demon K4499 to Sutton Bridge where, in the cold evening air of 24 January 1937, while out on a Direction Finding (DF) homing exercise, he failed to receive the radio signals and had to make a forced landing. Although he pulled off a reasonable landing in the gathering darkness, the aeroplane tipped onto its nose in boggy ground. A RAuxAF pilot since 1934, Skinner was called up when war broke out and flew with 604 throughout the Battle. It is ironic, that having flown and survived in combat, he should meet his death in 1942 as a sea-borne observer on the Dieppe raid.

Turning now to a happier topic, in 1936 RAF Sutton Bridge became a focal point for air displays in the district and for the next three years assumed the mantle previously held by the civilian air-pageant operators, who had themselves served the district exceedingly well in past years.

Providing light relief to both the participating stations and spectators alike, Empire Air Day air displays were the means by which the efforts of an expanding – and modernising – RAF were brought to the attention of the public. It was a way, too, for the government to show what the taxpayer was getting for his/her money. Proceeds from entrance fees were donated to the RAF Benevolent Fund, a worthy cause but was this not also just a thinly dressed-up ploy to ease the inevitability of war into the minds of the public? Whatever the motive, on Saturday 23 May 1936, 3 ATS, RAF Sutton Bridge, was one of forty-nine stations throughout the land throwing their gates open for the public to enjoy themselves. Attracting good coverage by local newspapers, according to the *Spalding Guardian*: 'All roads in the district led to Sutton Bridge' that afternoon. For the first time since Empire Air Days were instituted three years earlier, Sutton Bridge, now with the status of a permanent RAF establishment, was included in the open day list. Almost 3,000 people visited the station, availing themselves of an opportunity to wander through hangars and even climb into aeroplane cockpits. Pilots and ground crew were on hand to patiently answer questions from a curious public. Despite the far from ideal weather – occasional showers and blustery winds, relieved by the sight of the sun from time to time – it was possible to put on a varied and exciting programme.

Promptly at 2.15 pm three Bulldogs from 56 Squadron took to the air, giving a spirited aerobatic display to open the show. Fresh from past appearances at Hendon, three Fury aeroplanes of 25 Squadron thrilled the crowd with precision formation aerobatics. In those days of relatively slow speeds, aeroplanes like these could be thrown around 'on a sixpence' and low cloud was not a problem although the blustery wind would tax the pilot's skill during aerobatics.

Next came individual displays by various single Bulldogs, including one from 56's CO, Sqn Ldr Charles Leslie Lea-Cox (later Gp Capt), who seemed to have lost none of his mastery of aerial manoeuvres learned with the Sopwith Camel during his service on the Italian Front in the First World War. Fighter attack techniques, the basis of everyday life at Sutton Bridge, were ably demonstrated by a flight of Bulldogs, again from 56 Squadron, upon a drogue towed by a station flight Gordon. A comic interlude of crazy-flying was staged with a De Havilland Moth displaying 'L' plates. The stiff wind enhanced these hair-raising stunts but in the hands of Flt Lt D. B. McGill the little Moth appeared perfectly safe. Naturally everything stopped for tea; the first part of the programme being brought to a close by a sedate formation of three station flight Fairey Gordons flown by Flt Lt Palmer and Sgts Drake and Roberts.

A demonstration of air drill, with manoeuvres controlled from the ground by radio and relayed to the crowd via the loudspeaker system, was followed by a screaming, ear-splitting dive-bombing routine by three Hawker Furies opening the second half. Somewhat more gently, a Hawker Hind was put through its paces by Sgt Roberts, while the final item on the flying agenda was a mass formation flypast by nine aeroplanes; three each of Gordons, Furies and Bulldogs.

Meanwhile at ground level a Gloster Gauntlet was the focus of much interest as 'the latest RAF fighter'. Elsewhere the staccato rattle of machine gun fire rent the air as the twin Vickers machine guns of a Hawker Fury, propped up in front of the firing-butts, were made to turn streams of lead into fountains of sand, much to the delight of the watching crowd. Armourers demonstrated how to fill ammunition belts, assembled and dismantled machine guns, while aerial photographers showed pictures of local landmarks taken from the air. The intricacies of wireless telegraphy were explained by the signals section and aeroplane servicing workshops opened for closer inspection. All in all, there was much indeed for the visitors to see and enjoy that year.

In contrast, the weather for the 1937 RAF Sutton Bridge Empire Day was ideal. Attracting 5,000 people that year, the 4-hour programme included an even greater variety of aeroplanes. It was the turn of pupils from 5 FTS (RAF Sealand) to bring their Hart and Audax aeroplanes to the range for air firing practice in late May and early June 1937. They, too, supplied some of the thrills for the Empire Air Day held on 29 May; pupils from that FTS opening the busy programme with a formation flypast of five Harts. All went without mishap considering that during practice the previous day, two Harts collided during landing, luckily each sustaining only minor damage and causing no crash. Four Bulldogs flown by Flt Lt H. Eales in company with Sgts Smith, Wood and Stanford dived and wheeled repeatedly in simulated attacks upon a towed drogue target. Later, Sqn Ldr J. F. F. Pain displayed accurate low flying skill by dropping and picking up message bags using a hook attachment beneath his aircraft fuselage. Several solo aerobatic items were contributed by Flt Lts D. B. D. Field, N. H. Fresson, E. A. Springall and Plt Off James Douglas Ronald of 5 FTS; even the Station Commander, the irrepressible Wg Cdr Harry Smith, got in on the act with his own solo aerobatic effort. The inevitable comic turn was provided by Flt Lt Vivian Blackden, who made numerous flour-bomb attacks on an old car driven erratically at high speed across the airfield. His aim must have been pretty acceptable as Blackden rose to prominence in 1941 when, promoted Wg Cdr, he commanded 12 Squadron as they were re-equipping with Wellington II bombers. Sadly, however, Wg Cdr Blackden was lost on 9/10 April 1941 during his squadron's first operation with their new mount.

By mid-1937 the Westland Wallace had replaced the ageing Fairey Gordon and a splendid formation of these new target tugs, led by Flt Lt F. A. A. Strath, flew sedately over the airfield. A delightful show of synchro-aerobatics by Flt Lts Springall and J. C. Evans, in a pair of Furies, followed before the day's proceedings closed with a grand formation flypast. Three Wallaces, three Furies, one Boulton Paul Overstrand bomber from neighbouring RAF Bircham Newton and one Avro Anson provided that year's finale.

The final Empire Air Day at Sutton Bridge was scheduled for Saturday 28 May 1938. In common with other aerodromes throughout the country, that display suffered continuous rain all day causing practically all flying items to be scrubbed. Nevertheless, a substantial crowd gathered, despite inches of water on the grass and tarmac areas, particularly braving the weather to inspect what was described by the *Spalding Guardian* as 'the new type all-metal bombers in the aircraft park'. These were unnamed in the article but are most likely to have been Bristol Blenheims, some of which were based at nearby RAF Wyton at that time.

For most of the afternoon, with poor visibility and a cloud base of 400 feet, only one aeroplane at a time was allowed into the air for restricted aerobatics when the rain eased off. By tea-time however it was brighter, the clouds having risen sufficiently for nine fighters to carry out squadron air-drill in the form of Fighting Area set-piece manoeuvres of the sort mentioned earlier. A Hawker Nimrod from an unknown unit demonstrated the in-flight art of picking up messages from the ground. Despite the rain, visitors made the most of a similar range of ground attractions as in previous years – with the addition this time of anti-aircraft searchlights, sound locating gear and the parachute packing shed.

This was the end of an era in more ways than one, for RAF Sutton Bridge never opened its gates to the public again.

Following its performance at the 1937 air show, it can be established that 5 FTS remained at Sutton Bridge until at least 11 June that year because Air Ministry accident records show that on that date Act/Plt Off M. J. Earle in Audax K5161 undershot his approach, turning the machine onto its back when its nose dug into long grass just short of the field. Plt Off Earle walked away uninjured. He had also walked away from an earlier incident when he was training at Sealand. On a night-flying practice he became lost and force-landed. Aiming for the beach at West Kirkby he missed and landed in the middle of the Marine Lake by the promenade. Michael Earle did manage to complete his training and in 1939 was posted to 75 Squadron at RAF Feltwell to fly Vickers Wellington bombers – which he did successfully, and survived the war.

The next FTS unit to arrive for a stay at Sutton Bridge in July and August, 6 FTS from Netheravon, was not so fortunate. In rapidly deteriorating visibility Act/Plt Off Philip Herbert Bailey taxied out Audax K5253 with Act/Plt Off Douglas Leslie Parnell Bagot-Gray in the rear cockpit. It was 8.00 am on 4 August and one of the first air firing sorties of the day. Bailey took off but at only 200 feet altitude he entered early morning mist while still near the airfield. At this juncture he seemed, wisely, to decide to abort the flight and turned back towards the sanctuary of the airfield. There were only two civilian witnesses to what followed. Mr G. Kirk and Mr T. Tibbles were out hedge clipping on the banks of the River Nene.

'We are always interested in planes that fly past,' said Mr Kirk when interviewed by a reporter, 'and as we looked up to see this one passing overhead it swung round. Flying lower it dipped behind some trees and a large glasshouse. Just before it disappeared from view I could plainly see that the pilot was having difficulty in handling the aeroplane. I expected it to appear over the top of the glasshouse but instead I heard a most awful crash.'

Both men rushed to the scene and faced the grim task of extricating the unfortunate airmen from the crumpled wreckage, which fell on Mr Sole's farm some 400 yards from the airfield.

Boston Guardian newspaper of 6 August 1937 carried that story, together with another accident only four days earlier. Acting Plt Off Albert Edward Ralph Ferris, 11 FTS, misjudged his pull-out from a firing dive on a target and lost his life when the aeroplane, a Fury I K5666, crashed onto the shore at Holbeach range. Closing what was a sad catalogue of mishaps in so short a space of time, was yet a third crash, also on 4 August, this time at Gedney Dyke. Flt Lt Stephenson, whose unit was not stated, sustained minor injuries in this incident.

After this period, a tragic illustration of the high price of flying training in human terms, there was a lull in the accident rate for a few months. Evidence of the return to Sutton Bridge of front-line fighter squadrons later that year, together with the 604 Squadron crash mentioned above, indicates that the airfield and range was now in constant use during every month of the year.

Having completed his air firing exercise over Holbeach range, Sgt Rene Attilio Albonico (who was born in Surrey), from 1 Squadron based at Tangmere, was returning for a well-earned rest, his being the last sortie on 1 December. With twilight turning to dusk, a thick mist developed, obscuring the ground near the airfield. In his own words some fifty years later, Sgt Albonico wrote:

> I misjudged my height in the mist. My approach was fine until I realised I was actually still some way up in the air. The aeroplane stalled and crashed heavily, ripping off the main-planes, undercarriage and prop in the process. I scrambled clear, unhurt, but the aeroplane was a complete write-off. The aeroplane involved was Hawker Fury II, K8258.

Sgt Albonico continued to serve with 1 Squadron, being posted to France with the squadron in 1940. He flew several operational sorties in Hurricanes during the Battle of France before being shot down by flak on 18 May 1940 while escorting bombers near St Quentin. He crash-landed his Hurricane, L1865, and was made a POW for five long years.

Audaxes and Furies from RAF College (RAFC) FTS Cranwell were becoming regular visitors to the range from mid-1938. The senior term was now receiving advanced instruction designed to give them some working knowledge of subjects needed when they joined operational units. This included a period of five weeks during which the course members visited Sutton Bridge. Despite their firing practice being hampered by bad weather and unserviceability issues at the range, the cadets managed to blast off more than 68,000 rounds and drop 1,800 bombs in the time allocated – although, according to the College Commandant's passing-out report, while their theory was fine, practical results were somewhat mediocre! Inevitably these students encountered a few mishaps, too. With an engine derated for FTS use, the Audax, a general-purpose variant of the ubiquitous Hart, was used mainly by trainees destined for Army Co-operation or day bomber squadrons, while single-seat Fury IIs were allocated to those pupils displaying fighter pilot qualities. Fortunately, none of the RAFC accidents were fatal but one incident is noteworthy because it involved a cadet who, having survived it, carved out a reputation second to none in the Battle of Britain and its aftermath. Undergoing training since early 1936, Flight Cadet Charles Brian Fabris Kingcombe flew to Holbeach range on 27 June 1938 in Fury II, K8302. As he did so he made the elementary error of forgetting to change over his fuel supply from gravity to main tank *en route* and ran the tank dry. His engine stopped abruptly and unable to make it to the range landing ground, he was obliged to force-land. During his approach, however, he stalled and the Fury fell heavily into a sugar beet field, smashing the undercarriage. Flt Cdt Brian Kingcombe fortunately lived to fight another day. One month later, Kingcombe had completed his two-and-a-half years of training – a lengthy process for an RAFC cadet in those days – and was posted to 65 Squadron. When war came, he saw action over Dunkirk and then, posted to 92 Squadron, fought all through the Battle of Britain, being credited with eight, plus three shared, air victories. He held a number of senior operational appointments for the remainder of the war, finally retiring from the RAF in 1954 as a Group Captain DSO DFC*.

As a member of 87 Squadron's aerobatic team, Sgt Thomas Frederick Dowsett Dewdney was acknowledged by his peers as a skilful pilot. On 18 June 1938, for example, in company with Fg Off George Hermann Joseph Feeny and Plt Off Robert Lawrie Lorimer, their 'tied-together' aerobatics display in three Gloster Gladiators dazzled spectators at Brooklands Flying Club. For 20 minutes the three Gladiator pilots held the crowd in thrall with dives at the clubhouse, upward rolls, loops and half-rolls off loops and at no time did their formation vary in its shape and compactness – nor did the flagged cords ever look like being broken. This performance was repeated with similar success on 10 July before a French audience at the Fete de l'Air at Villacoublay airfield in Paris.

Just two months later, on 14 September, Sgt Dewdney was dead; killed at the controls of Hawker Hurricane L1620 when it dived headlong into Holbeach Marsh mudflats. While Sgt Dewdney was engaged in air to air firing practice, thick clouds rolled in across the range with a swiftness for which The Wash is noted. Strange to relate, in view of his undeniable flying skill, the Air Ministry record card (AM Form 1180) for Dewdney's accident indicates he had done little cloud flying (flying on instruments).

With the Munich crisis emerging into the light of day, the race was on to re-equip the RAF with modern monoplane, multi-gun fighters. Among the first to convert to Hurricanes, 87 Squadron was anxious to become fully operational and for all pilots this included firing the battery of eight Browning machine guns. Exactly what happened will never be known but perhaps being unfamiliar with the Hurricane – the squadron had only re-equipped between 12 July and 4 August – Dewdney may have stalled in that low cloud and was unable to recover in time. His thus became the first accident at Holbeach range to involve one of the new generation of monoplane fighters. It is also sad to relate that both the other members of that trio did not survive the war. Lawrie Lorimer was killed in action on 14 May 1940 while flying a Hurricane with 1 Squadron, near Sedan in France. George Feeny transferred to the Fleet Air Arm and having fought against the odds in a Gloster Gladiator during the Narvik campaign, died on 8 June 1940 when his aircraft carrier HMS *Glorious* was sunk off Norway.

It was an eclectic mix of biplanes and monoplanes to be seen wheeling over the range and the airfield during 1938 as evidenced by 3 Squadron's visit for annual firing practice that August. The squadron marked its stay when the pilot of Gloster Gladiator K7956 undershot his approach to land at Sutton Bridge and neatly somersaulted the aircraft. It was carted back to the squadron base at RAF Kenley for repair. The reason why 3 Squadron was still operating Gladiator biplanes in August 1938 was because after starting to re-equip with the Hurricane during March that year, the conversion process had to be halted in July while the runway at Kenley was extended to cope with the new monoplane fighter. The squadron thus reverted to the Gladiator until that work was completed a year later.

As Europe slid downhill to war, the year 1939 would bring many changes to RAF Sutton Bridge too. First of these occurred on 6 February when the station diary recorded: 'The station commenced to be re-equipped with Hawker Henley aircraft.' Underpinning this terse statement is a little-appreciated effect of the significant technological advance heralded by the latest monoplane fighters. Elderly Wallace and Gordon target-towing (TT) aeroplanes, in use for example over the years at Sutton Bridge, were by 1939 incapable of providing realistic air-to-air firing training conditions for Hurricanes, Spitfires and Blenheims now visiting the range.

Hawker's attempt to produce a monoplane light bomber – the Henley – was met with little enthusiasm by the Air Ministry and although production went ahead, it was converted for target-towing work. Fitted with a windmill-driven winding device mounted on the port side of the rear cockpit, the Henley TT III was limited in RAF service to a cruise speed of 220 mph in its target-towing role. In the transition period from peace to war and even on into the early war years, this speed restriction – apparently officialdom's attempt to reduce engine wear – was not the problem it was to become later. With Hurricane and Spitfire engines and airframes being developed to raise speeds ever higher, together with the advent of the next generation of fighters, even the Henley's performance was also found wanting.

The Westland Wallace TTs soldiered on into the era of the monoplane fighter before being phased out – although not before one of their number, K6067, came to grief on 24 January with tragic consequences. Air firing continued apace and Sutton Bridge station flight target-tug crews, flying flat out, day and night, must have been very weary under the constant pressure. Returning to the range from a night sortie, Sgt James Thomas Wyse undershot his approach and K6067 hit the raised road on the airfield's eastern boundary, overturned and burst into flames. Sgt Wyse died although his winch operator, LAC Edward Lawrence Wade, escaped with injuries. By no means the last accident, it was the last fatality to befall the station before the outbreak of war some seven months later.

One of the last squadrons to arrive for annual firing practice before war broke out, for example, was 25 Squadron, which operated the Blenheim IF. Arriving on 14 August 1939 and leaving on 22 August, seems to indicate that the annual firing practice camp had been reduced in duration from two weeks to one, probably to enable more units to squeeze in time to squeeze the trigger. Mishaps also continued unabated. On 16 August, Plt Off Aberconway John Sefton Pattinson was returning from the range after a camera-gun sortie for the benefit of his air gunner. He forgot to lower the undercarriage of Blenheim L1436 and the cockpit horn failed to work to warn him of his omission. In consequence, he belly-landed the Blenheim but fortunately without causing any injuries. He flew operational patrols with 23 Squadron (Blenheim) before being posted to 92 Squadron to fly the Spitfire. Pattinson joined 92 Squadron on 11 October and was killed in action the very next day during his first operational patrol.

Events began to rush one after another. On 8 August 1939 Wg Cdr John Melbourne Mason DSC DFC (later Air Cdre CBE), a First World War RNAS bomber pilot, took over command from Gp Capt Soden, who was posted to command RAF Finningley. Then 3 Armament Training School was transferred from RAF Sutton Bridge to RAF West Freugh near Stranraer in Wigtownshire, Scotland. On 2 September 1939, RAF Sutton Bridge was placed on a Care and Maintenance (C&M) basis, under the temporary command of Flt Lt R. P. Smillie and a small group of airmen. What a sudden come-down!

On 3 September – that fateful day – with only the C&M party remaining, war was declared and at 3.00 am the first air raid warning to be experienced by the station was sounded. One week later it was all change again when Flt Lt H. N. Hawker arrived with another small group of airmen to form the nucleus of 3 Recruits Sub-Depot. In common with several similar establishments, such as those at Catfoss and Finningley, hurriedly set up at the outbreak of hostilities, this unit was created 'For the purpose of accommodating and training recruits as per the War Syllabus'.

Administered initially by 24 (Training) Group, 3 Sub-Depot Sutton Bridge was affiliated to 2 Recruiting Centre, Cardington. Its aim was to train airman recruits in the essentials of Air Force discipline, kit them out, give them time to mark such issued kit, undergo medicals and variously integrate those raw recruits rapidly into the weird and wonderful ways of the service – including, it seems, digging pits and trenches for many obscure reasons.

In the case of Sutton Bridge, originally 336 recruits were to be accommodated for four weeks and the first – no doubt bewildered – batch of 144 arrived from Cardington on 11 September. Ten days later the unit was re-named 3 Recruits Training Pool and transferred to the jurisdiction of 25 (Armament) Group. A further 176 embryo airmen turned up on 30 September, bringing the total at the station to 320. In rapid succession new orders were received from Group to prepare to accommodate a total of 576 men, who were to be organised into a 'squadron' of four 'flights' each with 144 recruits all overseen by headquarters staff.

The initial intake completed its training by 27 October and during the next two days, with the exception of sixty-eight airmen, were all posted away. Having done its job, the unit was officially closed down on 29 October when the remaining recruits were posted. All, that is, except one solitary soul who according to the unit diary remained behind for reasons which were never recorded. As the final entry dated 16 November so eloquently puts it: 'With one exception, all recruits have been disposed of"!

Officers and airmen from both the C&M party and HQ 3 Recruit Pool continued to be posted into and out of Sutton Bridge station HQ in quick order during November. Did anyone know what they were doing? It soon became evident that the reason for this flurry of activity was to re-arrange enough manpower in such a manner as to produce an organisation capable of forming and administering two twin-engine fighter squadrons at the station. Now *this* was the real thing – and it needed a special sort of man to make it all work.

4

Battle of France

Squadron Leader Philip Reginald 'Dickie' Barwell was a fighter pilot and an outstanding leader of men. Born in Solihull, Warwickshire, in 1907, at the end of the First World War his family moved to a small-holding poultry farm at Swavesey in the Cambridgeshire fens from where, in 1925, he joined the RAF.

Philip Barwell first came to our attention earlier in this story as a trainee pilot using Sutton Bridge airfield and Holbeach range during its very first firing season back in 1926. He comes into prominence now as a fully fledged fighter pilot leading the Hawker Hurricanes of 46 Squadron into combat from RAF Digby. His gallantry in action on 21 October 1939 earned him a DFC for routing the first enemy air attack on a convoy off the Lincolnshire coast, during which Sqn Ldr Barwell displayed qualities of discipline, leadership and courage which were to become his trademark. Shortly after this incident – which became known unofficially as the Battle of Spurn Head – he was promoted and placed in command of RAF Sutton Bridge, where he was to oversee the formation of three new fighter squadrons. It is this early part of his all too short wartime flying career that will be outlined here.

Just after war was declared, RAF Sutton Bridge seemed to be drifting somewhat on the rising tide of hostilities; going through a period of abrupt re-adjustment – as no doubt was the rest of the war machine – until a new sense of purpose could be established. This new direction was not too long in coming for, on 1 November 1939, Sutton Bridge was transferred from Training Command to 12 Group Fighter Command and, a few days later, newly promoted Wg Cdr Philip Barwell DFC took command of the station. His family, of course, were also on the move again too and, according to his son John, they took up residence in the East Lighthouse, a couple of miles downriver from the station on the east bank of the River Nene outfall. This building, though not actually a lighthouse, was built in the style of one and, as we heard earlier, was, until just before the war, the home of Peter Scott, the naturalist and painter.

Postings to and from SHQ were designed to create a station establishment to support the formation and operations of 264 Squadron, under the command of Sqn Ldr Stephen Haistwell Hardy (later Air Cdre; CBE) and 266 Squadron under Sqn Ldr John William Arthur Hunnard. It was now up to the station commander, Wg Cdr Barwell, to see that these new squadrons were brought to operational readiness as rapidly and efficiently as possible. As we shall see, though, this was not going to be an easy task but he was the right man for the job.

264 Squadron officially came into existence on 1 November 1939 with the arrival at Sutton Bridge of Sqn Ldr Hardy. During the next week a number of pilots were posted in from 12 FTS Grantham and 14 FTS Kinloss, to be joined later by two flight commanders, Flt Lt William Arthur Toyne (later B of B, DFC) from 213 Squadron, Wittering and Flt Lt Nicholas Gresham Cooke (later B of B, DFC), 611 Squadron, Digby. As yet, no aircraft were allocated to 264 but three Miles Magisters (N3857, N3867, N3868) were collected from RAF Hullavington to enable the new boys of both 264 and 266 Squadrons to keep their hand in until their proper aircraft turned up. Dickie Barwell, always keen to add new types to his log book, also kept his flying hand in and made some local recce flights in these Maggies during November.

On 14 November, Fighter Command announced that 264 Squadron was to be equipped with Boulton-Paul Defiant fighters and a week later announced it would move out to RAF Martlesham Heath. This prompted Sqn Ldr Hardy, his two flight commanders and ground crew SNCO, Flt Sgt Lines, to visit Martlesham to inspect facilities preparatory to the move. That same day, 25 November, Sqn Ldr Hardy travelled on to RAF Northolt to scrounge a flight in a Defiant – for none had yet reached Sutton Bridge. Organisation? Cor blimey!

Finding something to keep these aircraft-less fellows occupied was difficult, resulting in numerous sightseeing visits to sector operations at RAF Wittering and further individual visits by squadron pilots to RAF Northolt to get the feel of a Defiant. This air experience was augmented by ground personnel being sent off to attend Boulton & Paul's Wolverhampton factory for a four-day Defiant servicing course. All in all, Sutton Bridge seemed to resemble nothing more than a hotel for transient 264 Squadron personnel. This period of relative inactivity came to an end, however, on 7 December 1939 when all air and ground elements of 264 upped sticks and left RAF Sutton Bridge bound for a new home at RAF Martlesham Heath, where – within days – Defiants began arriving from depots such as Brize Norton and Little Rissington. Ever eager to add a new type to his log book, Dickie Barwell flew over to Martlesham and went up for 20 minutes in one of the new Defiants.

Meanwhile, across the airfield, 266 Squadron had been stirring since 30 October when it began the process of forming under the command of Sqn Ldr Hunnard. In manpower terms the established size of this proposed two-seater squadron was declared as 13 officers, of whom 11 were pilots, and 204 airmen, of whom 10 were NCO pilots and 20 aircrew (air gunners). One of the most notable names to arrive at Sutton Bridge for flight commander duty with 266, was one of Dickie Barwell's old squadron colleagues, the diminutive Flt Lt Ian Richard ('Widge') Gleed, promoted and posted in from 46 Squadron, Digby. Experience and leadership were obviously the qualities most required to bring a squadron to an effective state quickly and it was for this reason that Gleed was selected for this job, with another old hand, Flt Lt James Baird Coward, formerly of 19 Squadron, Duxford.

Any aeroplane, let alone a real fighter, was hard to come by in those days of rapid expansion so 266 also had to settle for three Miles Magisters, collected from 10 MU Hullavington, on which to begin their work-up. With the arrival of the 'Maggies' on 11 October, local flying got under way, while the Link Trainer was also put to good use. The inevitable stand-by activity, those visits to sector ops at Wittering, still continued.

On 18 November word came down from on high that 266 Squadron was to be equipped with Fairey Battles instead of Blenheims as originally intended. At a guess, neither would have inspired these hopeful fighter tyros but it seemed to point to an intention to turn 266 into a single-engine unit eventually – most likely Spitfire – once the production lines moved into top gear. Accordingly, the squadron personnel was quickly scaled down as the air gunners were shipped out to pastures new.

It was not until 4 December, however, that the first three Fairey Battle I: L5348, L5350 and L5374, materialised at Sutton Bridge, flown in from 24 MU Ternhill by Hunnard, Gleed and Coward.

Within a couple of days, training began with these three, which were joined shortly after by a further batch comprising L5343, L5365 and P5244. A spell of fog, rain and low cloud hampered flying but soon the sky around Sutton Bridge echoed to the roar of six Battles doing everything from circuits and bumps to formation practice. It was not long before the first 'prang'. Finding the undercarriage of L5350 refused to lock in the down position, Flt Lt Coward, with Plt Off James Leon Wilkie in the back seat, had to belly-land on the airfield on 9 December, but both men emerged unhurt. James Coward fought in the Battle of Britain with 19 Squadron. He was shot down on 31 August, sustaining injuries that caused the loss of one of his legs but returned to flying training duties, for which he was awarded an AFC in 1954. James Coward died in 2012 aged 97. Plt Off Jim Wilkie was posted from 266 to 263 Squadron on 3 May 1940 to fly Gloster Gladiators in the Norway campaign. During a combat patrol on 2 June he died when his Gladiator was shot down by the German ace Lt Helmut Lent flying a Bf 110 (killed in action (KIA) in 1944 with 110 victories to his name).

Next day five more Battles (L5375, L5442, P5248, P5368 and P5369) were collected from 24 MU Ternhill by other squadron pilots: Plt Offs Wilkie, Williams and Bowen and Sgts Eade and Jones. Being December, the weather was a constant hazard and flying became subject to continual interruption. Plt Off Bowen bent the tail wheel of L5246 in a heavy landing on 12 December, but by now, the flow of aeroplanes and pilots was sufficient to cope with a few minor mishaps such as this. The cold, misty, damp month wore on. There was even formation flying practice on Christmas Day and by the turn of the year, the training programme included fighter attacks and longer cross-country flights. It is known that Plt Off Nigel Greenstreet Bowen was KIA in the Battle of Britain on 16 August, at the age of 20; Sgt Arthur William Eade fought in the Battle, was later promoted Warrant Officer (WO) and awarded an AFC; and Sgt William Ross Jones also fought in the Battle, was commissioned and retired as a Sqn Ldr, AFC.

Although on 31 December the flying strength of 266 Squadron stood at 20 pilots and 15 Battles, the ground echelon was desperately short of servicing equipment for their charges. In fact, if it had not been for the co-operation of RAF Upwood, 266 might well have been grounded as most of its aircraft were due for 30-hour inspections. To overcome the difficulty, Battles were flown, one by one, to RAF Upwood for vital servicing and repair until the arrival of ground equipment – yet another bottleneck in the system.

Despite day after day of severe frost during January 1940, 266 pressed on with its task, even managing to raise the daily totals of hours flown compared to previous months. In the end it all seemed worthwhile for, on 10 January, Fighter Command ordered the squadron 'to be re-equipped with Spitfires forthwith'. With renewed vigour the pilots continued to practise in all weathers, severe frosts, ground fog, snow and even blizzard conditions during which Plt Offs Wilkie and Mitchell in P5244 were forced down near East Kirkby, fortunately without either being hurt. Plt Off Philip Henry Gurrey Mitchell fought in and survived the Battle of Britain, flying with 266.

Finally, on 19 January 1940, the great day arrived. The first three Spitfire Mk Is were flown to Sutton Bridge by Sqn Ldr Hunnard and his two flight commanders, with a fourth arriving a day later.

The weather, though, did not relent. More snow fell daily until in the last week of the month, with more than 6 inches lying on top of the already frost-hardened grass airfield and as the temperature was below zero day after day, flying was abandoned. It was no better when February arrived either. A thaw set in and the rains came, turning the airfield into a quagmire. Not until 9 February was the grass surface sufficiently water-free for flying to re-commence and on this date, training with the new Spitfires began. Dickie Barwell pulled rank to go to the front of the queue to get his hands on a Spitfire and himself air tested N3175, 3092, 3120, 3175 and 3118 during the first week. Within days, most of the Battles had been exchanged for Spitfires, the former being flown to or collected by other squadrons, such as 234 and 245. By mid-February, 266 was up to strength with nineteen Spitfires on charge but one of these, N3120 which Dickie Barwell had flown on 14th, was written off by Flt Lt Gleed in a quite spectacular manner.

Part of the work-up process involved taking each Spitfire up to its rated altitude, in this case 18,000 feet. It was a test such as this that, on 18 February, very nearly brought to a premature and abrupt end the promising flying career of Ian Gleed. Airborne from Sutton Bridge, Flt Lt Gleed eased N3120 ever higher into the cold afternoon air, climbing in circles through one cloud layer after another until he broke out into bright sunshine. The official version of subsequent events states that the Spitfire was being air tested at 18,000 feet with all going well until the pilot throttled back into a gentle turn towards base. There is no suggestion in the report of any high-speed manoeuvre that might have led to over-stressing the airframe. Suddenly, there was a loud bang; Gleed found himself torn out of his harness and thrown clean through the cockpit canopy as the aeroplane began to disintegrate around him.

For a personal account of those events there is no better place to turn to than Ian Gleed's autobiography *Arise to Conquer* (London: Gollancz, 1942).

> As soon as I reached 18,000 feet I levelled out, checked all instruments and opened up to full throttle. Boost was OK, revs steady at 2,850, speed just right. She seemed to be flying a bit right wing low but we could put that right later. It was a bit nippy up there so I decided to go home. I nosed down into a gentle dive; the speed rose and I began a gentle left-hand turn, closing the radiator as I did so. CRACK! Christ! What was that?
>
> I was thrown forward, my harness just stopping me from hitting the dashboard. I tried to lift my head but could not. BANG! Blackness! Everything was black. Where am I? Christ! I must still be in the air! Oh God, where's the ripcord? Fumbling, at last, I found the metal square and tugged hard. Felt a jerk; then nothing.

Knocked semi-conscious when he left the cockpit, Gleed fell through the rarefied air and was fortunate indeed to recover his senses just sufficiently to pull his parachute ripcord with height to spare. In a daze he managed to release his 'chute as he was dragged along the snow-covered ground. He could not see for the coagulated blood from cuts to his head, one shoe was missing, his left arm and right leg were hurting, possibly broken. He lay shivering in a biting wind before hearing voices approaching. He heard one voice say that the doctor was on his way and that his Spitfire lay in pieces. After what seemed a nightmare of being carried and bumped about on foot and in vehicles, Ian Gleed finally arrived at hospital. He was operated upon and woke later to find himself flat on his back, weak; his left arm in plaster and his head and right leg swathed in bandages.

Spitfire N3120 had fallen to earth at Little Ouse, near Littleport, and as his first rescuer had remarked, it was in little pieces. Ordinarily that would mean just another load of scrap to be melted down but an odd coincidence concerning N3120 came to light in 1989, almost fifty years from that fateful day. During that year the author visited Kent Aviation Museum on the former Hawkinge airfield, near Folkestone. There, mounted on a wall, was the virtually intact starboard wing of N3120. Its route to Hawkinge was said to be via Woolwich Arsenal but no reason was offered for it being deposited with the latter. It can only be assumed that Air Ministry investigators, in view of the disturbing circumstances of this accident to a relatively early mark of Spitfire, may have gathered up wreckage and sent it to Woolwich Arsenal for technical examination. Perhaps only this major component survived and by way of some personal contact was scrounged by or donated to the embryo museum.

It was fully three months before Ian Gleed was passed fit to fly single-seat fighters again, by which time 266 had moved on and he was posted back to 46 Sqn to fly Hurricanes in France. He was lucky that day but recovered to carve out a reputation for aggressive leadership in the Battles of France and Britain and beyond, before being killed on active service in North Africa on 16 April 1943, by which time, at the age of 26, he was a Wing Commander, DSO DFC and credited with thirteen air victories.

In spite of the setback of the loss of one of its flight commanders – Flt Lt Sydney Howarth Bazley was posted in from 611 Squadron as replacement for Ian Gleed – 266 Squadron pressed on apace with war practice. Daily now the programme tested engine boost at rated altitude – fortunately without further mishap – formation flying, cross-countries, cloud penetration, battle climbs, fighter attacks and rapid refuel and re-arm exercises. This intense activity culminated in Fighter Command's acceptance, on 26 February, of 266's readiness to join the fray. On 29 February 1940 the squadron moved out of Sutton Bridge for a new home at RAF Martlesham Heath.

In these opening months of the war, the third flying unit to find its feet under Dickie Barwell's watchful eye at RAF Sutton Bridge was 254 Squadron. It actually re-formed at RAF Stradishall but, in need of time to become effective, was relocated from that operational station to quieter pastures at Sutton Bridge. Thus, on 9 December 1939, 254 arrived with just nine Blenheim Mk Is, which were intended to be converted to Mk IF night fighter standard. Only one of these was fitted out for dual control and all were sorely under-equipped, lacking such essentials as radios, oxygen apparatus and guns. Pilot training, begun at Stradishall, now ground to a halt through a combination of lack of the aforementioned equipment plus an acute shortage of aeroplanes themselves. Didn't anyone know there was a war on? By mid-December two Blenheims were grounded awaiting 360-hour engine inspections, three others would reach a similar position imminently and a further two were grounded for lack of spares. A sorry state indeed and only slightly relieved by a plea for the engine overhaul limit to be extended to 420-hours being accepted by Fighter Command. Even so, serviceability continued to be such a bind that on 10 January the only alternative was for the ground crews to work longer hours trying to cobble together sufficient aeroplanes to put just a few into the air each day.

HQ Fighter Command must have been equally exasperated for in mid-January 1940 it announced a change of heart. 254 was to be re-equipped with 'long-nosed' Blenheim Mk IV, 'for employment in trade defence.' This coincided with the return of ten Royal Air Force Volunteer Reserve (RAFVR) air gunners to the station from a gunnery course at RAF Evanton. The squadron diary lamented the fact that three months had elapsed since re-forming and it was still far from being declared operational. Blame was laid squarely on the appalling present equipment. There seemed no chance of the squadron crews reaching effectiveness until the unit was fully equipped with the new aeroplanes. Meanwhile, the Mk Is were still going out of service through lack of spares or plain mishaps. Among the latter was K7130 which, on 17 January, was landed by Plt Off Illingworth who then inadvertently selected the wrong lever and raised the undercarriage instead of the flaps. Sgt T. K. Rees had a lucky escape from death on 23 January while carrying out local flying practice in Blenheim K7132. For reasons best known to himself, Rees attempted a half-roll. Being at 7,000 feet at the time, he may well have had sufficient altitude but at 200 mph his speed was too high. He said afterwards that when he came to ease the Blenheim out of the inverted position, it would not respond. By this time, he was in a vertical dive towards Mother Earth, with the speed rapidly increasing and the altimeter rapidly unwinding. Frantically winding the tail trimmer back, while heaving on the control column, Rees finally regained control at just 200 feet altitude and with 320 mph on the clock. His troubles were not over yet, as further difficulty was encountered when he could not maintain control below 110 mph during landing approach. Having brought the machine to rest on the airfield, an inspection showed the damage list to be: starboard tailplane tip, lost; rivets securing the stiffening flange to the main tailplane, sheared; port tailplane tip, bent at right-angle; part of starboard engine cowling, missing; and during the landing run the port undercarriage axle gave way, causing each prop blade on that side to be bent as it touched the ground. No doubt Sgt Rees discovered the colour of fear that day.

Inexorably 254 Squadron was being reduced to a standstill by this attrition rate and in fact never became operational at Sutton Bridge. On 27 January 1940 the luckless squadron was ordered to transfer to Coastal Command and move immediately to RAF Bircham Newton, where it did eventually receive its Mk IVs, maintaining an anti-shipping role for the rest of the war. During its stay at Sutton Bridge, naturally Dickie Barwell managed a few trips in a Blenheim before the squadron left for pastures new.

While all these new boys were striving to become operational under all sorts of trying conditions, the regular trade of range firing practice continued to be provided by the station.

By early 1939 the Fairey Gordon target tugs had gone, being replaced by the Hawker Henley described earlier.

Sutton Bridge station flight, comprising the Henley contingent – and known locally as the Henley Towing Flight (HTF) – was integrated with 254 Squadron when the latter arrived. Space was at a premium on the airfield now that there were three fighter units in the process of working-up. From 16 December 1939, therefore, the HTF, comprising Plt Off N. L. Banks, Sgts R. F. Worsdell, M. U. Wilkin and J. M. Cockburn, together with four Henley aeroplanes L3310, L3320, L3335 and L3375, was attached to 254 Squadron for matters of maintenance and discipline. Naturally Wg Cdr Barwell made sure he put some time in on the Henley, too (L3335).

Foul weather prevented customers from visiting the range so there was little for the 'Henley Boys' to get worked up about. In fact, during the whole of January 1940 only two towing sorties, for the benefit of 254, were flown. For the remainder of the time, tug pilots used the station Magister for local flying practice. In common with other units at Sutton Bridge at that time, the Henleys also arrived with certain essential equipment unfitted. Radio sets, in particular, were missing and made early towing sorties fraught with problems due to the inability to communicate effectively in the air. That in itself made range control difficult – and not a little dangerous. However, the situation was resolved in early January when radio sets were finally installed. At the end of that month, the officer in command of Henleys, Plt Off Banks, was posted to Aston Down and Sgt Worsdell had to temporarily assume command.

With adverse weather conditions persisting into February, again only 2 hours local flying practice could be completed. By March the weather perked up so that an hour or two towing over the range could be achieved most days but it was more a case of lack of customers than problems within the HTF. Initially the flight served squadrons based at Sutton Bridge itself – 254 and 264 – but due to the poor serviceability encountered by these units, gradually other relatively local squadrons, such as 29 (Debden) and 213 (Wittering), seem to have been invited along.

At the beginning of April 1940, Henley L3335 was reallocated to RAF Acklington for towing duty at that station and L3375 came in as a replacement. In this month, too, Plt Off S. C. Sutton took up residence as the new OC station flight and perceptibly now, there was an increase in the towing hours flown.

It was now time for events at RAF Sutton Bridge to take another significant, historic, twist. This latest change of direction allowed the station to retain its niche as a vital component of that process – begun before the war – which enabled the Royal Air Force to engage the enemy in the air with growing confidence. On 3 March 1940 an advance party from 11 Group Pilot Pool arrived from far-off RAF St Athan in South Wales. This was the forerunner of what, one week later, became known as 6 Operational Training Unit (6 OTU), which would remain at Sutton Bridge for the next two years – training pilots to fly the Hawker Hurricane before they were sent into combat. Keen as ever to lead from the front, Wg Cdr Barwell managed 3 hours in some of the OTU Hurricane (L1895, L2011, N2356, N2616, N2617), Gladiator (K8020) and Miles Mentor (L4400, L4404, L4420) aircraft, using these familiarisation trips to make visits to Group HQ at Hucknall and to fly under the guise of carrying out local air tests.

But how did it all begin?

Formed originally at RAF Andover 14 January 1939, the purpose of what was then known as 11 Group Pilot Pool was twofold:

a) To bring pilots posted from FTS to 11 (Fighter) Group up to the standard of fully trained fighter pilots before their posting to service squadrons.

b) To train RAF Volunteer Reserve pilots who had completed 120 hours flying solo and who were willing to devote from two to six months to learn the operational side of work as a fighter pilot. This latter referred to a pre-war situation.

Equipment was to be the Hawker Hurricane for operational training, and the Fairey Battle (T) for dual flying instruction. Establishment in men and machines was to be equivalent to that of a front-line, single-seat, fighter squadron. After six months the Pool moved to St Athan in South Wales and it remained there until the move to Sutton Bridge, whereupon it also transferred to 12 Group.

Sqn Ldr John Rhys-Jones assumed command on 24 February 1939 and he was joined by Plt Off P. A. N. Cox, Fg Off P. C. Pinkham, Fg Off M. L. Robinson and Fg Off A. W. A. Bayne, as flying instructors. On 1 March, No.1 course of eight Volunteer Reserve pupils arrived. The reason for the somewhat limited quantity was that until 12 and 142 Squadrons moved out of Andover there was a shortage of accommodation. On 1 July, the Pool completed its move to RAF St Athan where temporary accommodation had been erected to allow the unit to operate at full strength. 'B' Flight was created under the command of Fg Off Michael Lister Robinson, assisted by Fg Off Alfred William Alexander Bayne, and on 10 July seven new RAFVR pupils were allocated to it (course No.2). The original eight pupils were allocated to 'A' Flight. On 25 August, 'C' flight was formed under the command of Fg Off Philip Anthony Neville Cox; and on 31 August, six North American Harvard dual-control trainers were allotted to replace the Fairey Battle (T) aircraft, considered by all to be a great improvement but the Harvards were slow in being delivered.

Upon declaration of war, on 3 September 1939, the unit itself was declared operational and it was written in the ORB that 'all aircraft possible [i.e. six Hurricanes] to be rendered fit for operational flying, guns loaded with live rounds and harmonised to a range of 200 yards.' There has been much discussion about gun harmonisation and it has been widely recorded that ACM Sir Hugh Dowding ordered that the fire-pattern from aircraft with multiple machine guns was to be set to converge at 400 yards (sometimes referred to as the 'Dowding spread'). It is therefore interesting to find reference to '200 yards' at this early stage.

On 2 September, fourteen RAFVR sergeant pilots and three officers reported to St Athan for training and these are believed to represent course No.3. With the departure of Sqn Ldr Rhys-Jones to 13 Group HQ on 22 January 1940, Flt Lt Philip Campbell Pinkham took command of 11 Group Pool. It was not until 1 February 1940 that the next group of twenty officer pupils arrived to mark the commencement of course No.4. Interestingly, only two days later, ten of this batch were posted away to make space for the arrival of twelve Finnish pilots who were being given high priority for Hurricane training. Finland was at war with Russia in what was later called the 'Winter War' and Finland struck a business deal with the British government to buy a dozen 'low-hour' Hurricanes – allegedly for the sum of £9,700 each. The political situation was considered of such importance that it prompted a visit to St Athan by HM King George VI and HRH Queen Elizabeth, on 9 February. The twelve Finns completed their course by 25 February, on which date a group of six of them, escorted by a Bristol Blenheim, each flew a Hurricane to RAF Wick, the point at which they were to leave British shores and ferry the Hurricanes to Finland. The remaining six Finns repeated this arrangement on 29 February. Two Hurricanes were written off during the ferry flight and the remainder never saw action in the Winter War because in the meantime,an armistice had been reached. On 1 March, Course No.4 officially ended at St Athan and shortly afterwards, on 4 March 1940, the advance party of 11 Group Pilot Pool ground staff – four non-commissioned officers (NCOs) and twelve airmen – left St Athan by train, bound for RAF Sutton Bridge in Lincolnshire, to be followed on 9 March by the main party of six NCOs and ten airmen in the charge of Fg Off Yeo.

Fenland climes may seem an odd choice to locate a fighter training unit, being close to the east coast and particularly in view of the vagaries of the weather around The Wash – already mentioned on many occasions in this narrative – and furthermore the decision, just six months earlier, to banish 3 Armament Training School to the far north. In fact, RAF Speke (Liverpool) and Hucknall (Nottingham) were both considered as potential homes for the Pool but the former suffered from a surfeit of balloon barrages and bad weather, while the latter had too many night-flying restrictions, so both possibilities were discarded.

However, on 6 March, 11 Group Pool was officially re-named 6 Operational Training Unit (6 OTU) and with a complement of seven Hawker Hurricanes, three North American Harvards, five Miles Mentors and one Gloster Gladiator, its aeroplanes and team of instructors under the command of newly promoted Sqn Ldr Philip Campbell Pinkham arrived at Sutton Bridge. On 11 March the first flying training course to be run at the new station, No.5 course, got under way.

At this time, the ORB gives the impression that the pace of life at the OTU was still quite leisurely. One day a week was designated as a day off – the station closed – church parade went on as usual and the station routine seems to suggest a 'nine-to-five' mentality. Serviceability of the woefully small number of Hurricanes was poor; on 31 March, for example, only five were available for flying and – bearing in mind there were twenty pupil pilots approaching – coupled with inevitable non-flying weather days, the progress of the OTU pupils was slow. Another issue at Sutton Bridge was the layout of the grass airfield itself. It was relatively long but quite narrow and as a consequence, flying was particularly influenced by the direction of the wind. For example, the ORB states: 'landing is difficult on this airfield when the wind is from the west. There is insufficient room to land across the aerodrome and therefore cross-wind landings have to be made.' On 27 March and 4 April, it was noted: 'the wind was from the north-west and no Hurricane flying was possible owing to the narrow width of the airfield in the NW/SE diameter.' Cross-wind take-off and landing – at least by the rookie pilots – was not encouraged; there were precious few Hurricanes as it was, without running the risk of unnecessarily bending any more of them.

Springtime 1940 arrived in the fens and with it the rain, fog, frost and snow, which had be-devilled previous months, faded into the past. Originally, each training course – intakes of recognisable batches of pilots – was scheduled to last six weeks, although of necessity this was much reduced as that fateful year progressed; eventually to as little as two weeks. In that length of time it was intended to teach pupils how to fly a Hurricane, hopefully without bending it too much; something of what to expect in an operational squadron situation, and perhaps some tips from the experts (instructors) on how to stay alive in battle. Sadly, though, many young men trained here were yet to lose their lives in combat, while others never even made it that far. The importance of their task, however, was emphasised during a visit, on 22 April, by the AOC Fighter Command himself, ACM Sir Hugh Caswall Tremenheere Dowding GCVO KCB CMG etc.

Commencing upon completion of the move, on 11 March 1940, seventeen students made up the first fighter pilot course, which graduated from RAF Sutton Bridge on 27 April after about seven weeks of training. This was followed on 28 April by the start of what was called No.6 course but, before long, batches of trainees became gradually less defined, at least until some groups of foreign pilots began to arrive. A sobering fact about the statistics of this period of RAF Sutton Bridge history is that the numbers are so small, yet every pilot in Fighter Command was so vital to the success or failure of the Battle of Britain. From the date flying training commenced at 6 OTU Sutton Bridge – 11 March 1940 – to the official end-date of the Battle of Britain – 31 October 1940 – a total of 525 pilots 'graduated' from the station. Of this number, 390 pilots flew with Fighter Command and met the criteria for the award of the Battle of Britain clasp.

Great Britain & Commonwealth	300.	
Poland	41	(145)
Czechoslovakia	39	(87)
France	6	(13)
Belgium	3	(29)
USA	1	(11)

The numbers in brackets above indicate the total number of fighter pilots from that country who fought in the Battle. To put this into context, in simple terms, according to data in the book *Men of the Battle of Britain*, 2,927 airmen (the Battle of Britain Memorial, London, lists 2,937) were awarded the Battle of Britain clasp and 544 of these men lost their lives during the Battle. It is appreciated that not all were single-seat fighter-pilots, such as the graduates of the fighter OTUs, but the latter figure, the loss, is a key statistic; the one that the graduates of 6 OTU – and indeed the other fighter OTUs operating during the Battle – had to replenish. During the period under discussion there were two other fighter OTUs operating in a similar manner to Sutton Bridge. 5 OTU at RAF Aston Down, formed 15 March 1940, was also equipped with Hurricanes but had some Spitfires, Blenheims and Defiants on charge. 7 OTU at RAF Hawarden, formed 15 June 1940, was originally equipped with Hurricanes and Spitfires but standardised on Spitfires by August 1940.

To cope with the rising tide of pupils, the equipment inventory of 6 OTU was expanded rapidly during May 1940 from an average of about half a dozen Hurricanes available to No.5 course, rising to an average of twenty available to No.6 course. The number of serviceable aircraft increased even more after the middle of the year to a respectable 34 Hurricanes, 4 North American Harvards, 8 Miles Masters, 4 Fairey Battles (TT) and 4 Miles Mentors, plus an unknown quantity of each type classed as temporarily unserviceable. The Miles M9 Masters were initially the Mark I version powered by a RR Kestrel engine. During the course of the war, however, these were gradually replaced by the Mark II

(Bristol Mercury radial engine) and Mark III (Pratt & Whitney Wasp Junior) versions. Among the Master Mark Is at Sutton Bridge have been identified a couple of the rare Miles M24 Master Fighter conversions. These unusual 'fighters' were the result of the Air Ministry making contingency plans in case production of Spitfires and Hurricanes did not keep pace with the rate of attrition during the Battle of Britain. It asked manufacturers to put forward ideas for a cheap and easy to produce an alternative fighter and the Miles Aircraft Company came up with the M24 modification of their Master trainer.

The rear seat and dual controls were removed and the rear cockpit glazing reduced. A gun-sight was installed in the remaining front cockpit and six .303-inch machine guns installed, three in each wing (the usual integral single machine gun was removed in this instance). Twenty-six conversions were built with serial numbers N7412 (prototype) N7780 to N7782 and N7801 to N7822. Fortunately, it turned out that a stop-gap fighter was not needed and these rare single-seat M24 Masters were dispersed among the FTSs and single-engine OTUs, hence some being found in 6 OTU inventory at Sutton Bridge. It is not known if they were modified in any way before issue to the OTUs. Evidence of their use can be seen from the following incidents. Sgt Francis John Twitchett, who was posted in to 6 OTU from 3 FTS South Cerney on 31 August 1940 for operational training, had just 1 hour's advanced flying under his belt when he took up Master Fighter N7805 on 3 September. The engine failed on take-off and he made a wheels-up forced landing in a nearby field, from which he emerged unscathed. Having qualified on the Hurricane, Twitchett was posted out to 43 Squadron at RAF Usworth on 29 September, then went to 229 Squadron at RAF Northolt during October where he survived the Battle but was not credited with any air victories. He held flying posts for the remainder of the war and into the peace-time RAF. Another M24 Master, N7803, was identified from an accident to Plt Off R. Barrett on 19 September. Taxying for take-off, his aeroplane was caught by a strong gust of wind and it tipped onto its nose. Plt Off Barrett was unhurt but eventually mastering the Hurricane and being posted to 615 Squadron on 5 October, he does not appear to have qualified as a Battle of Britain pilot.

The Hurricanes were of variable quality by the time they reached 6 OTU with many from the L- series and some still had Merlin II engines fitted with a Watts fixed-pitch, two-blade wooden propeller e.g. L1714, L1896, L1897. In 1939 metal, three-bladed variable-pitch (two-positions: coarse and fine pitch) props were fitted to Hurricanes, even those with the Merlin II engine, greatly improving its performance and this improvement was followed up by the introduction of the Merlin III, which was designed to utilise a Rotol constant-speed, three-bladed wooden propeller. Hurricanes with the Merlin III/Rotol propeller combination eventually made up the bulk of 6 OTU inventory.

In addition to a few remaining Fairey Battle (T) trainers, four Fairey Battle (TT) Target Tugs also appeared in the OTU inventory during July 1940. This seems to reflect the increased work load on Sutton Bridge station flight – which operated the Henley Tugs primarily for 'visitors'. Up to July, the Henleys also provided a service for OTU trainees when required, as well as towing sleeve or cone targets for any operational squadron wishing to book air-to-air firing time over Holbeach Marsh range – much as their predecessors had done in the pre-war years. Squadrons visiting between April and June 1940, for example, were 19, 23, 29, 32, 66, 213, 254, 264 and 61. It should be remembered, too, that air-to-ground firing continued apace on the range and it was even recorded, on 15/18/19/27 October and 3 November, that a cannon-armed Hurricane and Spitfire used Holbeach range for air-to-air and air-to-ground test firing. The Battle (TT) aircraft therefore were operated by the OTU, which allowed station flight to concentrate on operational units while the OTU dealt with its own target towing requirements. Similarly, the influx of so many aeroplanes caused another problem; how to accommodate upwards of fifty machines both for protection against the elements and for servicing purposes.

To cope with the ever-rising tide of pupils – 33 for example arrived to begin training on 17 August 1940 – the aeroplane inventory of 6 OTU was increased. Serviceable aircraft on that date included 34 Hurricanes, 4 Harvards, 8 Masters, 4 Battles and 4 Mentors. Similarly, the influx of so many aeroplanes caused another problem; how to accommodate upwards of 50 machines both for protection against the elements and for servicing purposes. To this end Wg Cdr Barwell constantly pressed his superiors for more hangar-age and at long last, on May 1, work began to erect a new Bellman hangar, the first of two such hangars built. These never resolved the matter entirely and though they eased the issue of servicing, the situation would become even more acute when the total quantity of Hurricanes at the station hovered in the region of 90 machines during 1941 and even later when Spitfires and Wellingtons occupied the airfield in its Central Gunnery School (CGS) days.

It did not escape the Station Commander's notice that, situated as it was, close to the east coast and within the potential invasion area, his airfield might attract hostile attention from the Luftwaffe. He surmised that the enemy might attempt to carry out attacks on the aerodrome either by dropping bombs or parachute troops and under certain circumstances, they might arrive over or in the vicinity of the aerodrome without having been intercepted by fighter squadrons. Being a man of action therefore, on 12 May, Dickie Barwell drew up his Operational Order No.1, the stated intention of which was: 'to provide from station resources air opposition to an attack on this station'.

Wg Cdr Barwell ordered the OC 6 OTU to detail one section of three Hurricanes to be brought to readiness:

a) Whenever air raid warning 'yellow' was received in daylight hours.

b) From half-an-hour before sunrise to half-an-hour after sunrise.

c) At other times as ordered by the station commander.

The readiness section, call sign 'Domino Green', must always be led by an instructor but the other members could be either pupils or instructors. Pilots were to be strapped in, ready for take-off with aircraft positioned on the leeward side of the airfield, fully armed and with starter batteries connected. As might be imagined, there was no shortage of volunteers! Wary of trigger-happy ground defences and for the well-being of his men, Dickie Barwell also took care to warn the section to be particularly careful how they returned to the airfield after a sortie. There was to be no high-spirited antics – 'a wide circuit at 1,000–1,500 feet altitude must be made, at a speed of 140 mph so that ground defences may have time to recognise friendly aircraft. Pilots must NOT approach at low altitude, high speed or by diving on the airfield.' It was made pretty clear that if they did so they risked getting their **** shot off!

Ground defence at that time was composed of light anti-aircraft (AA) weapons – 40 mm Bofors cannon and light machine guns – manned by 66 officers and men of 'D' Company, 1st Battalion Cambridgeshire Regiment, supported by a searchlight battery operated by 10 men of the Royal Engineers. The composition of these units changed from time to time as the war progressed, while in August 1940, at the height of the Battle of Britain, in addition to its transient pupils, RAF Sutton Bridge permanent staff numbered 386 officers and airmen and 54 civilians. In mid-June 1940 it was time for another change and Wg Cdr Barwell was posted to 12 Group HQ at Watnall (Nottinghamshire) and Group Captain Henry Dunboyne O'Neill AFC (Air Cdre, CBE 1946) was posted in from North Weald to take command of the station; this upgrade of rank signifying its rising status within the RAF.

Air fighting on the Continent, sporadic until then, was about to erupt over the Franco-German border area, culminating in the land invasion of France and the Low Countries on 10 May 1940 backed up by the Luftwaffe. The pilots of No.5 course, who had been posted out of Sutton Bridge on 27 April, were pitched headlong into the thick of the *Blitzkrieg* in France.

In the course tables that follow, the 'Posted To' squadron is that written against each name in 6 OTU ORB/Form 540. It is realised, of course, that these pilots may well have been posted subsequently – rapidly or otherwise – to other squadrons during their RAF service. Abbreviations used are:

KIA   Killed in action.

MIA   Missing in action.

POW   Shot down & prisoner of war.

KOAS   Killed on active service (e.g. non-op mishap).

MOAS   Missing on active service (e.g. non-op mishap, body not recovered).

BF   Fought in Battle of France.

BB   Fought in Battle of Britain.

6 OTU, No.5 Course (11 March to 26 April 1940).
All listed in ORB as posted to France.

Name	Posted to.	Notes
Plt Off Roland Harold Dibnah	1 Sqn	BF; BB; Survived war.
Plt Off George Ernest Goodman	1 Sqn	BF; BB; DFC; KIA 14 June 1941, 73 Sqn.
Plt Off Charles Michael Stavart	1 Sqn	BF; BB Survived war. AFC 1953.

Plt Off Hugh William Eliot	73 Sqn	BF; BB; KIA 4 March 1945. DSO DFC.
Plt Off Aubrey McFadden	73 Sqn	BF; BB; KIA 5 April 1942.
Plt Off Valcourt Desmond Meredith Roe	73 Sqn	BF; KIA 14 May 1940, Namur, France.
Plt Off Robert Durham Rutter	73 Sqn	BF; BB; Survived war. DFC 1944.
Sgt L. Y. T. Friend	73 Sqn	BF; Combat in France; no further information found.
Plt Off Denis Heathcote Wissler	85 Sqn	BF; BB; MIA 11 Nov 1940; 17 Sqn.
Plt Off Paul Leonard Jarvis	87 Sqn	BF; MIA 14 May 1940 France.
Plt Off Arthur Eugene Le Breuilly	87 Sqn	BF; MIA 14 May 1940 France.
Sgt Eric John Keith Penikett*	87 Sqn	BF; Survived the war.
Sgt Kenneth Norman Varwell Townsend	607 Sqn	BF; POW 12 May 1940 France.

*There appears to be some doubt about Sgt Penikett's posting. His name is found in the caption of a group photo of 87 Squadron pilots taken in 1939 but he is also known to have been posted to 6 OTU from 87 Squadron during March 1940. He is then recorded as being posted back to 87 Squadron but his name cannot to be found among 87 Squadron accounts of the Battle of France, nor has he been found in any Battle of Britain listing. However, he does appear to have served through the war in some unknown capacity, as his name appears in issues of *The London Gazette* both when he was commissioned and promoted to Flt Lt (13 June 1946) and when he received the Kings Commendation for Valuable Service in the Air, also in 1946. The conclusion here, therefore, is that he did not fly in either of the Battles.

In addition to the above thirteen names that were recorded in the ORB, four more pilots have been identified as belonging to the original intake for No.5 course, making a total of seventeen in all but, for a variety of reasons, these four were not posted out when the bulk of the course left Sutton Bridge on 27 April. Although the above pilots are recorded as leaving on 27 April, unfortunately neither the ORB for 11 Group Pilot Pool nor 6 OTU listed the names of all the pilots when they joined No.5 course. The four additional pilots identified are Sgt John Wright, Plt Off Owen Edward Lamb, Sgt Geoffrey Tock and Plt Off Johannes Jacobus ('Chris') Le Roux, whose stories follow below.

Sgt John Wright, BB, went to 5 Course at 6 OTU on 11 March. While at 6 OTU he became lost during a cross country flight on 22 April and crashed Hurricane L2009 in fog at 200 mph into a hillside near Dishforth, Yorkshire, sustaining what were described as minor injuries. Suitably recovered, he was eventually posted to 79 Squadron on 6 July, thus missing the Battle of France. He fought in the Battle of Britain with 79 and died of wounds sustained in combat on 4 September.

Plt Off Owen Edward Lamb, (NZ) BB, crashed Hurricane L1896 on 25 March at Sutton Bridge but was unhurt in the incident. His Hurricane was an early model fitted with an original two-blade fixed-pitch propeller and the pilot managed to stall the aeroplane just after take-off and crash-landed. On 13 April he was posted to 1 Air Armament School at RAF Manby for a specialist armament officer course. This kept him occupied until 31 August when he went to 5 OTU for a refresher course on the Hurricane, after which he was posted to 151 Squadron at RAF Digby on 18 September to play his part in the Battle of Britain at last. He was killed in action on 14 April 1941 while flying with 73 Squadron during the air defence of Tobruk in North Africa.

Sgt Geoffrey Tock had two mishaps; force-landing Hurricane L2073 on 4 April when loss of oil caused the engine to seize and on 25 April when he collected L2006 from RAF St Athan and used the return leg to carry out a cross-country exercise. He ran out of fuel due to him running the engine at too high boost setting and had to force-land 5 miles north of Wisbech. It is believed he was posted from 6 OTU to 7 Bombing & Gunnery School as a staff pilot since there is a pilot of this name recorded as being killed in an air accident on 4 March 1941, while at that unit.

Plt Off Johannes Jacobus ('Chris') Le Roux, a South African, comes to prominence at 6 OTU as a result of a court martial – his own! On 14 May 1940, in the midst of the dust-up in France, Plt Off Roland Dibnah of 1 Squadron reported in at RAF Sutton Bridge as a witness at the general court martial of Plt Off Le Roux, which took place at the station on 16 May to investigate a complaint of low flying against Le Roux. The charge was dismissed. Plt Off Le Roux was ordered to proceed immediately to Personnel Distribution Centre (PDC) Uxbridge on being posted to 85 Squadron (as recorded in 6 OTU ORB) while Plt Off Dibnah could now get back to more pressing matters in France. Accounts of Le Roux's early RAF service are riddled with vagueness. He is believed to have served in 73 Squadron in the closing stages of the Battle of France and this might be consistent with his departure from Sutton Bridge. Some accounts suggest he also flew during the Battle of Britain – even to the extent of claims that he was shot down no less than 12 times during 1940 – but there is apparently no mention in his service record of him doing so and – though not necessarily conclusive – his name does not appear in any of the several modern listings of Battle of Britain participants. Le Roux's service during the Battles of France and Britain period therefore remains something of a mystery. Nevertheless, no matter what he had got up to since 14 May it is undisputed that from February 1941 Chris Le Roux carved out a distinguished flying career with 91, 111 and 602 Squadrons, as a fighter pilot and squadron commander, for which he was awarded a DFC and two bars (DFC**) and credited with an undisputed eighteen air victories. He was posted missing on 19 September 1944 when he failed to complete a non-operational flight from landing ground B-19 in France to RAF Tangmere, during which he is believed to have crashed into the English Channel.

In France, such was the mounting loss rate in 1 Squadron that by 20 May, for example, less than a month after leaving Sutton Bridge, Charles Stavart and George Goodman were leading sections of aircraft on combat sorties several times daily in French skies, while Roland Dibnah, equally committed, was put out of the fight for three months with a thigh wound sustained in combat on 26 May.

Singling out one person does not detract in any way from the gallant actions of others, but the story of 19-year-old Plt Off Denis Wissler will serve to illustrate just what these young men – boys – were thrown into. From RAF Sutton Bridge, Denis was posted to 85 Squadron on Lille-Lesquin/Seclin airfield France on 27 April, where he was attached to 'B' flight. The balloon had not yet gone up and he was instructed by his CO, Sqn Ldr John Oliver William Oliver (later CB DSO DFC), to fly only to get himself accustomed to the local area. The CO considered there was no pressing need at the moment for Wissler to be put on operational patrols and he would be better occupied putting in some more hours on the Hurricane; familiarising himself with the squadron routines and generally making himself useful on the ground.

When all hell was let loose on the morning of 10 May, the airfield was bombed, causing many casualties on the ground but fortunately most of the pilots were already in the air on patrol. Left behind, Denis Wissler had to run for his life for a slit trench when the bombing started and soon found out what war looked like when he helped to rescue the casualties afterwards. With mounting pilot casualties, now the CO had no option but to commit Plt Off Wissler to operations and Denis took his place alongside his comrades in the air – and managed to survive. During his first operational patrol on 12 May, Denis became separated from his flight and got lost. Landing on what – fortunately – turned out to be a French Air Force aerodrome he had to ask for directions back to his own base. No sooner had he returned than he was airborne again for another patrol. That night Denis wrote in his diary (a document that has survived and is lodged in the archives of the Imperial War Museum): 'I now have had six hours sleep in last forty-eight hours and have not washed for over thirty-six hours. My God, am I tired? And I am up again at three am tomorrow.' Next day, 13th, he was indeed up at the crack of dawn for a patrol from which he returned safely. His second sortie of the day was part of a flight led by Sqn Ldr Oliver. They were jumped by enemy Bf 109 fighters and John Oliver was shot down but managed to bale out. Denis Wissler made a bee-line for the cover of clouds and emerging cautiously, found himself alone and unsure of his whereabouts – again. Landing on another French airfield, this time Cambrai, it was pointed out to him that his Hurricane was badly leaking oil. For once, he was able to sleep soundly in the French officers' mess while RAF ground-crew were sent to fix his aeroplane. Just four days had elapsed in which Denis had to try to learn to do all the things needed to get himself airborne from a bombed airfield, fly his Hurricane in combat, avoid being shot down and, as if that wasn't enough, then find home when he had spent most of his time pulling such tight turns that he hardly knew which way was up! Tired he was – weren't they all – but he survived until the squadron was withdrawn to England (Debden) on 22 May. But Denis was not quite done with France yet. At Debden he was posted to 17 Squadron on 8 June and it was still operating in France, covering the withdrawal while flying from Le Mans airfield. He flew out to join the squadron on 9 June and survived the last days of the RAF campaign in France, finally withdrawing once more to Debden on 19 June.

Denis Wissler remained with 17 Squadron during the Battle of Britain, scoring his first success on 29 July when he shared in the destruction of a Heinkel He 111 bomber. By September he could be now considered an experienced fighter pilot, but in combat with Bf 109s over the Thames estuary on 24 September, after shooting at one '109, he went for a gaggle of four more and his Hurricane took a cannon shell hit in the port wing. The explosion damaged the flaps on that side and a shell fragment wounded him in the left arm. Denis dived hard to escape the fight and flew back to Debden where he made a flap-less landing. His Hurricane ran into a pile of rubble, which added to his woes by causing cuts and bruises to his face. After a couple of weeks in Saffron Walden hospital, he returned to flying duties on 10 October.

In the closing stage of the Battle of Britain, 17 Squadron was moved to RAF Martlesham Heath, where Fate finally caught up with Denis. On 11 November 1940 he was shot down and posted as missing in action during an engagement with enemy aircraft off the Essex coast near Burnham-on-Crouch. Plt Off Denis Wissler had played a gallant part in Fighter Command's two most significant air campaigns of the Second World War: The Battle of France and The Battle of Britain; he was just 19 years old and his story is truly representative of the young airmen of his day. Sqn Ldr Oliver's DSO and DFC were simultaneously awarded at the end of May, following the squadron's return to England.

Between 6 March, the date 6 OTU began operating from Sutton Bridge, and 18 June, when the RAF pulled out of France, sixty-two of its 'graduate' pilots had been sent to fight in that battle.

Relations between 1 Squadron and 6 OTU were further cemented when that squadron was forced to re-organise in France in late May. Two worrying factors brought about this situation although it was the point at which members of Sutton Bridge's 5 & 6 courses won their spurs. Exhausted by incessant – though successful – air combat, mounting losses and a nomadic existence, 1 Squadron's CO, Sqn Ldr Patrick John Handy ('Bull') Halahan pleaded with higher authority to replace his dwindling pool of experienced pilots and return them to

England before they all succumbed to the inexorable attrition rate. Not only were combat losses among the pre-war trained pilots and early graduates from 11 Group Pool and 6 OTU robbing Dowding of his hard core of experienced men, but he was also short of replacements and equally short of men capable of teaching them how to stay alive in the air. RAF Sutton Bridge was now going to play a vital role in dealing with this situation.

5

Battle of Britain

In the cold light of reality, if Fighter Command was to have any chance of growing sufficiently to defend mainland Britain, there was no other choice but to send the new boys into the fray, thus releasing what was left of the weary old hands to inject backbone into new units and pass on their combat experience. The new boys, too, acquitted themselves with honour and many of those who survived also went on to play a key role in the next big battle – the Battle of Britain.

Halahan's recommendation was accepted and on 28 May 1940 the following pilots from 1 Squadron, all distinguished Battle of France veterans, each with many air victories to his name, reported to 6 OTU Sutton Bridge for duty as flying instructors:

Name	Notes
Fg Off John Ignatious Kilmartin DFC	Posted from 6 OTU to 5 OTU on 12 June
Plt Off Peter W. O. ('Boy') Mould DFC	
Flt Sgt Francis Joseph Soper DFM	later DFC
Plt Off Raymond Grant Lewis	Mention in Despatches.
Fg Off Cyril D. ('Pussy') Palmer DFC	
Fg Off William Hector Stratton DFC	later bar to DFC
Fg Off William ('Billy') Drake DFC	Wounded in France 13 May 1940, hospitalised in England, arrived at 6 OTU on 20 June, later bar to DFC and a DSO

Sqn Ldr Halahan with his remaining original members of 1 Squadron were posted to the other Hurricane OTU (5 OTU) at RAF Aston Down.

During its sojourn in France, Sous-Lieutenant Jean Demozay, a French Air Force pilot, was attached to the squadron as official interpreter. In the closing days of the French campaign, the squadron ended up on Nantes airfield from which all its remaining aeroplanes were flown back to England. When the last Hurricanes disappeared over the horizon, Demozay and a group of eighteen RAF ground crew were left to fend for themselves. The idea was for them to drive another 100 miles south to La Rochelle for evacuation – hopefully – by sea. Demozay was not enamoured by this proposal and spotted a Bristol Bombay twin-engine transport out on the field. A quick inspection established that it was topped up with fuel but due to a broken tail wheel assembly it had been left behind as useless. Some of the ground crew had other ideas though and set to work to put this defect to rights, whereupon Demozay offered to fly them all back to England. Assisted by the senior NCO, Demozay took off and set course for the South Coast, intending to land at RAF Tangmere. During a singularly uneventful flight – when they were not intercepted by any other aircraft – the NCO told Jean that most of his group lived in East Anglia and would he mind flying on to RAF Sutton Bridge? Readily agreeing he simply carried on northwards – still not intercepted – and duly delivered them to their preferred destination.

Several other veterans of the campaign in France are recorded arriving at Sutton Bridge for instructor duties during the summer of 1940. For example, Fg Off Harold George ('Ginger') Paul was posted in from 5 OTU on 12 June upon his safe return to England from combat flying with 73 Squadron in France. On 25 August, Ginger Paul was posted from 6 OTU to the Central Flying School to attend a flying instructor ('war') course.

Before being posted to 6 OTU, Plt Off Richard Frewin Martin also saw action with 73 Squadron in France and had survived a quite unusual experience while on ops. Scrambled on 8 November 1939 to intercept a high-flying enemy bomber, 'Dickie' Martin passed out due to oxygen failure at 21,000 feet. Recovering his faculties at very low altitude, he found he was short of fuel and made a forced landing on an airfield that turned out to be in neutral Luxembourg – and thus found himself interned. Undaunted, he succeeded in escaping and made his way back to his squadron, arriving on 26 December to re-join the fray. Dickie was in constant action, claiming several air victories before 73 Squadron returned to England. Awarded a DFC, he enjoyed a long and distinguished military and civil flying career.

A contemporary of Martin's, Plt Off Peter Vigne Ayerst, also with 73 Squadron in France, became the first RAF pilot to encounter the Messerschmitt Bf 109 in combat in late-1939, surviving that encounter to become an ace during the Battle of France. With several of his comrades, he was posted as an instructor, first to 6 OTU at Sutton Bridge on 14 June 1940 to pass on his hard-won experience, then to 7 OTU, a Spitfire-equipped unit based at RAF Hawarden, on 3 July. Flt Lt John Evelyn ('Ian') Scoular DFC, 'B' flight commander of 73 Squadron was another battle-hardened veteran of France (twelve confirmed kills) posted in to 6 OTU on 24 June as an instructor.

On its return from France, 79 Squadron, too, gave up some of its combat experienced pilots for instructor duties. For example, New Zealander Flt Lt C. L. C. 'Bob' Roberts arrived at Sutton Bridge on 18 June, staying until 28 August 1941 before being posted to 57 (Spitfire) OTU; while Fg Off Frederick John Lawrence Duus arrived a few days later, on 25 June. The instructor pack was shuffled again when, on 28 June, Peter ('Boy') Mould left 6 OTU to re-join his former 1 Squadron pals instructing at 5 OTU Aston Down. This move was followed next day by the arrival at Sutton Bridge of his replacement, Flt Lt William Arthur Toyne from 17 Squadron, yet another veteran of the French campaign who had tasted and survived combat and who remained at Sutton Bridge until 22 March 1941 when he was posted to CFS for a formal instructor's course.

While the next intake of ex-FTS pupils provided more replacements for the final weeks of the campaign in France, subsequent intakes helped rebuild depleted squadrons for the imminent Battle of Britain. No.5 course had a duration of six weeks but the intake of twenty-seven pilots for what was called No.6 course, which commenced on 29 April, were posted out in batches on 11, 12 and 15 May after barely two weeks, with about half of their number being sent to France, while the rest went to squadrons in England. Incidentally, it was recorded by the OTU that the total flying time achieved by the twenty-seven trainees of No.6 course during their time at Sutton Bridge was 669 hours – an average of 25 hours apiece. During that hectic summer, though, some pilots were posted to front-line squadrons after less than a week and/or with just a few hours flying a Hurricane at 6 OTU.

The next course of ex-FTS pupils for operational training (let us assume No.7 but it was not actually identified by a number in the ORB) appears to have begun assembling at Sutton Bridge with the arrival of four pilots on 14 May followed by a further fifteen on 18 May. With a week or less getting to grips with the Hurricane, all nineteen were posted out to squadrons on 24 May with five of them, even at this late stage, being posted to squadrons still in France. This 'course' comprised:

Name	Notes
Plt Off James Lockhart	85 Sqn; BB.
Plt Off Peter Leslie Gossage	85 Sqn; KOAS 31 May 1940.
Plt Off John Lawrence Bickerdyke (NZ)	85; BB; KOAS 22 July 1940.
Plt Off William Henry Hodgson (NZ)	85; BB (DFC); KOAS 13 March 1941.
Sgt John Hugh Mortimer Ellis	85; BB; KIA 1 Sept 1940.
Sgt Ernest Reginald Webster	85; BB.
Plt Off Charles Edward English	85; BB; KIA 7 Oct 1940.
Sgt Walter Reginald Evans	85; BF; BB.
Plt Off David Cooper Leary	17; BF; BB (DFC); KOAS 28 Dec 1940.
Plt Off Jack Kenneth Ross	17; BF; BB; (later DFC); KOAS 6 Jan 1942.
Sgt Desmond Fopp	17; BF; BB; (later AFC).
Sgt Glyn Griffiths	17; BF; BB (DFM).
Plt Off Hubert Weatherby Cottam	213; BB; KOAS 5 Dec 1941.
Plt Off Joseph Emile Paul Laricheliere (Can)	213; BB; MIA 16 Aug 1940.
Sgt George Downs Bushell	213; BB; KOAS 31 Dec 1940.
Sgt Ivor Kenneth Jack Bidgood	213; BB; KOAS 2 June 1941.
Sgt Ernest George Snowden	213; BB.
Sgt Harry Snow Newton	111; BB; (later AFC).
Sgt Richard Alfred Spyer	111; BB; MIA 22 March 1941.

In early 1941, as an experienced combat pilot, Sgt Bidgood was posted back to 56 OTU for a spell as an instructor. On 2 June 1941, he was flying a practice sortie from Sutton Bridge in company with another experienced Battle of Britain pilot instructor, Flt Sgt John

Craig DFM. During combat manoeuvres the two aeroplanes collided and crashed at Terrington St John, near King's Lynn, with the loss of both men.

In contrast to the ex-FTS pupils, other pilots were drawn from a variety of units and selected for rapid conversion to, or a refresher course on, the Hurricane, in a desperate attempt to top up the flow of fighter pilots to the front line. These further categories included:

a) Pilots posted in from existing front-line units who it was felt would benefit from a spell at the OTU before being pitched into combat and

b) More senior officers who were currently 'flying a desk' or holding non-operational posts and were considered suitable to take over command of squadrons that had perhaps lost their CO during the fighting.

On 27 May, for example, a former pre-war RAF College Cranwell graduate and subsequent member of the college staff, Flt Lt Henry Cecil Sawyer, was posted from the staff of 9 Bombing & Gunnery School (9 B&GS) at RAF Penrhos to 6 OTU for a flying refresher course. He was in line for promotion as the new OC 65 Squadron, which operated the Spitfire at RAF Hornchurch, so, having found his feet (or should that be his wings) again on the Hurricane, on 14 June he was sent to 7 OTU at Hawarden to convert to the Spitfire. Having completed that transition satisfactorily, Sqn Ldr Sawyer was posted to RAF Hornchurch on 2 July and took command of 65 Squadron on 8 July. Henry Sawyer was killed on active service on 2 August 1940 when he crashed during take-off for an operational night sortie.

Similar examples include Flt Lt George Douglas Morant Blackwood (of the Blackwood publishing company) who entered the RAF in 1932, and held a number of flying posts during the pre-war era, before re-joining the family business. Mobilised when war broke out, he found himself first in an instructor role then on the staff at 23 Group HQ, where he requested a move to operational flying. Blackwood was posted to Sutton Bridge on 20 May for a 'flying refresher course' to convert him to the Hurricane before being posted to command 213 Squadron on 5 June. At the end of June 1940, he was appointed as the first OC of 310 Squadron, the first Czech fighter squadron to be formed and which became operational on 17 August. He participated in the Battle of Britain and, surviving the war, he re-joined his family business once again. Flt Lt Wilfred William Loxton was posted to 6 OTU on the same day as Blackwood. Loxton came in from 1 FTS Netheravon where he was an instructor, also for a flying refresher course and he too was posted out on 5 June, taking command of 25 Squadron during the Battle until relinquishing that post on 24 September.

Emigrating to England from his native New Zealand in 1930, Terence Gunion Lovell-Gregg joined the RAF in 1931 and held many flying posts before the war. The outbreak of war found him in the operations room of RAF Finningley in Bomber Command from where, in January 1940, he moved to HQ 5 Group, Bomber Command. After requesting a posting to fighters, Lovell-Gregg got his wish and was sent to Sutton Bridge on 27 May for a flying refresher course and conversion to the Hawker Hurricane. He was posted out on 15 June to 87 Squadron, joining it at RAF Church Fenton as a supernumerary until he had gained some operational experience. Sqn Ldr Lovell-Gregg then led the squadron when it relocated to Exeter. Flying operations from that station, he was killed in action on 15 August 1940.

Much has been written about young replacement pilots – in both world wars – being pitched into the cauldron of battle with woefully little experience. Some lived, some died, but all were indeed brave young men. 6 OTU can provide examples of the contrasting stories of three such men who fell into the 'trawled pilot' category.

Commissioned on 26 May 1940, Plt Off Kenneth Maltby Carver was posted to 29 Squadron to fly the twin-engine Blenheim IF. His subsequent posting can be seen as an example of the policy of trawling multi-engine squadrons for potential single-seat fighter pilot material as the Battle of Britain gathered momentum and highlighted gaps in manpower. Sutton Bridge was to play a key role in this process, too.

Plt Off Carver, Plt Off Neville Solomon and Sgt Ronald Bumstead were three pilots from 29 Squadron detailed to report from their current station of RAF Digby to 6 OTU on 16 July for what was termed 'a flying refresher course'. This term differentiated those pilots being trawled from other units or even non-flying posts – who were felt either to have single engine fighter aptitude or already had previous experience which needed brushing up – from those new pilots fresh from the Flying Training Schools. The latter were usually referred to in the ORB as being 'posted in for operational training' but every few days from June 1940 and throughout that fateful summer, there was a constant trickle of two or three of the former, inter-mingling with the new boys as postings came and went. Although distinct groups of trainees can be detected among the new arrivals at Sutton Bridge, gone was the concept of numbered 'courses' (such as No.5 and No.6 mentioned above), now replaced by the necessity for a continual flow system as losses from the Battle mounted.

Kenneth Carver recalled turning up at RAF Sutton Bridge and being billeted in the local doctor's house. That same day he was confronted by his first Hurricane and swiftly shown over the controls. Climbing into the cockpit he took off gingerly only to be alarmed to find the windscreen gradually becoming obscured by leaking glycol (engine coolant fluid). Landing safely after 'a hairy flight' he was blithely informed he should not have been allocated that particular aeroplane as it had been declared unserviceable! The very next day, now considered capable of flying a Hurricane, he was posted out to join 229 Squadron at RAF Wittering!

Fortunately for Ken Carver, Wittering sector was pretty quiet and he had time to find his feet before 229 moved to RAF Northolt to take a more active part in the Battle. It was here that Plt Off Carver finally got to grips with the enemy but was shot up and badly burned on his hands and face during a combat engagement with enemy fighters on 11 September while flying Hurricane N2466. He baled out and survived his ordeal, returning to 229 Squadron in 1941 after many months of hospitalisation and retired after the war as a Sqn Ldr with the DFC.

Plt Off Neville David Solomon was less fortunate. He left Sutton Bridge bound for 17 Squadron at Debden after just three days trying to get to grips with the Hurricane. Debden, being closer to the action, offered no gentle breaking-in period but fortunately for him, Plt Off Solomon's woeful lack of experience was quickly recognised and his CO packed him off back to Sutton Bridge for more Hurricane training. It was 15 August before he returned to the squadron to take up his place in action alongside his hard-pressed comrades. On the day that historians now call 'The Hardest Day' of the Battle of Britain, 18 August, 17 Squadron was scrambled around 1.00 pm to intercept hordes of German fighters and bombers that were streaming back to their French bases having attacked the RAF airfields of Kenley and Biggin Hill. What a helluva day for Plt Off Solomon, in Hurricane L1921, to fly his first operational sortie. He was in Red section; three Hurricanes led by the squadron commander Sqn Ldr Cedric Watcyn Williams and they were after the bombers. Neville was the section 'weaver' whose job was to fly from side to side at the rear of the section guarding the tails of the two more experienced men. Sgt John Etherington was the other member of Red section and he recalled seeing what seemed to be hundreds of German aircraft of all types streaming past them. He said Solomon just disappeared and he never saw him go nor heard him on the radio. It was somewhere off Dover that a 109 must have got him and he was never seen again. Neville Solomon's body was washed ashore on the French coast and he is buried in the CWGC section of Pihen-les Guines cemetery, south of Calais.

Sgt Ronald Frederick Bumstead was also posted to 17 Squadron at RAF Debden on 18 July after just two days at Sutton Bridge, but he managed to stay alive – even moving across the airfield to join 111 Squadron on 26 August. Soon after, it is believed he was posted to RAF Kenley as an instructor at the Kenley Wing Training Flight before returning to 111 Squadron on 14 September, which by then had moved north to RAF Drem. He was commissioned in 1943, survived the war and was awarded an AFC in 1946.

Pressure such as this at OTU level brought accidents with it. The extent and frequency of mishaps varied from one group of trainees to another, with no discernible pattern except that most were due to errors of judgement or mechanical failures. For example, during the first course (No.5) six mishaps were recorded, all fortunately without fatal result while the second course (No.6) was completed with a clean record – although the latter was to become a rarity as will become apparent later. First of the accidents to result in a fatality for 6 OTU was that involving Sgt Charles Frederick Cotton, who arrived at Sutton Bridge on 2 June but lost his life in Hurricane L1897 on 25 June 1940 when it crashed near the village of Upwell. Tony Steer was 10 years old and living near Upwell at the time of the accident and he described what he saw that day:

The crash remains very vivid in my mind, happening at that impressionable age and living in an area much frequented by the aeroplanes from Sutton Bridge. My cousin and I were standing near a large, black, metal-framed bridge spanning Middle Level Drain. We watched this Hurricane following the drain, flying towards the bridge at about 60 feet above the water. I could see the pilot quite clearly, waving at us and we waved back. Approaching the bridge, which is about 40 feet high, the aeroplane suddenly climbed steeply. At a guess, when it reached between 1,000 and 1,500 feet it appeared to stop in mid-air then plunged nose down to crash into a wheat field at the side of the drain. The site was part of Low Farm, Upwell.

Running like mad to the field, at first sight there was no sign of the aeroplane. Everything was below the level of the wheat crop and all that marked the passage of the Hurricane was a relatively small crater with a little wisp of smoke rising from it. Hereabouts the soil is very soft, with a lot of peat and I think this would account for the Hurricane going in so far.

I remember being frightened by the thought of perhaps seeing a dead man so I held back from going any closer. That night, too, I overheard talk of removing the remains of the pilot to our farmhouse and had a nightmare about it. I never discovered if the pilot was found or what happened to him. Next day a 60-foot RAF recovery lorry arrived and tried to get close to the crash site but it was unable to do so because of the gateways from the river bank being too narrow.

During 1980 my cousin and I re-visited that field and found a few small fragments from all those years ago. We even found some pieces with blue and red paint on, probably from the roundels.

According to the Air Ministry (AM) accident record card (Form AM 1180), Sgt Cotton was authorised to carry out aerobatics in a low flying area but for unknown reasons appeared to have gone below the recommended height of 10,000 feet. It was considered that when he pulled up to avoid a bridge the aeroplane stalled and hit the ground before he had time to recover. Sgt Cotton was buried in his home town in Essex.

Having arrived in March with just a handful of Hurricanes, by the end of May the quantity of serviceable aeroplanes available at 6 OTU rose to a more practical 24 Hurricanes, 4 Harvards, 5 Mentors and 3 Gladiators. When the impact and lessons of the air fighting in France filtered down through the hierarchy of the RAF, it was clear that the 'nine-to-five' days were over. On 27 May at Sutton Bridge it was decreed that flying training would be carried out over longer working hours to increase the throughput of pupils. Two 'shifts' would be worked daily: 5.00 am to 12.30 pm and 1.30 pm to 9.00 pm. With effect from 9 June, to keep the supply of pilots flowing even more effectively, now that there were more Hurricanes and instructors available, flying training was again re-organised on a three-Flight basis: 'A' commanded by Flt Lt George Greaves (arrived 14 April), 'B' by Fg Off 'Pussy' Palmer, and 'C' by Fg Off Alexander Andrew Marshall Dawbarn. Sqn Ldr George Campbell Tomlinson DFC (OBE 1946), who had seen action with 17 Squadron during the Battle of France, was posted in on 3 June as officer in charge of (i/c) flying. Sqn Ldr Philip Pinkham was posted out to command 19 Squadron at Duxford, to be replaced by Wg Cdr John Humphrey Edwardes-Jones (later AM Sir Humphrey KCB CBE DFC AFC), who had been OC 17 and 213 Squadron during the Battle of France before taking over as OC 6 OTU on 9 June. The OTU was indeed well staffed by men with proven experience of combat flying.

In its time, RAF Sutton Bridge saw aircrew of all Allied nationalities pass through its gates. Polish pilots, the first of many batches of exiles destined for active service in the summer of 1940 – and beyond – arrived on 23 June complete with an interpreter. The latter was a highly necessary role in a potentially hazardous situation. Some of these fellows, in most cases already trained pilots (to varying degrees) and some even with combat experience, had little command of the English language, high performance aeroplanes in which all the knobs, levers and dials were labelled in a foreign tongue, or RAF radio procedures. 6 OTU was eventually to train these men with great success and many carved out distinguished war records with the RAF. It is not intended here to record in detail the wealth of individual careers and feats as these are far more adequately handled in books such as Kenneth Wynn's *Men of the Battle of Britain* (Norwich: Glidden, 1989); by Christopher Shores' *Aces High* and *Those Other Eagles* (London: Grub Street, 1994 and 2004 respectively) and by many websites that have sprung up both at home and abroad. Instead, a few examples will be outlined to illustrate the richness of activity at Sutton Bridge and some of the more prominent incidents that occurred. To say that these exiled patriots, be they Poles, Czechs, Belgians, French, Danes, Norwegians and others, simply 'arrived' at Sutton Bridge is to understate the tortuous journeys many of these individuals endured while fleeing across Europe. Some, in particular the Poles and Czechs, after fighting the Germans in the air with their respective air forces, undertook hazardous journeys to reach England in order to carry on their fight, but often ended up in filthy camps in Romania and even France. It should not be overlooked, therefore, that many Poles and Czechs who eventually flew with Fighter Command had faced not only the potential wrath of the Germans and Russians but, for purely political and racial reasons that will not be elaborated upon here, they were initially treated poorly by both France and Britain.

The first 'foreign' contingent which arrived on 23 June at Sutton Bridge, was also the first of five batches of Polish airmen to be posted in during The Battle.

Composition of first Polish pilot course at 6 OTU
Posted In: 23 June 1940. Posted Out: 16 July 1940.

Name	Posted To	Notes.
Plt Off Stanislaw Lapka	302 Sqn	BB Survived the war.
Plt Off Tadeusz Nowak	253 Sqn	BB KIA 21 Sep 1941.
Fg Off Antoni Ostowicz	145 Sqn	BB MIA 11 Aug 1940.
Flt Lt Wilhelm Pankratz	145 Sqn	BB MIA 12 Aug 1940.
Plt Off Edward Roman Pilch	302 Sqn	BB KOAS 20 Feb 1941.
Plt Off Wlodzimierz Michal Czech Samolinski	253 Sqn	BB MIA 26 Sep 1940.
Plt Off Virpsha	Retained as interpreter.	

The above group of six Polish pilots and an interpreter, was posted in from 18 OTU at RAF Hucknall, which, from 15 June 1940, was the new designation for the original Polish Training Unit. This unit was formed to train light bomber crews for Polish-manned Fairey Battle squadrons but 18 OTU later trained crews for Polish Wellington bomber squadrons.

These six pilots were the first Poles to join operational Fighter Command squadrons. Fg Off Antoni Ostowicz is generally credited as the first Polish pilot to claim an air victory during the Battle of Britain when, on 19 July, he shared in the destruction of a Heinkel He 111 bomber. He continued combat flying with 145 Squadron, although not adding to his score, until he was shot down on 11 August, near the Isle of Wight in Hurricane V7294 and posted as missing in action. Flt Lt Wilhelm Pankratz joined 145 Squadron at the same time as Ostowicz and he, too, was shot down and reported missing in the same area the very next day.

At RAF Kenley, 253 Squadron was having a very hard time of it, having lost three commanding officers and eleven pilots in the week prior to 26 September. Plt Off Wlodzimierz Samolinski had survived so far and made his mark, claiming a Bf 110 on 30 August; another 110 on 4 September and a share of a Dornier Do 17 on the 11th. On 26 September he was on patrol as wing-man to his new CO, Sqn Ldr Gerald Richard Edge, a highly experienced and successful fighter pilot. Around 11 am, out over the English Channe,l they were bounced by enemy 109s and both men were shot down immediately. Sqn Ldr Edge managed to bale out of his burning machine and, badly burned, was rescued from the sea by a British boat. It was November 1941 before he was fit enough to return to operational flying. Plt Off Samolinski's Hurricane V7470 was seen to dive into the sea and he disappeared without trace.

Composition of the second Polish pilot course at 6 OTU.
Posted In: 14 July 1940. Posted Out: 3 August 1940.

Name	Posted To	Notes.
LAC Zbigniew Urbanczyk	18 OTU	Ferry Pilot, 112 & 306 Sqns.
Plt Off Karol Pniak	32 Sqn	BB Survived the war. DFC.
Plt Off Jan Piotr Pfeiffer	32 Sqn	BB MOAS 20 Dec 1943.
Plt Off Boleslaw Andrzej Wlasnowolski	32 Sqn	BB KIA 1 Nov 1940.
Plt Off Michal Jan Steborowski	238 Sqn	BB KIA 11 Aug 1940.
Sgt Marian Boguslaw Domagala	238 Sqn	BB Survived the war.
Flt Lt Tadeusz Chlopik	302 Sqn	BB KIA 15 Sep 1940.
Plt Off Stanislaw Skalski	302 Sqn	BB Survived the war as Poland's most successful fighter pilot. DSO DFC**.
Fg Off Stefan Witorzenc	501 Sqn	BB Survived the war. DFC.
Sgt Antoni Glowacki	501 Sqn	BB Survived the war. DFM DFC.
Fg Off Witold Urbanowicz	145 Sqn	BB Survived the war. DFC.
Flt Sgt Josef Kwiecinski	145 Sqn	BB MIA 12 Aug 1940.

This second intake of Polish pilot trainees arrived on 14 July from 1 School of Army Co-operation at RAF Old Sarum where the ability and potential of pilots was assessed and graded. There was certainly some talent in this batch.

On 24 August 1940 Flt Sgt Antoni Glowacki, having already one confirmed victory to his name, achieved the distinction of becoming the first pilot to claim five enemy aircraft destroyed in a single day's flying, thus becoming the first RAF ace-in-a-day. He survived the Battle of Britain with nine confirmed victories and ended his operational flying with 303 Squadron and adding one more claim to his total.

LAC Zbigniew Urbanczyk had flown in action when the Germans invaded Poland in 1939 and was credited with shooting down one enemy Henschel Hs 126 and sharing a Heinkel He 111, all while flying the PZL P-7 fighter. He blotted his copybook three days after arrival at Sutton Bridge when he suffered a landing accident in Hurricane N2616. Coming in to land, he held off too high and the aircraft 'ballooned' as it touched down. Urbanczyk pulled the stick back sharply, the aircraft stalled, hit the ground hard and the undercarriage collapsed. The station commander, Gp Capt O'Neill, was not amused and wrote in his report that the accident was due to the pilot's lack of knowledge of English and his inability to fly the Hurricane successfully. He recommended that Urbanczyk be posted for further preliminary training and went on to say that in his opinion pilots should not be sent to OTUs until they had at least some command of the English language. LAC Urbanczyk left Sutton Bridge but continued to fly, first as a ferry pilot in the UK and then at RAF Takoradi in Ghana. In 1942, after a course at 71 OTU in the Sudan, he was posted to 112 Squadron to fly Curtiss P-40 Kittyhawks in combat in the North African desert campaign, sharing in the destruction of a Bf 109 during that period. After more ferrying work he was posted back to the UK to convert to the Spitfire at 58 OTU prior to joining 306 (Polish) Squadron in February 1943. Ironically, he ended his wartime RAF career as an instructor at 18 FTS and retired to Blackpool where he passed away in 1986.

In complete contrast, one of Urbanczyk's companions was Plt Off Stanislaw Skalski, who became a legend in the RAF and the top-scoring Polish fighter pilot in Fighter Command. Born near Odessa in Ukraine in 1915, in 1917 his mother took him to live in Zbarazh which was then in Poland. He joined the Polish Air Force in 1936 and flew the PZL P-11c fighter in action with 142 Eskadra when Poland was invaded, claiming at least four aircraft destroyed and a number shared, becoming the only Polish ace of that five-week campaign. He escaped from Poland to Romania, making his way to the Mediterranean and thence to France and finally to England, where he arrived in January 1940. Skalski volunteered for the RAF and with his experience, he was commissioned and posted to 1 School of Army Co-Operation at Old Sarum on 5 July, a holding unit for Polish pilots while their flying experience and potential were assessed. Graded as fighter pilot material, Skalski was posted to 6 OTU Sutton Bridge on 14 July and on 3 August he was posted to RAF Leconfield to join 302 Squadron, the first Polish squadron to be formed within RAF Fighter Command. 302, however, was not declared operational until 15 August and Skalski was posted on 12 August to 501 Squadron as a much-needed replacement, since 501 was in the thick of the action down at RAF Gravesend. Here he met up with Fg Off Stefan Witorzenc and Sgt Antoni Glowacki, who had been posted directly to 501 and it was not long before all three men were claiming several air victories each. Credited with seven enemy aircraft destroyed during the Battle, Skalski was shot down on 6 September and his injuries kept him out of action until 25 October. Various promotions, postings and gallantry awards (both British and Polish) came his way and his score continued to steadily mount. During 1943 he formed a special Polish Fighting Team, equipped with the latest Spitfire model, to operate as a roving combat unit in support of the Desert Air Force in North Africa. This was a great success and gave rise to the unit being known universally as 'Skalski's Circus'. He became only the second Polish pilot to command an RAF Squadron (601) and by D-Day in 1944 was Wing Leader of three Polish squadrons operating the North American P-51 Mustang over the Continent. In 1944 he attended command courses in the USA, returning to England in 1945. He opted to return to Poland in 1947 and served in the Communist-dominated Polish Air Force until he was arrested in 1948, tried for espionage, sentenced to death but incarcerated in a prison until released in 1956. He continued to fly as a civilian until his death in 2004 and he was greatly revered throughout the world of flying.

In 1930 Witold Urbanowicz joined the Polish Air Force, graduating in 1932 as a fighter pilot and during 1936 he demonstrated his potential by shooting down a Russian aeroplane that had strayed into Polish air space. At the outbreak of the Second World War he was a flying instructor and managed to escape the German invasion of Poland by fleeing to Romania, then to France and eventually to England where, in January 1940, he volunteered his services to the RAF. Having convinced the authorities of his considerable experience, Urbanowicz was sent to 6 OTU at Sutton Bridge on 14 July for conversion to the Hurricane. He was subsequently posted out to 145 Squadron on 3 August and claimed two air victories with the squadron. In September he was posted to 303 Squadron as officer commanding and added at least thirteen more 'kills' before being posted again prior to the end of the Battle of Britain. Sent to the USA, he fulfilled several public relations roles and also that of Assistant Air Attaché at the Polish embassy in Washington DC. His flying career took a new twist when he accepted an invitation to fly with the US 14th Air Force in China. While flying operationally with General Clair Chennault's Flying Tigers, he shot down two Japanese aircraft during December 1944. Returning to England in 1945, he was appointed Polish Air Attaché back in Washington; resigned from the RAF and returned to Poland. In common with many of his compatriots, Urbanowicz was arrested and imprisoned by the Communist regime but upon release emigrated to the USA where he spent the rest of his life as a US citizen. Wg Cdr Witold Urbanowicz DFC is credited with a total of at least eighteen air victories during his flying career.

The third group of Poles was six in number arriving on 18 July and being posted out to squadrons on August 17. All fought in the Battle of Britain – except for Plt Off Kazimierz Olewinski, who was killed halfway through his OTU course. Airborne at 7 am on 29 July in Hurricane L1714, Plt Off Olewinski was authorised to practise air combat and aerobatic manoeuvres above 5,000 feet altitude. His aeroplane was last seen by one of his comrades to begin a dive at 10,000 feet altitude from which it never pulled out, crashing deep into the earth at Walsoken, near Wisbech. Olewinski was buried in the cemetery of St Matthew's Church in the village of Sutton Bridge and although he was not the first fatality at 6 OTU (see Sgt Cotton 21 June 1940), he became the first of the long lines of wartime airmen's graves in that churchyard.

Central to the co-ordination of this embryo training system was SHQ RAF Sutton Bridge. It will be remembered from an earlier chapter that Wg Cdr Barwell was at the helm initially. Having got the three embryo fighter squadrons off the ground, leaving the way open for 6 OTU to take up residence, Dickie Barwell saw the OTU safely established then, on 13 June 1940, handed over command of the station to Gp Capt Henry Dunboyne O'Neill AFC (CBE 1946), a First World War RFC veteran. Barwell was subsequently appointed station commander of RAF Biggin Hill. Having made a practice of flying occasional operational sorties, consistent with his policy of leading from the front, it was on one such patrol, 1 July 1942, that Wg Cdr Philip Barwell lost his life, shot down in error by a rookie Spitfire pilot who made a tragic error of identification.

Sandwiched between the second and third Polish intakes it was the turn of a group of twelve Free French airmen to arrive on 20 July, followed ten days later by three Belgian pilots and the fourth group of eleven Poles. These were followed on 17 August by the first group of twenty Czech trainees and the second, smaller group of five Frenchmen.

First French intake.

Posted In: 20 July 1940. Posted Out: 10 Aug 1940 all to FAFL RAF Odiham.
(Ranks are those recorded by 6 OTU)

Name	Notes.
WO Albert Littolff	KIA 16 July 1943 in Russia.
WO Georges Francois Marie Gérard Grasset	Survived the war.
WO James Georges Denis	DFC; survived the war.
WO Roger André Edouard Speich	Survived the war.
WO Louis Ferrant	Survived the war.
Flt Sgt Adonis Louis Moulénes	Survived the war.
Flt Sgt Robert Grasset	KIA?
Sgt Robert Guédon	MIA 25 April 1941 Tobruk.
Sgt Xavier Albert Marie Esprit de Scitivaux de Greische	Survived the war.
Sgt Noel Michel Castelain	KIA 16 July 1943 in Russia.
Sgt Jules Paul Marie Joseph Joire	KOAS 18 March 1944 in Russia.
Sgt Claude A. D. Deport	Assigned to 6 OTU 30 Sept 1940 as instructor; to 213 Sqn 14 Dec 1940; survived the war.

Following Général de Brigade Charles de Gaulle's impassioned radio broadcast from England on 18 June 1940, these former French Air Force pilots, who had escaped to England when France fell, were among the first exiled Frenchmen to rally to the cause of de Gaulle, the self-exiled and self-declared leader of Free France. Upon reaching England and volunteering for service with the *Forces Françaises Libres* (FFL) as pilots, they were posted with other potential French aircrew to RAF St Athan. The flying ability of this first dozen – with their claims of substantial experience – was checked out at St Athan and found to be as good as claimed and then, mindful of de Gaulle's great impatience to get the contribution of the FFL to the war effort under way, they were deemed suitable candidates to be trained rapidly for that purpose.

This background accounts for them now being despatched to 6 OTU at Sutton Bridge 'for operational training' but, unlike other intakes, these French pilots were not posted out to operational RAF squadrons. On completion of their time at Sutton Bridge, all twelve were posted to RAF Odiham, designated as the operational and training base for the Free French Air Force (*Forces Aériennes Françaises Libres* or FAFL), where they formed the fighter element of *Groupe de Combat Mixte 1* (GMC 1) the first mixed (fighters, bombers, reconnaissance) unit of de Gaulle's embryo air force. By opting to fight with the Free French Forces instead of returning to France to serve the Vichy Government these pilots faced the prospect of execution as deserters if captured by Germans or Vichy forces on future operations. As we shall see later, by no means all escaped Frenchmen and women were supporters of General de Gaulle and during 1940 there were other exiled French pilots who preferred to serve with the RAF rather than with de Gaulle's FAFL. Among all the exiled patriots passing through Sutton Bridge, this first batch of Frenchmen shows just what these men had to go through to reach what they saw as freedom and then how far and wide they served to fight for their chosen cause.

When de Gaulle broadcast his 'Free France' appeal, James Denis was an instructor at the *Ecole des Radio-navigants 1* (1 Wireless School) at Saint Jean-d'Angely airfield, near La Rochelle. He decided to escape to England and on 20 June, with nineteen like-minded compatriots, they hi-jacked an obsolete Farman 222 four-engine bomber from the servicing hangar and Denis flew it to England. Among his passengers that day were Roger Speich and Louis Ferrant, who were also experienced pilots on the Wireless School staff. After volunteering for the FAFL – and being carefully 'vetted' in case they might be German/Vichy agents – they were posted to 6 OTU at Sutton Bridge as part of the above first French intake. Speich completed his OTU course but was considered unsuited to fighters and joined GMC 1 at Odiham as a Blenheim bomber pilot. James Denis and Louis Ferrant were graded as fighter pilots.

General de Gaulle was desperately keen to undertake distinct FFL operations with his meagre resources on as many fronts as possible and particularly in the French colonies. In September 1940 he persuaded the British to convey GMC 1 to the Vichy-supporting French West Africa (modern Senegal) as part of an expedition to 'persuade' the colony to back Free France (and the Allies). James Denis, Roger Speich and Louis Ferrant were among pilots of four FAFL Blenheim and Lysander squadrons sent out on what became known as Operation Menace or the Dakar Expedition – a substantial sea and air operation that turned into an Allied failure.

These three airmen then spent some time in French Cameroon, which had declared for the Free French side, then went their separate ways. James Denis was posted to command the first FAFL fighter unit, EFC 1 (French Fighter Squadron 1), flying Hurricanes in Greece, Egypt in defence of the Suez Canal and Libya in defence of Tobruk during 1941/42. At this time, EFC1 was attached to 73 Squadron RAF and the French pilots operated as its third Flight. He was credited with six 'kills' and awarded a British DFC, then posted to command the 'Strasbourg' Squadron of Free French Fighter Group 'Alsace', flying operations in the French protectorates of Syria and Lebanon during 1942. From 1943 James Denis undertook a number of air-staff posts with the FFL in the Middle East and in liberated France until the end of the war.

Roger Speich flew operationally in Gabon, Eritrea and Libya during 1941. He helped to set up the French Military Airline (LAM) and flew transport missions until late-1944 when he was posted to command the 'Arras' Escadrille (flight) of the 'Artois' Coastal Reconnaissance Group, flying operations in French Central Africa (Congo). After the war, with more than 10,000 flying hours to his name, he flew med-evac operations in French Indo-China.

Louis Ferrant also flew combat sorties over Tobruk, scoring two confirmed air victories before eyesight problems took him off operations. He held instructional posts in Egypt and Lebanon and continued in staff and command roles in the post-war French Air Force until his retirement as a lieutenant-colonel in 1957.

Albert Littolff had combat experience before he escaped to England, having shared in the destruction of six German aircraft (one Junkers Ju 88 and five Henschel Hs 126) in June 1940 while flying Morane-Saulnier MS 406 fighters during the Battle of France. Just before the

Franco-German armistice was signed, his squadron was re-equipped with Dewoitine D.520 fighters but the unit was languishing on its airfield waiting for new orders. In response to General de Gaulle's broadcast, Littolff with Sgt Adonis Moulénes and Lt André Feuillerat, now based at Toulouse, stole three new D 520s and on 25 June flew them to England where they joined the FAFL. Adonis Moulénes had seen action with GC III/7 during May, claiming two air victories while flying Morane MS 406 fighters. Albert Littolff took part in the ill-fated Dakar expedition, then, after a spell in Gabon, flew Hurricanes on operations with EFC1 in Greece and Egypt, then over Crete and Tobruk with the Alsace Groupe (GC1) during 1941/42. He is credited with one air victory over Crete (Ju 88) and three over Tobruk (one Ju 87; two Bf 109).

The influence of General de Gaulle again came to bear when he insisted, as part of his desire for Free Frenchmen to be seen to be engaged on all fronts, that he would commit his FFL to fight with the Russians on their home front. The only practical way for this to be achieved was with air power, so he ordered a new FAFL unit to be formed: the *Normandie Groupe* (GC3). In September 1942 Albert Littolff volunteered for service with GC3 in Russia and travelled there on a circuitous route from England via North Africa, Iraq and Persia (Iran), arriving in November 1942. The *Normandie Groupe* was based initially at Ivanovo, 150 miles north-east of Moscow, where it was equipped with the Yakovlev Yak-1 single-seat fighter. Declared operational in early 1943, GC3 moved to the Central/Kursk front, 100 miles south-west of Moscow where Littolff, leading the 2nd Escadrille, soon built a reputation as a skilled combat pilot. He claimed four 'kills' (one Hs 126; one Fw 189; two Bf 110) and flew 371 combat hours in 218 sorties in support of several major ground battles. On 5 July 1943 the *Groupe* was re-equipped with the very effective Yak-9 fighter and it was while flying this fighter that Albert Littolff was shot down on 16 July 1943. Flying from a field at Khationki, he was leading a patrol of eight Yak-9 fighters escorting fifteen Russian bombers over the Krasnikovo district when they were intercepted by German fighters. In the ensuing dogfight, Albert Littolff disappeared and it was presumed he was shot down and killed. His wingman that day was Noel Castelain – a fellow Sutton Bridge OTU trainee – who had joined the *Normandie Groupe* at the same time as Littolff – and indeed his war-time career had followed a similar path. Castelain, too, was shot down in the same engagement and posted as MIA.

By this time, he had flown 129 operational sorties and claimed six air victories.

In circumstances that are not clear, the aeroplane and body of Albert Littolff were discovered on the former battlefront some ten years after his death and although he was originally buried in Russia, his remains were repatriated to France in 1960.

Another Sutton Bridge old boy is Jules Joire, who also volunteered for service with GC3 (Normandie) but his flying career took a very tortuous path before he made it to Russia. He flew Curtiss H-75 Hawks with French Air Force GC1/4 during the Battle of France, claiming six victories in eighty operational sorties. Wounded on his last sortie, he absconded from hospital and escaped to England on a fishing boat with more than a hundred other airmen. After leaving Sutton Bridge, he was involved in the Dakar fiasco and was actually captured by Vichy forces when he (with others) flew from the British aircraft carrier HMS *Ark Royal,* in some Caudron C 270 trainer aircraft, on a mission to Dakar airfield. They made an ill-conceived attempt to talk the local Vichy forces into changing sides and were taken prisoner for their troubles. He suffered great hardship while in prison in Dakar but was sent back to France in December 1940, where he was fortunate to be released from custody in January 1941. Joire made several unsuccessful attempts to escape to England during the next two years, one of which saw him reach North Africa via Spain, but his luck ran out and in January 1943 he was detained by Francoist authorities and imprisoned in Spain. Released but under house arrest, he absconded to Gibraltar, finally reaching England in May 1943. He joined the FAFL, volunteered for combat with GC3 (Normandie) and reached Tula, Russia, in October 1943. However, while training prior to joining GC3 at the front, on 18 March 1943 he was involved in a mid-air collision with Maurice Bourdieu. Although he baled out, his parachute became snagged on the aeroplane and he fell to his death. Bourdieu was also killed.

By mid-1944, in a series of huge battles, Soviet forces had rolled a large part of the German army back to the River Niemen. Due to its magnificent performance in general and particularly during this recent series of battles, Joseph Stalin conferred the honour of Soviet Regimental status on GC3 and ordered it should henceforth be known as the Normandie-Niemen Regiment. By the end of the war, GC3 (Normandie-Niemen) had lost 42 pilots out of the 97 French pilots posted to the unit and claimed 273 air victories.

By way of contrast, the second batch of French trainees is mentioned here because, upon completion of their training, these five were all posted to RAF squadrons and fought in the Battle of Britain.

Second French Course at 6 OTU.
Posted In: 19 August 1940. Posted Out: 11 September 1940.

Name	Posted To	Notes.
Sgt Maurice Philipe Cesar Choron	242 Squadron	BB 64; KIA 10 Apr 1942.
Sgt Henri Gaston Lafont	245 Squadron	BB 615; survived war.
Sgt Xavier de Cherade de Montbron	242 Squadron	BB 64, 92; POW 3 July 1941; deied in air accident 21 April 1955 with French AF.
Sgt Rene Gaston Octave Jean Mouchotte	245 Squadron	BB 615, DFC; KIA Aug 1943.
Sgt Georges Camille Perrin	245 Squadron	BB 615, 249; survived war.

While all these men were fiercely patriotic, from this second French group the charismatic Rene Mouchotte rose rapidly to prominence as a gifted fighter tactician. These qualities saw him rise first to become OC 65 Squadron and earn a DFC, then to command 341 (Alsace) Squadron as part of the famed Biggin Hill Wing, with which he was to lose his life in 1943.

By mid-August 1940 the air battle over Britain was heating up and with replacements for pilot casualties urgently needed, this was reflected in the reduction in the turn-round time for those airmen arriving at 6 OTU; for example, three weeks for the second French batch and just two-and-a-half weeks for the first Belgian pilots. Belgium had a small number of aeroplanes in its air force and these were virtually wiped out, together with the loss of twenty-eight pilots, when the Germans invaded the Low Countries on 10 May 1940. While more than 100 Belgian aircrew managed to escape to England, it is believed only 15 pilots and 14 navigators or gunners actually fought in the Battle of Britain and they were posted to serve in RAF squadrons.

Composition of first Belgian course at 6 OTU.
Posted In: 30 July 1940. Posted Out: 17 August 1940.

Name	Posted To	Notes
Plt Off Baudouin Marie Ghislain de Hemptinne	145 Squadron	BB KIA 5 May 1942.
Plt Off Alexis Rene Isidore Ghislain Jottard	145 Squadron	BB MIA 27 October 1940.
Plt Off Jean Henri Marie Offenberg	145 Squadron	BB KOAS 22 January 1942.

All three men were in the Belgian Air Force before the war began and having enlisted in 1929, by February 1940 Baudouin de Hemptinne was an experienced pilot and an instructor at a service flying school. When the Germans invaded Belgium, that flying school, complete with de Hemptinne, was evacuated first to France and then to Oujda in French Morocco. When France capitulated, he and many of his compatriots decided to escape to England, arriving in Liverpool via Casablanca and Gibraltar on 17 July. He volunteered to join the RAF as a pilot and was gratefully accepted, commissioned and packed off to 6 OTU for operational training – all in the space of two weeks. He was posted to 145 Squadron at RAF Drem in Scotland, which was resting after a gruelling spell of combat operations in the south of England and on 30 August moved to RAF Dyce, from where on 2 October de Hemptinne shot down a Heinkel He 115 that was shadowing a convoy off the coast. The squadron moved south to Tangmere to rejoin the fray on 9 October 1940 and he survived the Battle without scoring further. He was posted to 609 Squadron in 1941, claiming one Bf 109 before moving to 64 then 122 Squadron as a flight commander. It was while flying a 'Circus' operation to Lille on 5 May 1942 that Baudouin de Hemptinne died when his Spitfire was shot down.

With Belgium rapidly knocked out of the war, Alexis Jottard and other pilots flew their Fiat CR 42 biplane fighters to a French airfield and offered their services to the French Air Force, which was still fighting the Germans. The Belgian pilots were put on airfield defence duties at Chartres and experienced combat when they intercepted and damaged a Dornier Do 17 on 3 June. By mid-June the writing was on the wall for the French too, so Jottard and his friend Jean Offenberg decided to make a break for freedom while they still had time. They stole (liberated?) two Caudron C 635 Simoun light communications aircraft and flew them from Chartres to Corsica, refuelled, then flew on to Philippeville in Algeria and thence to the same Belgian training school at Oujda in Morocco to which Baudouin de Hemptinne had escaped. Jottard, Offenberg and de Hemptinne felt there was no future for them at Oujda so took a train to Casablanca, where they stowed away on a ship bound for Gibraltar. There they found passage on a British ship bound for Liverpool, where they arrived on 16 July 1940. By 30 July they were in the RAF and learning to fly the Hurricane at Sutton Bridge. Jottard was posted to 145 Squadron on 17 August and flew operationally until 27 October, when he was shot down into the Channel by a Bf 109 south of the Isle of Wight and posted as MIA.

Third in this Belgian trio was Jean Offenberg. He already had one shared Dornier Do 17 and claimed to have destroyed another on 10 May. As outlined above, with his two compatriots he then found his way to England. From Sutton Bridge he was posted to 145 Squadron at RAF Drem. He claimed a Do 17 and a Bf 109 together with some shared claims during the latter part of the Battle of Britain. His score rose when the RAF went onto the offensive over the Continent in 1941 and this brought him an award of a DFC. He moved to 609 Squadron at Biggin Hill in mid-1941 as a flight commander. At the end of 1941, 609 moved to RAF Digby in Lincolnshire and it was here that Offenberg died in a flying accident on 22 January 1942. He was airborne in a Spitfire near Digby, showing a new pilot the ropes with some combat manoeuvres when another Spitfire, from 92 Squadron also based at Digby, joined in. There was a mid-air collision at low level between Offenberg and the 92 Squadron aircraft which cut off the rear fuselage of Offenberg's machine. He died in the resultant crash. Flt Lt Jean Offenberg DFC was credited with five confirmed kills, five probables and seven damaged.

The next intake of foreign pilots to arrive at Sutton Bridge was the fourth batch of Polish pilots, which arrived on 1 August and thus overlapped the third Polish batch, the French and the Belgians. It was indeed a real cosmopolitan crowd that walked the streets and drank in the pubs of Sutton Bridge village during that hot summer.

It was, though, a time of intense activity at the station and in the air. The Battle of Britain was reaching its height and the cry was for pilots – more pilots. Such intensity brought with it the spectre of air accidents and the unit ORB records these occurred with regular frequency. Few days passed without one or more

Hurricanes being damaged and as many as five accidents have been noted on more than one day. In the air the biggest risks came from engine failure, oxygen failure or collision, and it was during the tenure of the fourth batch of Poles that the first mid-air collision at 6 OTU occurred on 18 August. It resulted in two fatalities: Sgt Dudley Malcolm Peter McGee in L2082 and Major (Sqn Ldr) Kazimierz Ludwik Niedzwiecki, a Polish pilot in 324, one of the ex-Canadian Hurricanes mentioned below in more detail. Twenty-one-year-old McGee arrived on 3 August from 10 FTS at Ternhill along with a batch of British trainees from an assortment of schools such as 6 FTS, 14 FTS, 15 FTS and some pilots sent by operational squadrons, such as 32, 43, 111, 238 and 615 for more training. The squadron pilots were posted out on 24 August, while the FTS trainees stayed on until 31 August, but all of them saw action in the Battle of Britain.

Major Niedzwiecki was one of eleven Polish pilots to arrive for operational training on 1 August from 15 EFTS at Carlisle, a test and grading school for Polish aircrew. At 42 years of age, he was an experienced flyer, having been a pilot in the Polish Air Force since the late-1920s; known, for example, to have held the rank of captain in 1933, when he was a contemporary of the famous Polish aviator Jerzy Bajan in the 2nd Aviation Regiment. All his experience was of no consequence as the two Hurricanes jousted in the bright morning sky near the airfield. Losing sight of each other – or perhaps one man was blinded momentarily by the sun – the two aeroplanes collided and fell to the ground, claiming the lives of both pilots. McGee's L2082 crashed on Petch's farm, Walpole House Farm at Walpole Cross Keys and Niedzwiecki's 324 (ex-L1887) fell on Roland Dennis's farm, Westfield House, Terrington St Clements, both roughly 2 miles east of Sutton Bridge airfield. In 1980 Fenland Aircraft Preservation Society (FAPS; now Fenland and West Norfolk Aircraft Preservation Society: FAWNAPS) recovered some small artefacts from the site of L2082 and the smashed remains of Merlin II No.2175, with evidence of a two-blade wooden prop, was recovered in 1982 from the crash-site of 324.

Sunday 18 August was a significant day in the Battle of Britain, too. The Luftwaffe made three very large separate attacks on southern England and many air battles, large and small were fought by the RAF in an effort to stem the onslaught. That day the RAF lost at least 136 aircraft in the air and on the ground and the Luftwaffe suffered at least 100 aircraft lost or damaged. During the Battle of Britain no other day had been, or would be, as expensive for either side as this one; in later years it would become known as The Hardest Day. Winston Churchill was at Chequers working on a speech he was to deliver to the Commons on 20 August. He received reports of the air fighting that day and was moved to include the now immortal passage of thanks to the aircrew of the RAF:

> The gratitude of every home in our island, in our Empire and indeed throughout the world, except in the abodes of the guilty, goes out to the British airmen who, undaunted by the odds, unwearied in their constant challenge and mortal danger, are turning the tide of the world war by their prowess and by their devotion. Never in the field of human conflict was so much owed by so many to so few.

The use of the word 'British' in this context of the RAF is all embracing and not in any way meant to overlook the role played by the exiled patriots.

As far as Hugh Dowding, C-in-C Fighter Command, was concerned the practical, present situation was that he needed pilots. He had lost 105 killed, wounded or missing in just the past nine days and he estimated that, at this point, Fighter Command was 209 pilots short of what it needed. In addition to the normal output of the FTS he asked for more pilots to be 'trawled' from other Commands and that the 'foreign' pilots were to be pressed into operational service as quickly as possible – and the output of 6 OTU is evidence of what was happening in this respect.

Now it was time for the arrival of the first of four batches of Czechoslovakian pilots to train at Sutton Bridge before the end of the Battle.

Composition of first Czech pilot course at 6 OTU.
Posted In: 17 Aug 1940. Posted Out: 11 Sep 1940.

Name	Posted To	Notes.
Sqn Ldr Jan Ambrus	312 Sqn	BB Survived the war. OBE.
Plt Off František Fajtl	1 Sqn	BB Survived the war. DFC.
Plt Off Stanislav Fejfar	310 Sqn	BB KIA 313 Sqn, 17 May 1942.

Plt Off Jaroslav Himr	79 Sqn	BB KIA 24 September 1943. DFC.
Plt Off František Kordula	1 Sqn	BB Survived the war.
Plt Off Jiri Jaromir Machacek	145 Sqn	BB MIA 8 July 1941.
Plt Off Karel Mrazek	43 Sqn	BB Survived the war. DSO DFC.
Plt Off Rudolf Bohumil Rohacek	238 Sqn	BB KOAS 27 April 1942.
Plt Off Karel Jan Vykoukal	111 Sqn	BB KIA 21 May 1942.
Plt Off František Weber	145 Sqn	BB Survived the war.
Sgt František Antonin Bernard	601 Sqn	BB Survived the war.
Sgt Vaclav Eric Cukr	43 Sqn	BB Survived the war. DFC.
Sgt Jaroslav Hlavac	79 Sqn	BB KIA, 56 Sqn 10 October 1940.
Sgt Vladimir Horsky	238 Sqn	BB KIA 25 September 1940.
Sgt Vaclav Jicha	238 Sqn	BB KOAS January 1945. DFC AFC.
Sgt Jiri V Kučera	238 Sqn	BB Survived the war.
Sgt Václav A Kopecký	111 Sqn	BB Survived the war, DFC.
Sgt Jindřich Poštolka	311 Sqn	Pilot with Polish bomber squadron. Survived the war.
Plt Off Josef Bryks		Posted to 12 OTU on 1 October 1940 then to Ferry Pilots Pool. Posted to 242 Sqn; shot down 17 June 1941; POW; multiple escapee. Survived war. MBE. Died 11 Aug 1957.
Sgt Karel Stibor		Killed in mid-air collision at 6 OTU on 3 September 1940.

The note that a pilot 'survived the war' might suggest that they enjoyed all that the peace brought with it. However, it should be remembered that for many Czechs and Poles, the peace in fact brought with it a so-called – some might say infamous – repatriation to their native countries, which were now occupied by the Soviets and governed under Communist doctrines. For reasons far too complex to dwell upon here, this had dire consequences for many former RAF pilots who were arrested by the Soviets, often humiliated by being allowed to pursue only menial work or, even worse, incarcerated in prisons or labour camps, often for many years under inhumane conditions that in some cases resulted in their death.

Plt Off Josef Bryks was one of the latter and his story is as harrowing as it is truly remarkable. As a former Czech Air Force pilot and without a clear plan, he left occupied Czechoslovakia on 20 January 1940 to join the Allied cause. Travelling through Hungary, Yugoslavia, Greece, Turkey and Syria, he reached France in May 1940 just in time to have to escape its capitulation a month later. Bryks escaped by ship to England where he volunteered for the RAF. First posted to 310 Squadron, he needed more training and was sent on 17 August to Sutton Bridge, from where he went to 12 OTU, on 1 October. His next posting was to HQ Ferry Pilot Pool at Kemble for a time, before going to 6 Maintenance Unit on 1 January 1941 as a test pilot. On 23 April 1941, at last Josef managed to get into action when posted to 242 Squadron to fly Hurricane IIs on daylight 'Circus' operations over the Continent but he was shot down on 17 June 1941 and was made a POW. Fearing, as a Czech, he would be treated harshly or even killed, he used his fluent command of English to brazen it out as a British pilot named 'Joseph Ricks'. Moved around several prison camps he reached Oflag VI-B at Warberg, where he and two other Czech pilots and three Poles escaped by tunnel on 20 April 1942. Bryks evaded capture until, ill with dysentery and suffering from lack of food and water, he was picked up near Stuttgart on 30 April and returned to Oflag VI-B. On 17 August he escaped again and was on the run until 8 September. Back in Oflag VI-B he was transferred to Oflag XXI-B, 120 miles west of Warsaw but escaped from there on 4 March 1943. This time he was on the run for three months during which time he reached Warsaw and became involved with the Ghetto Uprising. Betrayed to the Germans, Bryks was re-captured and in an SS prison in Warsaw endured two months of interrogations, beatings, starvation and death threats before he was sent to Stalag Luft III at Sagen in Poland. Severely injured during his time in prison he underwent surgery and recuperation in a

British prison hospital at Stalag VIII-B until returned to Stalag Luft III in December 1943. Bryks helped with preparations for the Great Escape of 24 March 1944 but was 100th in the queue and thus did not get out that night. He did, however, make another escape attempt on 27 March but was quickly recaptured. The Germans discovered his real, Czech, identity in July 1944 and sent him to various prisons in Prague during September for interrogation by the Gestapo, who sentenced him to death. This was not carried out and, after representation by the Red Cross on behalf of the British Government, Czech POW aircrew who were serving in the RAF were released by the Gestapo to various POW camps. Bryks went to Stalag Luft I on 22 September. On 7 November 1944 he was transferred to Oflag IV-C – Colditz Castle – still with a pending death sentence. Relief came when Colditz was liberated on 16 April 1945 and Josef Bryks was repatriated to England. Miraculously, he had survived the war!

In August 1945, back in England, he had more surgery on the injuries sustained at the hands of the Germans, as well as the removal of a piece of shrapnel from his mouth – a wound received when he was shot down. By this time, his wife had divorced him and remarried. Josef Bryks also remarried in England and he and his second wife returned to Czechoslovakia on 6 October 1945 where, unfit to fly due to his injuries, he continued to serve in the Czech Air Force as a ground instructor. All went well until the Soviets took control of the country in February 1948. Because of his past service with the British and the RAF, Josef Bryks was deemed as politically unreliable and removed from his Czech Air Force post. It was indeed for that past service that he was awarded an MBE but he was not permitted to leave the country to receive it. Arrested by the Soviets in May 1948, he was dismissed the Air Force, reduced to the ranks, stripped of his medals and sentenced to ten years hard labour. Sent to various prisons and labour camps he constantly resisted the authorities and plotted escapes, for which he was harshly punished. During 1952 he was sent to a uranium mine complex in north-west Czechoslovakia but still valiantly resisted all attempts to destroy his will. With declining health, he finally succumbed to a heart attack in the prison hospital on 11 August 1957 at the age of just 41 years. This hero had spent thirteen years of his life in prisons – four years as a POW after fighting to free his homeland and another nine years in prison as the result of fighting for his homeland. His wife Trudie was allowed to go to England at the start of his incarceration by the Soviets. It was not until 2009 that

Czech historians discovered his ashes had been interred in Prague and his wife could visit his grave for the first time. In the post-Soviet era the name of Josef Bryks is now both remembered and revered.

In many respects the story of Plt Off František Fajtl follows similar lines and it certainly echoes the indomitable spirit that resounds through the stories of all those men who are the 'exiled patriots' of this narrative.

Fajtl was a linguist, fluent in English and German, competent in Russian and French, and he had travelled widely in Europe. He was commissioned in the Czech Air Force in 1935 and was still serving when the Germans invaded in 1939. Fajtl escaped via Poland to France and was allowed to join the French Air Force, serving with *Groupe de Chasse III* (Fighter Group III) but without any combat success. Upon France's capitulation he escaped to England via Oran in Algeria and Gibraltar. Like many of his compatriots, on 6 August 1940 he was sent to 310 Squadron at Duxford but in need of conversion training he was packed off to 6 OTU at Sutton Bridge on 16 August. Training on the Hurricane kept him busy until 11 September, when he was posted to 1 Squadron at Northolt, then on 25 September, to 17 Squadron at Debden. He claimed a couple of 'shared' Dornier Do 17s and one 'damaged' during the Battle. Flying 'Circus' operations with 312 Squadron in 1942 he claimed one Bf 109 shared and one damaged, then in March 1942 he took command of 122 Squadron and claimed one more Bf 109 destroyed. On 5 May 1942 Fajtl was shot down near Hazebrouck. Evading capture, he reached Paris within eight days and worked his way down the escape lines into Spain, where he was arrested and put in a prison camp for a couple of months until his release was arranged by the British Consul in Madrid. He then travelled to Gibraltar – once again – but this time was flown back to England. After recuperation, Fajtl took up a number of staff jobs and became station commander of RAF Church Fenton, then RAF Skeabrae before moving to RAF Ibsley, where he led 313 Squadron on operations until the end of 1943.

Fajtl's career then took a novel direction when he volunteered for service in Russia, travelling there with a party of twenty-one Czech volunteers with whom he formed and commanded a squadron. His Czech squadron operated with the Russian Air Force on the Eastern Front; in the Carpathian region of Czechoslovakia and over northern Moravia and Silesia, flying Lavochkin LA-5 fighters. At the end of the war he went to Prague and was greeted as a hero but when the Soviets took over the country in 1948, despite his wartime operations with the Russians, he became another of the Czech pilots who, having flown with the RAF, was to be persecuted as politically unreliable by the Soviet regime and dismissed from the Air Force. He was permitted to do only menial jobs and in 1950 was arrested and sent to a labour camp for eighteen months. After this he worked as a bookkeeper until 1964 when the Soviets partially rehabilitated him as an air accident investigator. In the post-Soviet era, František Fajtl DFC regained his old Air Force status and his rightful position as a national hero. At the time of his death in Prague in 2006, Lieutenant General František Fajtl DFC was the last surviving Czech Battle of Britain veteran.

Vaclav Eric Cukr also led a charmed flying career. Already a Czech Air Force pilot when Germany invaded Czechoslovakia in 1939, he escaped through Poland to France where he enlisted in the French Air Force and was posted to GC II/3, a fighter unit equipped with the Dewoitine D 520. When the Germans invaded France in May 1940, Cukr was in the thick of the air action and is credited with destroying or sharing at least eight enemy aircraft up to the date of the French capitulation in June. He was shot down and wounded during June and evaded capture by fleeing to North Africa then to England via Gibraltar. Having recovered from his wounds, he volunteered for the RAF and on the strength of his combat claims he was posted to 6 OTU Sutton Bridge. He saw action during the Battle of Britain with 43 Squadron but did not add to his air victories. Cukr was then posted to 253 Squadron but during 1941, as a result of his earlier injuries, he was declared unfit to fly operations and took up an instructor post. Having experienced a second severe flying accident in 1943 he spent the rest of the war in rehabilitation and was finally invalided out of the RAF when the war ended. He returned to the Czechoslovakian Air Force but had to flee the country when arrest by the Communists seemed likely. Returning to England, he took up British citizenship then, in 1959, emigrated to New Zealand, where he died in 1989.

Of course, interspersed between all the exiled patriots was a steady flow of British and Commonwealth pilots too, a further illustration of how the courses overlapped across 6 OTU's three Flights to keep the momentum going. For example, on the day of the arrival of the first group of Czechs, a batch of thirteen English pilots also appeared; three from 9 FTS and ten from 10 FTS. Among their number was one,

Sgt Frederick John Howarth, whose name would be forever linked with the Czechs due to a mid-air collision near the station.

The accident, which occurred at 8.30 am in the bright sunlight of 3 September 1940, seems to have been due simply to an error of judgement by one or both pilots during an authorised combat flying exercise between aircraft from two flights. Perhaps in that bright sunlight – mentioned by an eyewitness on the ground – they momentarily lost sight of each other with fatal consequences. In the opinion of that same eyewitness, 'both aircraft seemed to be stunting in an effort to gain an advantage one over the other and collided at about 700 feet altitude.'

At this stage of the air war – it was the height of the Battle of Britain – there were not enough instructors to accompany pupils on a regular or individual basis, therefore trainees were sent off in pairs to practise combat tactics among themselves. Training course lengths were being cut to the bone and once a pupil could be trusted with a Hurricane, he was shown the ropes then left to get as much air experience as the time permitted. Frederick Howarth, in L1654, fell about half a mile from Czech Sgt Karel Stibor, in L1833, into a plum orchard at Saddlebow, near the village of Wiggenhall St Germans. At the time, a minimum of site clearance was carried out – just enough to recover the bodies of the unfortunate airmen and clear the farmer's property of ordnance and surface debris. It was not until the early 1970s that the site of L1833 was excavated by the landowner to remove the engine and other major components. The site of L1654 was left undisturbed until September 1985 when the Fenland Aircraft Preservation Society undertook an extensive and successful excavation, in what was now arable land, during the course of which the Merlin III and other artefacts were recovered on 6 October 1985. Now twinned with Sutton Bridge, a delegation from the Czechoslovakian town of Sedlec-Prcice, current home of the Stibor family, visited the graves of all the Czech pilots buried in St Matthews cemetery. Among the guests at the memorial service was pensioner Karel Stibor, nephew of the man who died in 1940, fulfilling a lifelong dream of paying his respects to his war-hero uncle, after whom he was named.

Next to go was a pilot from the second Czech group, Sgt Jan Kurka, who died on 30 September. Airborne in Hurricane L1986, Sgt Kurka apparently became alarmed when his engine began to fail and at the appearance of smoke and/or glycol fumes in the cockpit. Deciding to bale out rather than make a forced landing, he pulled the aeroplane into a climb then rolled it over in order to get out more easily. As he left the cockpit he may have hit some part of the machine, because his parachute did not function properly and is thought to have fouled the tailplane. The Hurricane was completely wrecked when it crashed at Walton near Peterborough. Sgt Kurka is buried in St Matthew's cemetery, Sutton Bridge.

Plt Off Desmond Crighton Brown arrived at 6 OTU on 1 October 1940 and just one week later he was dead. This tragedy unfolded late in the afternoon of 8 October when Plt Off Brown was detailed to carry out a low-flying exercise in Hurricane L2083. Immediately after take-off the engine failed and caught fire and Brown attempted a quick circuit with the wheels still down. He throttled back on approaching the airfield boundary, then, rapidly losing height and still short, he opened up again.

On the ground, Sgt Albert Norton, an armament fitter, watched in horror.

> The Hurricane came in streaming black smoke and it hit the ground travelling fast; ran on for 100 yards, cartwheeled and came to rest upside down on fire. A group of us ran to the Hurricane but in seconds it was blazing furiously. We tried lifting the tail so that the pilot could be rescued. He was still alive because we could hear him shouting but lifting the tail only increased the ferocity of the flames. The whole fuselage was burning and now the ammunition started to explode. It is a part of my memory that, after all these years, remains clear. I often wonder if we could have done more.

Having died on the aerodrome, within two or three days of the accident Plt Off Brown was buried in St Matthew's cemetery, Sutton Bridge. There is an entry dated 9 October 1940 naming Plt Off Brown in local undertaker Goddard & Son's 'funeral book'. It would seem, however, that his parents Archibald and Jean may not have been consulted about his interment. When they were informed, they set about seeking permission for him to be exhumed and re-buried in his home town of Southend. This train of events is outlined in a letter to the vicar of St Matthew's church, dated 18 May 1942, in which Archibald Brown explains that they were in the long and difficult process of having him exhumed and they were doing so because they wished him to be buried in Southend alongside three other deceased pilot officers who were his friends. From the date of this letter and the fact that his father hoped the matter would be resolved 'shortly', the process seems to have taken about two years for Plt Off Brown's parents to succeed in having him exhumed, since he is indeed now buried in Southend-on-Sea (Sutton Road) cemetery.

Part of a group of Czech pilots that arrived at 6 OTU on 15 October – but did not leave until November – Plt Off Tomas Matĕj Patlejch was one who, sadly, remains at Sutton Bridge forever. Ordered to carry out an altitude test in Hurricane L1851 on 1 November, Plt Off Patlejch called his base to report he had reached 25,000 feet as instructed. He then asked permission to dive on the airfield for his descent but this request was refused. Shortly afterwards Patlejch's aircraft was seen to dive into the ground at Strawberry Hall, Tydd St Mary, killing the pilot. The subsequent accident enquiry could not ascertain if the crash was as a result of disobedience of orders or of oxygen failure disabling the pilot. As might be imagined, from that altitude the crash made a large crater but in the soft blue clay subsoil little of the aeroplane was recovered. What remained of poor Tomas Patlejch was interred with due military honour in St Matthew's cemetery.

Every week from the end of April to the end of October 1940, pilots were being posted from 6 OTU to operational squadrons throughout the country. This unit (along with, let us not forget, its contemporaries 5 OTU and 7 OTU) was doing a vital job providing a steady flow of fighter pilots trained on the Hurricane to join the fray during the most crucial period of the air war. By the close of the Battle of Britain, no fewer than 525 pilots had passed through Sutton Bridge before the official closing date of the Battle on 31 October.

An analysis of those 525 pilots posted into and out of 6 OTU at RAF Sutton Bridge between 10 March and 31 October 1940 (*see* Appendix) produced the following result.

Pilots who fought ONLY in the Battle of France	17
Pilots who fought in BOTH the Battle of France and the Battle of Britain	45
Pilots who fought ONLY in the Battle of Britain	345
Pilots who fought in NEITHER Battle	118

By September 1940, contrary to the enemy's belief that the RAF was a depleted force on the edge of collapse, the supply of pilots from the OTUs was steadily increasing. For example, pilot fatalities in combat during September 1940 totalled 173, while 6 OTU alone (not forgetting there were two other OTUs working flat out, too) posted out 123 pilots during that month. Furthermore, during October, 6 OTU posted out 42 pilots between the 1st and 9th, then 28 pilots to squadrons on the 14th, and another 34 on the 28th. The OTU system had proved it worked; allowing front-line squadrons to get on with the job of engaging the enemy without being diverted by flying training issues or having to organise the supply of replacements.

6

A Foreign Field and English Sky

It has already been shown, and will be reinforced below, that RAF Sutton Bridge and 6 Operational Training Unit (later known as 56 OTU) played host to budding fighter pilots of virtually every nationality serving with the RAF. Indeed, the degree of multi-nationalism and multiculturalism pervading the RAF in those days should be the envy of modern campaigners. What is not generally appreciated though is that during 1941, this catalogue of nations also included citizens of the USA at such an early stage of the war. America officially entered the war on 7 December 1941 but long before United States Army Air Force (USAAF) personnel officially arrived in England during 1942, American pilots were already serving – and dying – in the RAF. Some American nationals are known to have flown in the Battle of Britain, although the exact figure still remains a source of debate – varying between seven and eleven, depending on the source of the information and/or the definition of 'American'. For example, Friends of the Battle of Britain Memorial in London list nine, while Kenneth J. Wynn in *Men of the Battle of Britain* lists eleven.

There is, however, clear evidence of at least one American pilot who flew in the Battle of Britain – who appears in all of the lists – being trained at 6 OTU prior to the influx of what will be generically labelled 'Eagles' arriving at the station from March 1941 (*see* below). This man was Plt Off John Kenneth Haviland, who was born in New York State of an American father and an English mother. Educated in England, he was already at university here when war broke out and having joined the RAF Volunteer Reserve as a pilot in 1939, he was called up to complete his flying training at 10 FTS. Posted to

1 School of Army Co-operation (1 SAC) – used as a holding unit – at Old Sarum, on 4 September 1940 along with half-a-dozen other pilots from 1 SAC, he was then posted to 6 OTU Sutton Bridge for operational training on the Hurricane. Having completed his OTU course, he was posted on 21 September to 151 Squadron at RAF Digby. Just three days later he narrowly escaped death when, on the 24th during a formation practice flight in V7432, he collided with P3306 flown by Sgt James McPhee. McPhee baled out safely and Haviland managed to force-land his aeroplane at RAF Waddington. It was this period of service with 151 Squadron which qualified him for the Battle of Britain Clasp. John Haviland is known to have still been with 151 Squadron during 1941 because he filed a report for a night combat on 12 September 1941. By then the squadron had moved to RAF Wittering, where it operated a mixed inventory of Hurricanes and Defiants in a night-fighter role. In a Defiant, Plt Off Haviland and his air gunner Sgt Richard Grange Stolz-Page (KIA 3 December 1942; 103 Sqn), intercepted a Dornier Do 215 near North Luffenham, but having fired several bursts at it, the bomber escaped, although it was claimed as damaged. John Haviland survived the war and died in the USA in 2002.

With publicity about the air war in Europe gathering momentum within the United States, although the Battle of Britain was over, civilian pilots were still keen to get a slice of the action by joining the RAF and soon the North American drawl joined Continental accents in the pubs and homes of rural Lincolnshire. Some – but not all – of these Americans went on to become members of the famous Eagle Squadrons of the RAF (71, 121 and 133 Squadrons). What follows below outlines this unusual story and looks in particular at the first group of RAF Sutton Bridge's fledgling Eagles who arrived at the station on 6 March 1941.

Helped by such men as the American adventurer Colonel Charles Sweeny some 'early birds' found their way to France with the intention of joining that country's air force. Frustrated in this aim by the collapse of France in 1940 before they could see action, the handful that managed to escape to England were welcomed by the depleted RAF and some saw action in the Battle of Britain itself. It was, however, Colonel Sweeny's nephew, Charles Sweeny Jr, an Anglophile businessman who was resident in England, who introduced and energetically pursued the propaganda-led idea of a single American-manned fighter squadron in the RAF to the British Air Ministry and for which approval was rapidly given. Operating inside the USA, he then recruited and financed American volunteers who, augmented by some of the 'early birds', formed the nucleus of 71 (Eagle) Squadron RAF. Having achieved his personal objective, amid considerable self-publicity that was frowned upon in official circles back in Britain, Charles Sweeny pulled away from further direct involvement with Americans in the RAF. However, emerging in parallel with Sweeney's work was another organisation that would consolidate, and then far exceed, the concept pioneered by Charles Sweeny.

In violation of the code of neutrality, under constant scrutiny by the FBI but with the US government contriving to maintain a blind eye, an organization known as the Clayton Knight Committee recruited civilian pilots throughout the USA for service with both the Royal Canadian Air Force and the RAF.

It should be borne in mind that not all of the American volunteers reaching the RAF actually passed through the Clayton Knight or Sweeny schemes and nor did all of them actually serve in those three particular squadrons (71, 121, 133) and thus qualify to be called Eagles. Furthermore, sixteen British pilots also served with RAF Eagle Squadrons.

So, who was this mysterious Clayton Knight? Born in 1891 in Rochester, NY, he joined the Aviation Section of the US Signal Corps during the First World War and having been sent to England for advanced flying training was, in 1918, a pilot attached to 206 Squadron RAF, in France. His war flying ended abruptly on 5 October 1918 when the Airco DH 9 aeroplane he was flying was shot down behind enemy lines. Severely wounded, Knight managed to crash-land, saving his own life and that of his observer, Second Lieutenant Perring RAF. Hospitalised in Belgium, Knight came close to losing a leg but survived his wounds and his captivity. Back in the USA between the wars Knight found fame as an aviation artist and writer, becoming widely respected, particularly for his distinctive illustrations, such as those he created in *Pilot's Luck* in 1927 and *Ace Drummond,* a hugely popular American cartoon series of the 1930s. He also wrote and illustrated books such as *The Story of Flight,* published in 1954.

When the Second World War broke out, Canada put its First World War hero Air Marshal 'Billy' Bishop VC in charge of recruitment for the RCAF. Realising that red-blooded Americans might try to enlist as 'Canadians' to get into action both with the RCAF and the RAF, Bishop actively encouraged this process inside the USA by asking Clayton

Knight – of whose reputation he was aware and with whom he was acquainted in the war – to set up an organisation to screen volunteers.

Knight was assisted and financed by Homer Smith, a wealthy Canadian and their main US office was in New York's Waldorf Astoria Hotel. Word spread like wildfire among the prolific US civilian pilot fraternity and applications were so great that they had to establish more offices in major cities across America: Memphis, Cleveland, Chicago, Kansas City, St Louis, Dallas, San Antonio, Oakland and Los Angeles.

To be considered, volunteers had to be aged between 20 and 30, have a high-school diploma, good eyesight, a Civil Aeronautics Authority (CAA) licence and about 200 or more flying hours in their logbook. Accounts vary on these criteria but applicants also had to have a medical and take a flying check at a local airport. The standards set were frequently not rigidly adhered to, nor were they as demanding as those required by the USAAF, whose lengthy, thorough – but slow and over-subscribed – training programme was less attractive than the prospect of adventure in England. There is also anecdotal evidence that some candidates' claims as to their hours of experience may have been doctored – but the need was pressing and the planned flying training courses in the USA would soon sort out those who could not make the grade.

By mid-1940 the Clayton Knight organization had vetted thousands of applicants and Knight returned to Ottawa with an initial list of 300 selected volunteers, most of whom would be destined for RAF fighters. The Clayton Knight Committee, later renamed the Canadian Aviation Bureau, continued its work, recruiting thousands more aircrew in the USA for service with the RCAF and RAF as single- and multi-engine operational and instructional aircrew. The British Empire Air Training schemes that were gathering momentum across the Commonwealth at this time, for example, had a voracious appetite for instructors and nowhere more so than in Canada.

In the second half of 1940 Clayton Knight contracted three US civilian flying schools to train pilots for the RAF from those applicants. Representing the RAF, Sqn Ldr Randolph Mills DFC was posted to Washington to help establish the schools, their flying programme and monitor standards. The courses were known in the USA as British Refresher Courses and the schools were located at airports in Dallas, Texas, (Dallas Aviation School); Tulsa, Oklahoma, (Spartan School of Aeronautics); and Glendale, near Oakland, California, (Polaris Flight Academy). In early 1941 a fourth school was established at

Kern County Airport, Bakersfield, California. Although there was an effort to establish a standard training scheme, in reality, for many months these schools offered widely varying flying curricula, had a variable quality of instructors, a wide mix of aircraft and inadequate accommodation. It was late into 1941 before these issues were overcome.

The first American volunteers were called in small batches for basic service flying training with the above schools. If they survived and passed the course, they were usually commissioned as officers in the RAF and on arrival in England, their new uniforms proudly bore RAF pilot wings. The problem of swearing allegiance to the British Crown and thereby potentially forfeiting the right to US citizenship, was overcome by special wording approved by the British Privy Council and in the USA, ways were also found to circumvent difficulties associated with the US Draft Board and of entering a war zone. The US government quietly made it known that volunteers would not forfeit US nationality and could elect to transfer to the USAAF if America joined the war.

Those early arrivals, through both the Sweeny operation and some 'independent travellers' – about nineteen in all – are believed to have been trained on the Hawker Hurricane fighter at 5 (later 55) OTU, based at RAF Aston Down (it re-located to Usworth later). They were posted to the first Eagle Squadron, 71, between October and December 1940. However, most of Clayton Knight's recruits selected for fighters during 1941 found themselves posted to 56 OTU Sutton Bridge and it is the first batch of these fellows in particular that we will look at more closely as an excellent photograph exists to provide evidence of their time at Sutton Bridge. At RAF Sutton Bridge, they too were to learn to fly the Hurricane and soon the North American accent joined the ones from occupied Europe in the pubs and homes of this small rural town.

With more to follow over a few days, the first thirteen Americans arrived at Sutton Bridge on 6 March 1941 and among these was 25-year-old Plt Off William Lee Davis, a native of St Louis, Missouri. Bill Davis was an aviation enthusiast since childhood and by December 1940, had accumulated 225 private flying hours. According to his college friends, Bill had a good light-operatic singing voice and he tried to break into the 'big time' in New York but he returned home, just before the war, quite demoralised by his lack of success. In January 1941, spotting an advert in his local paper, adventure in the RAF beckoned and quitting his job as salesman with a cork insulation firm, he signed up for a flying course through the Clayton Knight Recruiting Committee.

After a four-week training course at Love Field in Dallas, Texas, intended to take the place of the RAF Service Flying Training School (SFTS) stage and including about 40–50 flying hours, Bill left for Canada by train on 13 February 1941. *En route*, the train made a short stop in St Louis where he had just 25 precious minutes to say hello to his father and his girlfriend, Marian Gall, and to do a hurried interview with a *St Louis Post-Dispatch* reporter. As he was about to leave Union Railroad Station for the last time, he said: 'I consider joining the RAF is a matter of sentiment and heritage as my grandfather was an English Army officer who fought in the Boer War.' Once off American/neutral soil, Bill was commissioned into the RAF in Ottawa but curiously Bill's name does not appear in the Eagle Squadron Association's 'Boat Lists', although he arrived in England on the same date as some compatriots on the MV *Georgic*. Upon reaching England, in his only cablegram to the folks back home, Davis wrote to Marian Gall: 'Everything fine, England very beautiful, love you and miss you, wish you were here.' There was also confirmation of his arrival in England when, in a letter to Marian dated 12 March and written from Sutton Bridge, he said he had 'arrived a week ago', making that date 5 March. Did he also travel on *Georgic* or not? Perhaps the answer to this question lies within the 13 February *St Louis Despatch* article itself, where the reporter wrote: 'Upon completion of his course he was ordered to Ottawa where he will be formally commissioned [and] in a few days he will depart for England on a flying boat.'

The war waited for no man and so, having soloed in a Hurricane and already with a minor landing mishap in P5192 to his name on 17 March, Bill was sent off the next day (18th) on a routine map-reading exercise in P5195. Becoming lost beneath a rainy overcast, the flat featureless fenscape must have seemed miserable, uninviting and a million miles from home. Almost out of fuel he opted to land with the undercarriage down in a field at New Leake Fen, near Boston, Lincolnshire – but his luck ran out. Soft ground made the wheels dig in as the Hurricane touched down and, in an instant, it flipped over onto its back. The crashed Hurricane was found by local Observer Corps personnel who reported the sad fate of its occupant to RAF Sutton Bridge. Bill Davis died from a broken neck, the first American fatality at Sutton Bridge and the first St Louis son to be killed in the war. He is buried in St Matthew's churchyard, Sutton Bridge as an officer of the RAF and the headstone gives no hint of his US nationality.

Thus, by careful examination of little-known documents called 'Boat Lists', compiled by the Eagle Squadron Association after the war – and by reference to many publications and the wonders of the World Wide Web – it has been possible to untangle a little of the web of names and arrivals in England of American volunteers from those US flying training courses. William Lee Davis and Virgil Willis Olson were not recorded on any of the Boat Lists, yet they appear in the photograph of that first American course at Sutton Bridge. It seems Virgil was an early Sweeny candidate who, having reached France in early 1940 – hoping (unsuccessfully) to join the French Air Force in battle – escaped to England during May; then, although recorded on an initial roster of 71 Squadron in October 1940, he disappears until he turns up at 56 OTU in March 1941. Bill Davis, as we saw above, appears to have crossed the Atlantic in a flying boat.

One of Bill Davis' buddies, Carroll 'Red' McColpin, survived the rigours of OTU, RAF, USAAF and USAF service, rising to the rank of Major-General in command of the US Fourth Air Force in post-war years, before retiring in 1968. Of his entry into the RAF and his time prior to becoming an Eagle Squadron ace, Red McColpin recalled: 'we sailed with ten [sic] other Yankees ... having been provided with one-way ship tickets to England.'

Eagle Boat No.8; MV *Georgic* depart Halifax, Canada 24 February 1941. Arrive Liverpool 5 March 1941.
61923 J. E. Durham
61924 H. S. Fenlaw
61925 L. L. Laughlin
61926 C. W. McColpin
61927 T. P. McGerty
61928 E. T. Miluck
61929 C. C. Mize
61930 W. Pendleton
61931 L. F. Read
61932 F. Scudday
61933 T. M. Wallace
61934 J. M. Hill

Eagle Squadron Association's 'Boat Lists' show the ships carrying American volunteers to UK during 1940 and 1941. Some vessels crossed the Atlantic in convoy, others sailed independently.

Sailing Number	Depart Canada	Ship Name	Airmen on board.
1	30 July 1940	*Duchess of Bedford*	3.
2	13 August 1940	*Duchess of Richmond*	6.
3	27 August 1940	Not known	4.
4	6 September 1940	*Erin*	5.
5	27 September 1940	*Duchess of Atholl*	3.
6	2 November 1940	*Duchess of Atholl*	1.
7	17 February 1941	*Johan Van Oldenbarnevelt*	4*.
8	24 February 1941	*Georgic*	12*.
9	25 March 1941	*Jean Jadot*	11.
10	20 April 1941	*Alaunia / Royal Ulsterman*	4.
11	30 April 1941	Not known	2.
12	23 May 1941	Not known	10.
13	6 June 1941	*Bayano*	26.
14	19 June 1941	Not known	14.
15	27 June 1941	*Olaf Fostenes*	8.
16	6 July 1941	Not known	2.
17	10 July 1941	*Mosdale*	9.
18	22 July 1941	Not known	9.
19	4 August 1941	*Madura*	6.
20	15 August 1941	Not known	2.
21	25 August 1941	*Fort Richepanse*	11**.
22	26 August 1941	Not known	4.
23	26 August 1941	*Manchester Division*	8.
24	27 September 1941	*Bayano*	19.

Notes for Table:

1. * These two batches made up the first distinct American course
    at 56 OTU RAF Sutton Bridge. *Johan Van Oldenbarnevelt*
    was part of Convoy TC9; *Georgic* sailed independently
    Halifax to Liverpool.
2. ** Four airmen from this batch drowned when ship was sunk
    by U-567 on 3 September 1941.
3. Most of the pilots on Boats 1 to 5 attended 55 OTU RAF
    Aston Down while those on Boats 6 to 16 and 19 to 24 went
    to 56 OTU RAF Sutton Bridge.
4. Volunteers on Boat 17 went to 52 OTU, RAF Debden; those
    on Boat 18 went to 55 OTU, RAF Usworth.
5. Volunteers on boats subsequent to No.24 were distributed
    among several OTUs. For example, sixteen Americans on
    Emma Alexander, dep Halifax 21 November 1941 went to
    53 OTU RAF Llandow.

Another aspect of this thirst for action is illustrated by Sgt Hubert
'Bert' Stewart's story. He travelled to Canada under his own steam to
join the RCAF and recalled his own highly dubious onward journey
to England in the company of Plt Offs Ward, Coen and Hall, without
official knowledge, sanction or ticket. At his Canadian training station,
Bert constantly pestered his instructors to post him to fighters but was
equally continually told he was likely to go to bombers or become an
instructor himself. He would not accept this fate and while travelling
between postings, fell in with Oscar Coen and Bill Hall at a railroad
station. They explained how it could be done legally but instead Bert
decided to just tag along with them and bluff his way to England – and
it worked, too.

> Eagle Boat No.7; MV *Johan Van Oldenbarnevelt*. Depart Canada
> 17 February 1941. Arrive Clyde 27 February 1941.
> 61920 R. C. Ward
> 61921 W. I. Hall
> 62244 O. H. Coen
> RCAF H. L. Stewart

Most of the early American arrivals went to RAF Uxbridge (later
to 3 Personnel Reception Centre, Bournemouth) and it was here
that Bert Stewart was rumbled and detained while the authorities

checked him out. Ward, Coen and Hall, meantime, were posted to RAF Sutton Bridge, leaving Bert to plead his case to be a fighter pilot all over again. So determined was his pleading that the RAF authorities gave in and on 7 March, he too was sent to 56 OTU – to become a fighter pilot. Ward, Hall and Coen are also in the first course photo – taken outside the Officers Mess – but Sgt Bert Stewart is not; which suggests that either he had not yet arrived or, being the only NCO among the Americans, he was simply left out, which seems a mite unfair.

Pilot Officers Bill Hall, Rufus Ward and Tom Wallace were at RAF Sutton Bridge for about six weeks and after 35 hours flying Hurricanes they were posted to 71 Squadron on 19 April. Bill gained the dubious distinction of being the first Eagle to be shot down and made a Prisoner of War during a fighter sweep in July 1941, while Rufus survived the war and returned to the USA.

Although 'washed-out' of a USAAF cadetship (a frequent source of Knight's recruits), all Eddie Miluck, a professional basketball player from Mandan, North Dakota ever craved was 'to fly airplanes, see the world and have adventure'. For Eddie, the tiny advert he spotted in a Dallas newspaper about the Clayton Knight Committee was a heaven-sent opportunity. He applied and was accepted. Although on Boat No.8, Miluck missed the photo session because he was in the station hospital at the time. Eddie went through 56 OTU without mishap though and was initially posted to 121, then 71 Squadron, volunteered for an overseas posting and completed his RAF service flying Curtiss P-40 Kittyhawks with 250 Squadron in the North African desert.

After postings to 43, 121 and 133 Squadrons in England, Fred Scudday also opted for overseas service and in July 1941 found himself with 129 Squadron in the thick of the air battles over Malta. He then saw action with 4 Squadron SAAF in the Western Desert where he claimed two air victories against Bf 109s during 1942. Following a posting to 92 Squadron, Fred transferred to the USAAF in 1943, first serving as an instructor before being posted to 449 FS, 51 FG at Kunming, China, to fly the P-38G Lightning in combat against the Japanese. Moving to Suichwan airfield, Jiangxi province, in February 1944, 1/Lt Fred Scudday was credited with one 'probable' on 6 May and one air victory, a Nakajima Ki-43 'Oscar', on 12 May. Shortly afterwards he fell ill with pneumonia, from which he died on 16 June 1944.

After about 40 minutes of dual training in a Miles Master, moving onto the Hurricane fighter proved to be quite a handful and several more of that first batch of volunteers had narrow escapes during this vulnerable period.

Plt Off Red McColpin is recorded in the station war diary as having a minor mishap in Hurricane L2006 on 2 April. Its engine failed and caught fire and he was obliged to force-land at Peters Point, just west of the airfield. He was at 56 OTU for five weeks before being posted to 607 Squadron. McColpin later joined 121 Squadron, the second of the Eagle Squadrons, in May 1941, and went on to serve in each of the other two Eagle squadrons, rising to command 133 just before it was absorbed into the USAAF (as the 336th Fighter Squadron of the 4th Fighter Group). He is credited with at least twelve air victories while serving in the RAF.

On his first solo flight, in Hurricane P1935, Plt Off Oscar Coen escaped unhurt on 14 March when it bounced on landing, dropped hard onto the port wing and caused the undercarriage to collapse – a very common mishap among OTU trainees! Posted to 71 Squadron, Oscar was shot down over France on 20 October. Evading capture, he was passed down the Resistance chain, reached Gibraltar and returned to England on 28 December 1941 for operations once more. He retired from the USAF in 1962.

On 14 March also, Plt Off Virgil Olson 'bent' Hurricane N2341 in a landing accident at RAF Sutton Bridge. Virgil followed Coen into 71 Sqn in April but lost his life in action on 19 August 1941 while on a bomber escort sortie.

This ability of most OTU pupils to have close shaves (e.g. twenty-six American mishaps at Sutton Bridge during 1941) put Plt Off Hillard S. Fenlaw, into the mishaps listings. Mixing up the undercarriage lever with the flap lever, he managed to fold up the undercarriage of Hurricane N8021 while taxying out for take-off on 4 April. Posted to 71 Squadron he, too, was killed in action on 7 September 1941 soon to be followed by Tom McGerty who died in action with 71 Squadron on 17 September.

Loran Laughlin 'pranged' Hurricane N2341 at Sutton Bridge on 14 March, in a heavy landing from which he walked away but his luck eventually ran out too. Posted initially to 607 Squadron, then to 121 Squadron on its formation in May, Loran became 121's first casualty when he lost his life in a training accident in June 1941.

Sgt Bert Stewart didn't get off scot-free either, since 56 OTU war diary records his Hurricane W9114 as suffering an undercarriage collapse while landing on 8 May. Bert was posted to 121 Squadron, which formed at RAF Kirton-in-Lindsey, Lincolnshire that same month – and was commissioned.

Of the others in the photo, Lawson Reed and Collier Mize both went to 43 Squadron before postings to 121 in May and both survived the war. Joe Durham left 56 OTU in June to join 121 Squadron at Kirton in Lindsey, transferring later to RAF Coastal Command. Wendell Pendleton became an Eagle with 71 Squadron when he left Sutton Bridge but is believed to have transferred to Ferry Command and eventually returned to the USA. Plt Off J. M. Hill did not become an Eagle, as he was posted to 111 Squadron at RAF Dyce.

By the date when the three RAF Eagle Squadrons transferred to USAAF control in September 1942, a total of 244 American pilots (a generally accepted figure) had served in them; the Clayton Knight Committee being responsible for recruiting more than 90 per cent, while Sweeny and the 'independent travellers' accounted for the remainder. The enormous contribution made by 56 OTU at RAF Sutton Bridge was to train 144 of these American volunteers on Hurricanes between March and December 1941, of whom 87 went on to serve with an Eagle Squadron and the remainder with other RAF units. At a time when RAF Fighter Command was recovering from the Battle of Britain and stepping up its cross-channel air campaign, these Yankee volunteers proved themselves able and courageous fighters who provided an invaluable boost to RAF fighter pilot resources. It is a sobering fact too that 63 American Eagles were killed in action, 35 five were made POWs and 42 died in training or other mishaps during the Second World War.

After the war Clayton Knight returned to his writing and illustrating work and in 1946 was created an Officer of the Most Excellent Order of the British Empire (OBE) for his outstanding services to Great Britain in both World Wars.

Americans, Dutchmen, Norwegians, Danes and Indians mingled with British and other Commonwealth pilots, all keen as mustard to fly fighters. From February 1941 onwards, though, it becomes far more difficult to identify trainees and their progress because the Sutton Bridge Form 540/ORB – with all but a very few seemingly random instances – ceases to show the name/rank/number of the trainees arriving or departing, merely recording the quantity of postings in or out, and broken down into officers and NCOs – with the names of those who had 'prangs'.

Sgt Arthur Lowndes was a typical example of the British pilots who were posted to Sutton Bridge during 1941. Having undertaken

elementary flying training to 'Wings' standard on the De Havilland
(DH) Tiger Moth and Hawker Hart, Arthur was selected for fighters
and found himself walking over Cross Keys bridge on a frosty day in
February 1941 to begin his encounter with the Hurricane:

> I spent five weeks at Sutton Bridge and found the Hurricane
> difficult to cope with, being my first solo encounter with a
> monoplane that was at least twice as fast, or more, than the Hart.
> I spent most of my time in a state of high apprehension; generally
> oblivious to what was going on around me!

Reference to Arthur's log book shows what the flying routine was for
an OTU pupil. Starting on 24 February, Arthur had one dual sortie
in a Harvard with Flt Lt Greaves, followed by two dual trips in a
Master, each with Plt Off John Edward Sulman on the 26th and 27th.
After that he was sent off on 2 March for his first solo in a Hurricane.
He was in good hands, because John Sulman was a 607 Squadron
Battle of Britain veteran and a prime example of the unsung majority
of dependable squadron pilots so typical of that time. Sulman came
through the Battle having seen several months of action, with two air
victories plus one shared and two damaged. He had this spell with
56 OTU to pass on his knowledge, before being posted later that
summer to 238 Squadron in the Western Desert, where he died in
action on 8 November 1941 aged 25 years.

Up to this point Arthur had flown a total of 105 hours (46 dual;
59 solo). On the first day Arthur's flying course began, the availability
of serviceable aeroplanes was: 35 Hurricanes, 4 Harvards, 8 Masters –
but these figures fluctuated daily – not least due to anything up to
four 'prangs' a day! During his course a new intake of 10 officers and
14 sergeants – all un-named – arrived on 3/4 March with 9 officers and
23 sergeants being posted out on the same date and it is also of note that
the first intake of Americans (*see* above) also arrived from 4 to 6 March.

Sgt Arthur Lowndes flying programme at Sutton Bridge.

Date (1941)	Aircraft	Exercise flown	Hours. Minutes flown.
24 February	Harvard 7179	Ex.1 Dual instruction	1.00.
26 February	Master 8672	Ex.1 Dual instruction	1.15.
28 February	Master 7960	Ex.1 Dual instruction	0.20.

2 March	Hurricane 1917	Ex.2 First solo	1.00.
3 March	Hurricane 2328	Ex.3 Flying practice	1.35.
5 March	Hurricane 5192	Ex.4 DF homings	1.30.
5 March	Hurricane 1917	Ex.15 Map reading	
		Ex.18 Cloud flying	
		Ex.19 Low flying	1.25.
7 March	Hurricane 1706	Ex.18 Cloud flying	
		Ex.19 Low flying	
		Ex.20 Forced landings	1.30.
7 March	Hurricane 2328	Ex.15 Map reading	
		Ex.18 Cloud flying	
		Ex.19 Low flying	
		Ex.20 Forced landings	1.10.
13 March	Hurricane 5195	Ex.7 High flying	
		Ex.14 Firing guns	1.55.
13 March	Hurricane 2341	Ex.5 Formation flying	1.20.
14 March	Hurricane 5195	Ex.13 Aerobatics	1.45.
14 March	Hurricane 2328	Ex.5 Formation flying	0.55.
15 March	Hurricane 2328	Ex.5 Formation flying	0.50.
17 March	Hurricane 5192	Ex.16 Navigation	
		Ex.19 Low flying	1.30.
18 March	Hurricane 2365	Ex.5 Formation flying	0.50.
19 March	Hurricane 2502	Ex.5 Formation flying	
		Ex6(i) Individual attacks	
		Ex.8(i) Dog fighting	1.35.
19 March	Hurricane 2502	Ex.13 Aerobatics	
		Ex.19 Low flying	
		Ex.20 Forced landings	1.40.
20 March	Hurricane 2502	Ex.5 Formation flying	1.40.
20 March	Hurricane 4217	Ex.16 Navigation	1.30.
21 March	Hurricane 1732	Ex.18 Cloud flying	
		Ex.19 Low flying	
		Ex.20 Forced landings	1.30.
22 March	Hurricane 1951	Ex.5 Formation flying	1.30.
23 March	Hurricane 3854	Ex.5 Formation flying	1.30.

23 March	Hurricane 230 (320?)	Ex.5 Formation flying	1.10.
25 March	Hurricane 1706	Ex.18 Cloud flying Ex.19 Low flying Ex.20 Forced landings	1.40.
30 March	Hurricane 3210	Ex.5 Formation flying	1.20.

Sgt Arthur Lowndes total time in Hurricanes at OTU:
   32 hours 20 minutes.

On 31 March, aircraft serviceability at 56 OTU was 42 Hurricanes, 2 Harvards, 8 Masters. On that date 19 officers and 17 sergeants (including Sgt Arthur Lowndes) were posted out to squadrons and another batch of 14 officers and 24 sergeants posted in.

Among the new arrivals posted in while Arthur Lowndes was at Sutton Bridge was Canadian Plt Off Hugh Constant Godefroy who arrived with the intake of 4 March 1941. Born in Java in 1919 of a Dutch father and Canadian mother, Hugh had Canadian citizenship and was educated in Canada. Enlisting in Toronto on 22 June 1940 he was accepted for flying training, which he completed to 'Wings' standard at 7 EFTS at Windsor, Ontario, and 1 SFTS Camp Borden, also in Ontario. Commissioned in January 1941, Plt Off Godefroy sailed for England where he was posted for fighter pilot training at 56 OTU and his view of RAF Sutton Bridge in winter paints a chill picture of wartime austerity. The officers' mess was a draughty wooden building in which the only warm place was directly in front of the small coal fire. He considered the mess to be a socially depressing place that was bound by too many petty rules and he spent as little time as possible inside its dingy interior. Meals were unappetising and sandwiches at high tea each afternoon – if any could be captured before being devoured by other airmen – were regarded as a 'main' meal. Often all he could find was 'wrinkled-up bread, thinly spread with Marmite'. Hugh was billeted a mile-and-a-half from the station where he occupied a room in the house of a widow in the village of Sutton Bridge. It was a clean and tidy place and he slept in a feather bed, something he had never experienced before. His room was always cold and had a damp feel to it but his landlady always placed a stone hot water bottle in the bed, which made it more bearable – and stopped his chattering teeth. Each day she would wake him at 6.00 am with a cup of tea and he was by then reluctant to leave the luxurious warmth of the bed to get dressed in the cold morning air. He said it was only the prospect of flying a Hurricane that spurred him to dress quickly and set off on foot, whatever the weather, to the camp for breakfast. This also opened new vistas for Hugh Godefroy when he encountered the British kipper for the first time – and was not impressed. It was no substitute for bacon and eggs – of which he could only dream. He consoled himself by filling up with toast and jam, and drinking tea because the coffee, he said, was undrinkable. However, it was the Hurricane that drove him to live with these disappointments. In his opinion, with their flaking paint and patched fabric, the 'veteran' in these war-weary fighters rubbed off on their rookie pilots.

Hugh had 176 hours in his logbook when he made his first trip in a Hurricane. He was given a pre-flight briefing about what to expect and then sent off to do it. He reckoned that the key to not making a hash of it was to open the throttle slowly, while countering the torque effect of the Merlin by pushing the right rudder pedal fully forward. It was also light on the tail, so don't put too much forward pressure on the stick or you would end up ignominiously with the prop chewing a b***y great hole in the ground! Braking, too, was different from the toe-brakes fitted to the American types on which he had trained; on the Hurricane, they were controlled by a hand-lever on the control column and differential direction was applied by appropriately moving the rudder bar.

Hugh experienced the usual difficulty during 'clean up after take-off' when it was necessary to change hands to manipulate the 'H' box flap/ undercarriage lever. On his first take-off he was taken aback by the power surge and by the time he had the under-cart up and the canopy closed he was miles from the airfield. Keeping calm, he found his way back to the airfield to try a landing but, looking down, he saw several aeroplanes dotted along the landing line in various 'pranged' states, while another Hurricane about to land was given a red Very light to go round again. This latter aircraft and Hugh circled the airfield for half-an-hour while the wrecks were removed then received a green Very light to land. He had been warned that the Hurricane could drop a wing if the speed was too low so, with plenty of speed in hand, flaps and wheels down, he made an uneventful first landing in a Hurricane. Now he had to master RAF radio transmission procedure, spending many hours trying to memorise all the code words and phrases that were strictly adhered to in the air.

On 15 April, after 35 hours on the Hurricane, Hugh was declared to be operational and posted from Sutton Bridge to 401 Squadron, where his natural flying ability and leadership qualities took him on a path to distinction. By the end of the war he was a Wing Commander DSO DFC*, credited with destroying seven enemy aircraft in combat while serving with 401 and 403 Squadrons and as 127 Wing Leader. After the war Hugh Godefroy entered the medical profession, practising as a physician until his retirement. He died in 2002.

Among the 'random name' exceptions mentioned in the ORB are two Dutch pilots who arrived on 1 June 1941, Plt Off John Willem Yoshitaro Roeper-Bosch and Plt Off Ritsaert (Dick) van den Honert. Van den Honert fought with the Dutch Army until the Germans overran Holland, then he escaped through Belgium to France before finding passage to England in a fishing boat. Although both men had volunteered for the RAF, had undergone some elementary flying training and had been assessed as potential fighter pilot material, upon arrival at 56 OTU their ability was found wanting and they were packed off to 8 FTS at RAF Montrose for a couple of weeks instruction on the Miles Masters. It is known they were back at 56 OTU by 18 June, because Van den Honert had a landing accident in Hurricane P3114 at Sutton Bridge – one of four accidents on that date. It is not known when they left Sutton Bridge but both men were posted to 611 Squadron to fly the Spitfire. Roeper-Bosch was lost during a fighter sweep over Northern France on 21 October 1941 when his Spitfire Vb, W3227, was shot down into the sea 4 miles off Boulogne. His body was washed ashore and buried at Berck-sur-Mer but after the war was repatriated for reburial in The Hague. Van den Honert, on the other hand, survived 114 operational sorties in Spitfires while flying with 611 and 167 Squadrons before he, too, was shot down in action on 30 April 1942. He managed to survive and ditched his aircraft in the sea, swimming half-a-mile to the English shore. During the engagement, however, he sustained a severe eye injury that left him with visual problems and an onset of sinus trouble left him unable to fly fighter operations any more. He continued to fly as an air-sea rescue pilot, flying the Supermarine Walrus with 275 Squadron and rescued several downed pilots in difficult conditions, for which work he received a Mention in Despatches and later a DFC. After the war he flew as a commercial pilot with KLM airline and died in 1995.

Shortly after the Dutchmen, three Norwegian pilots identified as Plt Offs Marius Eriksen, Werner Christie and Rolf Arne Berg arrived on 22 June 1941, described as being posted in from Toronto. Christie and Berg trained as pilots before the war but when the Germans invaded Norway in May 1940 all three men fled their homeland, making their way over time and by various routes to join exiled Norwegian forces in England. Christie travelled through Sweden, Russia, Japan and the US to reach Canada, while Berg took a more direct route across the North Sea but had to be rescued from his ship when it was torpedoed on its way to England. Set ashore in Scotland, he found his way into the Norwegian training 'system' and travelled to Canada.

Leaving Norway in November 1940, Eriksen also crossed to Scotland by ship, then made his way to Canada. The Norwegian government in exile – in much the same way as the De Gaulle's French forces had done – wished to operate its pilots as an independent Royal Norwegian Air Force unit. As volunteers for flying training, these three airmen (and many others in due course) were sent to Canada where, under an agreement with its government, they underwent flying training at the Norwegian Army Air Service flight training school that the Norwegians had been allowed to establish at Toronto Island airport in southern Ontario. Known as 'Little Norway', it opened on 10 November 1940. When these three airmen arrived, the base was equipped with Fairchild PT-26 basic trainers and obsolescent Curtiss Hawk 75 fighters that were used as advanced trainers, all purchased from the USA. Being selected for fighters saw them posted to 56 OTU at Sutton Bridge where, for the next nine weeks, they converted to the Hawker Hurricane. It appears they were also joined by three more – unnamed – Norwegians, as on 2 September 1941 the ORB records that six Norwegians were posted out. They were all went to 331 (Norwegian) Squadron, an RAF unit primarily manned by Norwegian pilots and which operated Hurricanes before being re-equipped with Spitfires in November 1941.

Marius Eriksen also served with the second Norwegian Squadron (332) and scored nine 'kills' before he was shot down and made a POW in May 1943. He was awarded a DFM and after the war he became a champion skier and a film star in his native Norway. He died in 2009. Werner Christie DSO DFC rose to command 332 and 234 Squadrons and, as a Wing Commander, led 150 Wing, achieving nine confirmed 'kills'. He flew a total of 244 operational sorties before being shot down and made a POW in April 1945. After the war Christie held a number of posts in civilian and military aviation until his retirement from the Norwegian Air Force as a major-general in 1977. Rolf Berg DSO DFC* led two Norwegian and two English squadrons while rising to the rank of Wing Commander with five confirmed 'kills' to his name. About to be 'tour expired', on 3 April, he led his fighter wing on a routine sweep, which was to be his last operation before being rested. It was uneventful but when his deputy was ordered to lead a second sweep that afternoon, Berg got permission to go along. Over the target his aeroplane was hit by ground fire, crashed and he was killed.

Like their forefathers in the First World War, thousands of men from the Indian sub-continent volunteered to fight for King and Country during the Second World War. By 1945, more than 17,000 Indians had served in the RAF and a further 25,000 had joined the Indian Air Force (IAF). In common with other Commonwealth countries, the Indian government – and indeed the airmen themselves – were keen to contribute men to the air battle raging over Britain. With this in mind, twenty-four recruits that comprised No.4 Course at the Initial Training Wing (ITW) in Lahore were, upon completion, commissioned into the RAFVR on 8 August 1940 and posted to England to pursue their flying training with the RAF. The men in this little group were aged between 19 and 25 and some had private flying experience. One of this select band was Plt Off Mahinder Singh Pujji, who would pass through 56 OTU Sutton Bridge on his way to becoming one of the most famous Indian fighter pilots of the Second World War. After studying law at college in Lahore, Mahinder – in his words – found a well-paid job with the Shell Oil Company and in his spare time qualified as a private pilot at Delhi Flying School in 1937. Although eligible to join the Indian Air Force, when war broke out he saw a newspaper advertisement for pilots to join the RAF so, seeing this as an opportunity to go abroad, he promptly applied to join the RAFVR, was accepted and began his 'great adventure'.

In September 1940 the party of twenty-four would-be pilots, referred to as 'X-squad', sailed for England aboard the troop ship SS *Strathallen* (23,700 tons) a former P&O cruise liner, arriving in Southampton on 8 October 1940. There they entrained for grey, war-torn London *en route* to 1 RAF Depot Uxbridge where, muffled up in overcoats and scarves they must have wondered what the hell they had let themselves in for. In November they were all sent even further north to begin their flying training on the DH Tiger Moth at 12 EFTS Prestwick – a chilling prospect compared to the sunny climes of India.

Selected for fighters, Plt Off Pujji was posted for advanced tuition to 9 SFTS Hullavington, where he graduated to 'Wings' standard on 16 April 1941. Successful completion saw a parting of the ways, with some of his countrymen selected for fighters and some for Bomber or Coastal Command. Pujji's next posting was to 56 OTU Sutton Bridge in May, to get to grips with the Hawker Hurricane.

Of the original twenty-four X-squad recruits, six did not reach a high enough standard during flying training in the UK and were posted to non-flying duties. Of the remaining eighteen, seven were selected for fighters and eleven for bomber/coastal command. While the eighteen were serving in Europe, two were killed on operations. From 1942, the remaining sixteen returned to India to serve operationally with the IAF for the remainder of the war – and into the post-war era too. A total of eight of this original batch of twenty-four died in operations in Europe and the Far East.

Mahinder Pujji himself had one mishap while at Sutton Bridge, in Hurricane P2717 on 16 May 1941. On approach to land, he flattened out too low and the undercarriage struck the ground a glancing blow. When he opened up the throttle, the aeroplane stalled and crashed but he managed to walk away from the wreck with only his pride damaged. He was in good company, though, because just a few days earlier, on 11 May, his fellow Indian, Plt Off Edwin Nazir Ullah (post-war Sqn Ldr, Pakistan Air Force), had been flying an exercise of aerobatics and practice forced landings when the engine of his Hurricane, N2457, failed and he was obliged to make a real forced, wheels-up, landing at Horseshoe Hole farm, Terrington Marsh. In a true 'East-meets-West' incident, there is also an AIR 81 casualty file for 15 May reporting that Plt Off Ullah baled out of Hurricane W9207 after a mid-air collision with P3221 flown by Plt Off R. F. Patterson, both Hurricanes crashing near King's Lynn. Ullah dislocated his shoulder upon landing but Patterson escaped unhurt. Plt Off Richard Fuller Patterson was an American citizen from Richmond, Virginia – a Princeton graduate and heir to the Lucky Strike Tobacco Company. He enlisted in the RCAF in 1940 and having completed basic flying training in Canada, sailed to England 'legitimately' – that is by comparison with the Sweeney/Knight pilots mentioned above. With his American roots he was posted from 56 OTU to 121 Squadron and thereby became an Eagle Squadron pilot. Robert Patterson was KIA on 7 December 1941 during a 'Rhubarb' operation over Belgium with 121 Squadron. His Hurricane, P3221, was a Battle of Britain 'veteran', having served with 145 Squadron, where it was flown variously by Jean Offenberg, Baudouin de Hemptinne and Alexis Jottard, all Belgian former pupils at Sutton Bridge during 1940.

Plt Offs Ranjan Dutt (later AVM, IAF) and Hukum Chand Mehta (KOAS, 11 November 1941) are also known to have trained at Sutton Bridge but even though the names of all of the original twenty-four Indians are known, other than those four mentioned above, the identity of the other three with Pujji at Sutton Bridge is not known. Posted to 43 Squadron, Hukum Chand Mehta died in an air accident during a formation training flight over Northumberland on 3 November 1941.

Mahinder Pujji took his Sikh faith very seriously and insisted right from the outset of his training that he was allowed to wear his turban even while flying, indeed it is believed he was the only fighter pilot to do so. He had a special strap made to hold his earphones and oxygen mask in place over his turban and said he even took the precaution of carrying a spare turban with him on flights in case he was shot down and lost one the one he was wearing.

Plt Off Pujji and his compatriots were posted from 56 OTU on 4 June 1941. Pujji and Mehta are known to have gone to 43 Squadron, but on 26 June Pujji transferred to 258 Squadron at RAF Kenley. There he flew convoy and defensive patrols and it was during 'sweeps' over France, escorting bombers on 'Circus' operations, that he had many combat engagements and narrow escapes. Once, when his Hurricane was badly shot up and in danger of crashing into the English Channel, he stuck with it and managed to coax the stricken aircraft to stay in the air just long enough to crash land inland of the white cliffs of Dover. He said:

> I was hit from behind by a burst which shattered the instrument panel and hit the engine. One bullet went clean through my jacket but I managed to glide back to England with black smoke pouring from the engine.

Force-landing near Dover, he was knocked out but saved from serious injury by his turban, which became soaked in blood. When the aeroplane burst into flames, rescuers dragged him clear before he was engulfed. After seven days in hospital he was back flying operations again. Pujji is credited with two confirmed kills and three damaged while flying Spitfires before his first tour of operations came to an end. His second tour was in the North African desert theatre, where he was shot down for a second time – but unhurt; his third tour found him back in India, flying Westland Lysanders on operations against rebels rampaging near the Afghanistan border. His fourth and fifth tours took him to the jungles of Burma where, in November 1943, he was posted to 6 Squadron of the Indian Air Force as a flight commander flying Hurricane FR IIbs on photo reconnaissance and ground attack sorties. In April 1944 he was posted to 4 Squadron IAF, first as a flight commander then took over Squadron Leader when its CO failed to return from an operation. He recalled one particular operation:

> A column of 300 West African troops under American command had gone missing in the jungle after an offensive operation. All efforts by the Americans and the RAF to locate them had failed and they were at risk from enemy forces sighted in the area. My squadron had earned a reputation as 'the eyes of the army' and General 'Bill' Slim

the local commander called me to ask if my boys could help find the missing column. I said yes and flew the sortie myself. The area to be covered was very close to enemy lines. I planned to approach from the Japanese side so they would not expect me and I flew low and far out to sea to come in from the enemy's backyard. My plan worked and after a while I spotted a likely clearing. As I circled, soldiers in Allied uniform ran out of the trees and started waving. The missing column was found – and subsequently rescued intact. I was thanked personally by AM Sir John Baldwin and awarded a DFC. After this I went off to attend the Military Staff College in Quetta.

Mahinder left the IAF in 1946 due to ill health, having contracted TB. He stayed in India where he recovered from his illness, married and had several civilian flying jobs until returning to England in 1974. He retired to Gravesend in Kent remaining there until his death in 2010 aged 92. He is greatly revered in his native country as the most prominent Indian pilot of the Second World War. In 2014 the contribution made by all Indian air crew personnel during the Second World War was recognised in the form of an 8-feet tall memorial bronze statue, cast in the likeness of Mahinder Singh Pujji, which was unveiled in St Andrew's Gardens in Gravesend, Kent.

7

Hurricane Harvest

For Englishman Sgt Peter Montgomery, the summer of 1941 was, in his words, a halcyon one. Four-and-a-half months of blazing Canadian prairie sunshine had provided him with 60 hours of Tiger Moth flying, 100 hours on the Harvard and his RAF pilot wings. Travelling by train across Canada, two weeks in a troopship and a week's leave had barely taken the shine off his brevet when he reported to 56 OTU RAF Sutton Bridge in mid-October 1941 to learn to fly the Hawker Hurricane fighter.

By now, the courses were numbered once more and composed of quite distinct groups. Sgt Montgomery joined No.38 Course with 44 other pilots, a quarter of whom were officers and the remainder sergeants. This was a large course compared to that first (No.5) back in April 1940, which had just 17 pilots. It was also a mixed bunch of nationalities – but typical of the time: Americans, Canadians, New Zealanders, Australians, Indians and one Dane, as well as British airmen – who stepped onto the platform at the tiny railway station. For a different pupil's eye-view of life at RAF Sutton Bridge, some years ago Peter Montgomery wrote an account of his experiences at 56 OTU which, with his permission, is drawn upon here.

Before tackling the mighty Hurricane, the new boys were first given a dual check flight in a two-seat Miles Master. In Peter Montgomery's case his log book shows 35 minutes dual with Sgt Staniforth in Master I, N7567, on 12 October, followed the next day with a 1-hour solo in Master I N8022. Confrontation with a Hurricane (P3039) came the day after, initally just for 50 minutes to get the feel of her, then for a few local area flights each lasting about 1½ hours during the days that followed. One flight per day seems painfully slow but the combination of two overlapping courses, less than 100 per cent aircraft serviceability as the norm, the notorious English weather and being kept busy in the classroom, tends to sum up the situation quite well. Visits to sample the sparse social amenities of the village across the river were few in number and usually meant going to one of the pubs but only after a long day and at that time of year, in darkness. Occasionally a bus would run these boys to King's Lynn for a Saturday night out.

Food and accommodation at the camp itself was 'reasonable in the prevailing circumstances but we gave it little thought as we were all keen to get the course over and go on to a squadron.' This suggests that conditions at the camp must have improved a little in the year since raw New Zealand pilot, Sgt (later Gp Capt DSO OBE DFC) Desmond Scott, first sampled the delights of 6 OTU in late 1940. Scott and his group were posted from RAF Uxbridge like a bunch of schoolboys, each clutching a rail warrant that would take them to RAF Sutton Bridge. His lasting impression was that it was one of the most uninteresting parts of England he ever served in. The countryside was cold, low-lying and wet, and the station's domestic complex was very austere, resembling rows of aircraft crates all camouflaged in black and green paint, each hut being occupied by about twenty pilots. The beds were iron stretchers that concertinaed into a third of their length when not in use. Instead of a mattress on each bed, there were three square, canvas-covered squabs, filled with sawdust. Sheets were not issued so it was virtually impossible to keep the squabs in line or together on the bed. Being winter-time, many pilots woke up with their backsides between the squabs and resting on the cold iron slats that took the place of bed-springs. Such discomfort could be partly overcome by laying thick wads of newspaper beneath the squabs and then sleeping in an overcoat. Sgt Scott often wondered how many young lives were lost through lack of sleep. Apart from this jaundiced view though, Sgt Scott appears to have followed a similar training pattern to that of Sgt Montgomery.

For Peter Montgomery, it was back to the Master in week two for a spell 'under the hood' practising instrument flying. Again, once checked out, at this stage it was quite usual for one pupil to fly under the hood while another pupil acted as safety pilot, keeping a sharp lookout for other aircraft. Sgt Montgomery accumulated 4 hours in Master I T8342 during this phase before graduating to cloud-flying and map-reading exercises in various Hurricanes. He recalled that when taking off dual in the Master, the rear seat was raised and the top of the canopy angled up to form a windshield. The pilot/ instructor, in the back seat, could then see over the head of the man in front and correct any swing that might develop during a 'blind' take off. Once airborne, however, stress on the canopy mechanism became excessive at speeds above 120 mph so it was necessary to lower the rear seat and close the canopy. Apparently, it was as well to remember to carry out both actions in the right order otherwise one's forgetfulness was rewarded by a right old bang on the head, proportional to the airspeed!

For those trained on the Harvard the change to a British design such as the Hurricane also brought the need to remember that its wheel brakes were operated by a hand lever rather than toe-brakes generally found in the American types. More than one pupil taxying for take-off had to be pulled up by the duty pilot who spotted smoke curling from the brake drums. Another significant difficulty for pilots such as Peter, who trained in the Canadian prairies during high summer, was getting used to the cloud and poor visibility over England in early winter, factors which could lead to dire consequences for the unwary.

Week three saw pupils gaining in confidence; doing everything from battle climbs to 25,000 feet, aerobatics, low flying (authorised!), formations and pin-point navigation exercises, rounding off the week by air-to-ground firing at Holbeach range and a few air attack manoeuvres.

After relatively sedate training aeroplanes these new Hurricane pilots found the kick in the back, as the throttle was pushed forward, most impressive – both Desmond Scott and Peter Montgomery made reference to this sensation – and the ground dropped rapidly away. On the Mark I, though, it was an awkward handling job to get the wheels up. With the left hand on the throttle for take-off and the right hand on the stick, it was necessary to change hands on the stick to be able to reach the undercarriage selector lever, located on the right-hand side wall of the cockpit, with the right hand. This lever, however, also operated the flaps by working through an 'H'-type gate so, in order to avoid the embarrassing situation of lowering the flaps just after take-off it was usual for a new boy to look down to make sure the lever went into the right position. Unfortunately, the combination of changing hands and taking an eye off the horizon usually resulted in the nose dropping followed by a sudden over-correction as earth seemed to replace sky through the windscreen. This sequence might well be repeated if wheels-up was not quite selected the first time. In consequence many first-time solos on the Hurricane often began with the aeroplane disappearing, from the view of those on the ground, in the manner of a fairground Big Dipper!

Once airborne and 'clean', Peter considered the performance and handling characteristics were excellent, although the early marks had only a fixed rudder trim tab rather than an adjustable one. This was bent manually by the ground crew to compensate for torque at cruising power but it was a bit of a strain on the right leg after an hour or so in the air trying to counteract with rudder the additional torque encountered at higher speeds.

After the long tarmac runways of Canada, landing a Hurricane on Sutton Bridge's small undulating grass field was quite exacting, too, and despite the robustness of its undercarriage, it could not absorb as much rough handling as the Harvard. In an effort to stabilise the grass surface there is evidence that Pierced Steel Mat (sometimes called pierced steel track or PST) was laid at Sutton Bridge sometime during late 1942 as an outcome of a visit by AMWD inspectors on 14 July 1942, when the ORB recorded the 'proposed installation of runways [sic]'. Air Ministry Directorate of Works drawings certainly show clearly that the inter-locking steel track was laid over an area of 1,150 yards by 50 yards on the 080/260 run, together with another 800 yards of wire-mesh Sommerfeld Track running at right-angles from the former's northern end on the 130/310 run.

Watching other pupils landing, Peter saw many Hurricanes bounce rather too high, hit harder the second time and descend a third time with their undercarriage legs swinging free because the locking strut joints had broken on impact. On such occasions, naturally the wheels folded on final touchdown and the aeroplane skidded along on its belly showering wooden propeller splinters in all directions. There was usually no injury to the pilot – except perhaps his pride – and he had more to fear from the subsequent sticky interview with the Squadron Leader (Flying). An analysis indicates that the litany of bent undercarriages or worse, sustained by 6/56 OTU Hurricanes in the hands of erstwhile fighter pilots, exceeded 200 incidents in the two years it was at Sutton Bridge.

It was November 1941 now and poor weather made it difficult to get time in the air. During the next two weeks Peter Montgomery managed only 6 hours in Hurricanes, most of which was on aerobatics and formation flying and 2 hours instrument practice in a Master. One week of the course was spent attached to the Gunnery Flight. With just over 1 hour on air-to-ground gunnery and a mere 15 minutes air-to-air firing at a drogue, Sgt Montgomery's limited experience included using a Hurricane fitted with an early experimental gyro gunsight. Whether the shortcomings of this instrument were responsible, or whether the entry reflects the standard of air-to-air firing at the time, he did not know but, in his recollection, he scored no hits at all on the drogue although his gunnery efforts were still assessed as 'average' in his log book!

During one lecture on combat tactics it was pointed out to the students that German fighters had fuel injection systems enabling them to be nosed over from level flight into a dive without any loss of power or speed. Our own engines, on the other hand, had normal float carburettors which, when subjected to the same negative 'G' manoeuvre, would interrupt the fuel supply and the engine would cut. Pupils were told that the way to deal with this situation was to half-roll the aeroplane, then pull the stick back to maintain positive 'G' and keep the fuel flowing in the ensuing dive.

Curiosity about this technique got the better of Peter one day. After firing practice, he climbed to 15,000 feet and with 350 mph on the clock he rolled the Hurricane over and pulled through into a dive. With the aeroplane in a vertical dive and 500 mph indicated airspeed, the control column became solid and immoveable. He realised many years later that he had experienced the onset of compressibility but little was known of such things in those days, least of all by curious trainees. Hauling with both hands on the stick for all he was worth and with Mother Earth gaining rapidly in clarity, gradually it moved and the nose came up. At this point he blacked out and when the blackness turned red then pink then blue, he found the aeroplane travelling vertically but this time upwards. A hasty glance at the ASI showed the needle dropping past the 100 mph mark so in order to avoid a stall, which seemed imminent, Peter kicked on rudder to get the nose down onto the horizon. Much to his consternation the ASI needle continued to rotate rapidly anti-clockwise and it was only as the zero figure was left behind that he realised he had misread the wretched instrument and it had another complete circuit of the dial to go before flying speed would have become critical. Much enlightened and sobered he returned to Sutton Bridge and kept quiet about his little escapade but it said much for the inherent strength of the Hurricane and the reliability of the Merlin engine.

Many and varied were the mishaps to befall these OTU pupils; four of Sgt Montgomery's course were killed in separate incidents, one was seriously injured and numerous others suffered forced landings or undercarriage collapses of the type mentioned earlier. In human terms his No.38 Course (6–9 October to 14 November) would become the costliest ever for 56 OTU.

Plt Off Norman John Choppen was first to go on 20 October. He was flying a formation practice in V6690 when its engine began to lose power. Pulling away from the formation he approached the ground in a shallow dive but was seen to crash when the Hurricane went into a steep turn close to the ground, south of Reffley Wood near King's Lynn. Plt Off Choppen was killed and he remains forever at Sutton Bridge, after being laid to rest in St Matthew's church cemetery.

30 October was a particularly unfortunate day for Canadians Plt Off McKillop and Sgt Zadworthy who, with Sgt G. A. Johnstone each wiped the undercarriage off P3888, P3039 and P2992 respectively. Three in a day, however, was not at all unusual at the airfield. Plt Off Hosking did the same to R4076 on 3 November while later that day American Plt Off James A. (Jim) Gray took the undercarriage off Master T8286 on his first solo on the type. On 6 November, Sgt D. C. Goudie, a Canadian, force-landed on Carter's Farm, Burtoft, when the engine of P2814 failed while he was on a map-reading exercise. During 1942, Goudie was posted to 57 OTU, a Spitfire unit at RAF Hawarden, where he had the misfortune to have to bale out of Spitfire IIa P7533 when it suffered engine failure on 14 October 1942. He survived that episode and went on to fly operations with 253 and 421 Squadrons. Becoming lost was a frequent occurrence, too, with Indian pilot Plt Off Tarlochan Singh making a hash of things on 9 November when he strayed as far north as Yorkshire before Hurricane P3656 finally ran out of fuel and he had to force-land near Skipton.

Peter also recalled that one of the small number of Danish fighter pilots in the RAF, Sgt Jens Ipsen, was badly injured the same day, when his Hurricane, V7004, broke up after hitting a tree in a steep turn during low flying practice. It will come as little surprise to discover that Jens' adventures during his quest to reach England can match any of the other exiled pilots about whom we have heard so much already.

In a small cemetery in the village churchyard of Upwell St Peter in the Cambridgeshire fens a small group, including the author, gathered on 26 September 2012 to pay their last respects to Jens Ipsen. He died at the ripe old age of 98 and had instructed his sons John and Alan to bury his ashes not in his native Denmark but in England, the country he had come to love through his service with the RAF. Furthermore, he told them to find a churchyard closest to the site of his near-fatal crash back in 1941. So, that is how the story ended in Upwell St Peter, but Jens Ipsen's remarkable story began before the war had even started.

Graduating with a business degree from Aarhus University in 1937, Jens attended a trade exhibition in Paris that year. Something, though, pulled him towards adventure rather than a mundane life in business and he made a decision, there and then, to join the French Foreign Legion. Not long afterwards he found himself in an outpost of the French Empire deep in the Syrian desert – real *Beau Geste* stuff! Hearing news of the outbreak of war and the German invasion of Denmark, Jens was stirred to return to Europe and fight for the freedom of his country. The collapse of France made up his mind to desert from the Legion and head for England. Walking for two days without food or water, he crossed the Syrian border into Palestine where he convinced the British military authorities to ship him to England, arriving in mid-1941.

Having volunteered for flying duty with RAF, he was accepted and, on 27 July, he arrived at 5 (P)AFU, RAF Ternhill. Selected for fighters, he was posted to 56 OTU Sutton Bridge in October, with two other Danes: Jorgen Thalbitzer and Aksel Svendsen. All was going well for Jens until, with the grand total of 10 hours on the Hurricane, he was sent off in Hurricane V7004 on 6 November 1941 to carry out an authorised low-flying exercise. It was exhilarating to be allowed to cavort down on the deck where the sensation of enormous speed and power was at its most evident. Until, that is, one runs into a tree! Jens always maintained it was a miracle he ever survived the crash. His Hurricane ended up a tangled heap in a field at Low Fen Farm (now Cock Fen Farm), near Upwell and Jens spent the next six weeks in RAF Ely Hospital. Sgt Ipsen was declared fit to continue his flying training at 56 OTU Sutton Bridge early in 1942. It was during these months of illness and recuperation that he developed an affinity for the people in this rural countryside that was to make a lasting impression on him.

He is believed to have completed his OTU course before 56 OTU moved out of Sutton Bridge on 26 March and, on 27 May 1942, Jens was posted first to 118 Squadron then, very soon after, to 234 Squadron. There he finally caught up with his friend Plt Off Thalbitzer (POW 27 July 1942; died while escaping 29 March 1943). Meanwhile Aksel Svendsen had been killed in action on 24 April 1942. Jens served with 234 Squadron from 7 June 1942 until 4 January 1943, flying 57 operational sorties. His next posting was to Malta, from February to September 1943, where he flew 109 sorties with 126 Squadron. After the war Jens returned to Denmark and served as a pilot in the Danish Naval Air Service, then in the Danish Air Force until 1955. His time in England was very special to him and during a visit in 2003 he tried, unsuccessfully, to find his crash site. However, in 2005 he returned to search again and this time, with the help of FAWNAPS he found the site. It was at this point – he was 91 by then – he told his sons that, when the day came, his ashes were to be buried at St Peter's, Upwell, which was done on 26 September 2012.

Two Canadians went next: Sgt David Lawrence Meisner, from Nova Scotia, died on 7 November, followed on 11 November by Sgt Michael Thomas George Willson, from Vancouver Island. They crashed in separate accidents, Meisner in Hurricane V6735 and Willson in Master N7960 – the latter with Plt Off John Richard Sale who also died when their aeroplane spun in near Wayland, Thetford, in Norfolk. Meisner and Willson are buried in St Matthew cemetery, while Sale was cremated at the Norwich & Norfolk crematorium.

Few days elapsed without incident but the worst during Peter Montgomery's course occurred on 24 November. It was a dull, cloudy morning with a grey stratus layer covering most of The Wash area. A close friend of Peter Montgomery, Sgt George Arthur Johnstone, who had already come to grief in an earlier mishap, was sent off in Hurricane I, V6864, on what was intended to be one of his last exercises on No.38 Course. Sadly for Sgt Johnstone, this time it would be very final indeed.

During that morning a flight of Avro Manchester bombers from 97 Squadron (Coningsby) was cruising in formation, just below the cloud base, not far from the Sutton Bridge circuit. Flying above the unbroken cloud layer was Sgt Johnstone being homed back to base by radio. Nearing the airfield, he was instructed to descend through the cloud and on breaking out below flew bang into the centre of the bomber formation, colliding with Manchester R5792 flown by Fg Off Henry Thomas Hill. From the tangled mass of wreckage, there were no survivors. Fg Off Hill's crew who perished with him were Flt Sgt Arthur Carriss Smith (2nd pilot); Sgt John Newton (Observer (Obs)); Sgt Francis Edward Martin (Wireless Operator/Air Gunner (Wop/AG)); Sgt Ernest Charles Hutton (Aus) (Air Gunner (AG)); Sgt Jesse Few (AG). Both aeroplanes fell to earth near the village of Walpole St Andrew and Sgt Johnstone, too, was laid to rest in St Matthew church cemetery. Fg Off Hill is buried at St Andrew's Church, Chesterton, Cambridge. By the end of Peter Montgomery's six-week course at 56 OTU four (10 per cent) of his fellow pupils had been killed without ever reaching a squadron, a loss rate by no means untypical of the time at training units.

The last sortie of Peter's OTU course was 45 minutes of night flying in V7645 and then graduation day, 24 November 1941, arrived. To its collective surprise, on 14 November, No.38 Course had the honour of being inspected by no less a person than AOC-in-C Fighter Command, AM Sir William Sholto Douglas KCB MC DFC – much 'bull' that day! Finally came the postings. These were avidly scrutinised before the mad dash to go on ten days' leave. Sgt Montgomery found himself posted to a Defiant night fighter squadron but returned to Hurricanes with an AA Co-operation Unit later in the war.

Little opportunity for the station readiness section presented itself for, although there were plenty of air raid warnings, even 'red' ones, with very few exceptions these occurred in the hours of darkness. From mid-June 1940 for example, there was an air-raid warning at Sutton Bridge every night until the month end. A similar situation continued throughout July and August, with alerts sounding at intervals of every two or three nights. Anticipating attacks by the Luftwaffe against RAF stations, in 1940 the Air Ministry implemented its plan for decoy airfields and other deception devices. Among these were 'Q' sites, an arrangement of night flare-path lights or Drem-type circuit lights erected some distance, perhaps 4 to 5 miles, from a parent airfield. In the case of RAF Sutton Bridge a 'Q' site was established on farmland at the inland edge of Terrington Marsh, on the northern outskirts of Terrington St Clements village. Located in fields to the north of the old Marsh School building – now a private residence – it was within (but not entirely) the area roughly bounded by Bentinck, Greenmarsh and Balaclava Farms. It was composed of electric night landing lights and obstruction lights, the intensity of which could be adjusted to simulate, for example, an oil-burning 'gooseneck' flare-path as well as more substantial runway lighting schemes. It did its job well.

The Luftwaffe took its first crack at RAF Sutton Bridge on the night of 30/31 August 1940 and proved the effectiveness of the Terrington 'Q' site. In the early hours of the 31st, farms in the vicinity reverberated to the crump of four high explosive (HE) bombs exploding about 1,000 yards north-west of the glimmering 'flare-path'. A few minutes later, fifteen explosions heralded the arrival of more bombs, this time falling in a line 1,000 yards to the south-east of the site. Casualties were limited to one farm horse killed and a greenhouse damaged, but the raid would not have done much for the nerves of the good farmers of the district.

Three weeks later the Luftwaffe tried again, equally unsuccessfully. At ten o'clock on the evening of 22 September those tempting lights at Terrington did their job again by persuading a single raider to unload seven HE bombs near the 'Q' site. The lights were doused when the first bomb exploded and the remainder landed 1,000 yards south-west. Five minutes after the enemy aeroplane departed the lights were turned on again but attracted no more customers. Again it was the horse population that suffered with the loss of another one and two more injured by shrapnel. A number of windows in Bentinck Farm house were broken by the blast. Perhaps it was this latter occurrence that finally prompted residents of Terrington district to send a petition on 4 October to RAF Sutton Bridge, pleading for the removal of the 'Q' site from their locality.

By now Gp Capt O'Neill had been posted away to HQ Fighter Command after only a few months as Station Commander and his place was taken on 17 August by Wg Cdr Bruce Bernard Caswell, formerly of RAF Acklington. How Wg Cdr Caswell dealt with the petition is not recorded but one might guess that while being sympathetic, he would hardly be keen to give up such obviously effective protection – nor could he anyway. No doubt he would also consider two dead horses and a few broken windows in so sparsely a populated area a small price to pay. As if to back up such a view 'Jerry' paid two more visits during the night of 28 October when the 'Q' site collected more bombs. At 7.40 pm thirteen HE bombs whistled down at the lights and half-an-hour later another five dropped a quarter-mile from the site. Fragments found later suggested these were of 100 kg size and all fell into open fields. The residents would not be amused though, as one house had a ceiling damaged by blast. There was a little respite for a while at night while the Luftwaffe directed its Blitz efforts elsewhere but occasionally daylight brought trade for the local fighter squadrons, much to the chagrin of the 6 OTU Readiness Flight. One such foray by the Luftwaffe into the fens, however, resulted in Sutton Bridge getting the closest possible sight of enemy aircrew.

Based at RAF Wittering, 1 Squadron engaged the enemy on a number of occasions in late October 1940 when raiders entered its territory. For example, at dusk on 29 October three Spitfires, which had been scrambled to investigate a hostile raid believed heading for Sutton Bridge or one of the other airfields in the vicinity, intercepted Dornier Do 17s near Sutton Bridge. In the melee that followed, Blue section leader Sgt W. T. Page claimed to have damaged one of the Dorniers before his own aeroplane, P3318, was hit by return fire.

Glycol fumes forced him to attempt to return to base but he had to force-land at Orton near Peterborough.

Re-emphasising that invisible bond between Sutton Bridge and 1 Squadron, there came a most interesting engagement the next afternoon. Another section of three Spitfires caught a Ju 88 – later found to have been making its way inland for an armed recce of the Metro-Vickers plant in Salford. Plt Off G. E. Goodman (in P2877), a graduate of the very first 6 OTU course at RAF Sutton Bridge, Plt Off R. G. Lewis (P3229), back with 1 Squadron after his spell of instructing at 6 OTU, and Sgt Vaclav Jicha, a graduate of the first Czech course at Sutton Bridge, were directed onto a raider heading in from The Wash.

Coming at it head-on, Goodman mistook the aeroplane for a Blenheim and did not open fire. Recognising it as a Ju 88, the other two half-rolled and pulled up to attack from the rear. Lewis opened fire from 200 yards, broke away and then Sgt Jicha put in a short burst before it disappeared in cloud. The Ju 88 had turned south before the attack and now heading towards Sutton Bridge, two of the enemy crew baled out. They landed at Lovell's Hall, Terrington St Clements where, slightly hurt on landing, they were captured by soldiers from 374 AA Battery, taken to RAF Sutton Bridge and thence to a POW camp in Dunstable. Post-war research shows this enemy aeroplane to be Junkers Ju 88A-1, Werk Nr 5008, L1+GS from 8/LG1. The pilot was Uffz W. Arndt who, with Uffz A. Bronner, stayed in the aircraft to crash-land it at Middle Fen, Stuntney, near Ely, while the two who baled out were Ogefr P. Flieger and Gefr W. Kellner.

On 1 November 1940, officialdom decreed that all OTUs were to be re-numbered by having '50' added to their existing unit numbers and thus 6 OTU now became 56 OTU, still under the command of newly promoted Gp Capt Caswell.

Back came the Luftwaffe in strength on the evening of 14 February 1941. It had been a fine day for flying, after a spell of changeable weather and limited activity. Between the staff, pupils and 50 aeroplanes on the station at that time, 122 hours of flying had been crammed in that day. A juicy target indeed! By dusk the station was in darkness but with the 'Q' site at Terrington Marsh lit up. At 7.50 pm the first of an estimated 12 enemy aeroplanes unloaded the first of 47 HE bombs, 1 oil bomb and about 1,000 incendiaries in a concerted attack directed at the Terrington decoy. Many fell among farm buildings but only one house was hit and no casualties were reported. The only other damage was to yet another greenhouse and a minor road.

It would be quite reasonable by now for the Germans to believe they had dealt Sutton Bridge a serious blow and that it might no longer constitute a worthwhile target. A reconnaissance sortie would no doubt provide confirmation. With a daylight recce likely to be repulsed, just such a raid was mounted the very next night – 15/16 February – when an estimated six enemy aircraft (E/A) dropped numerous parachute flares around the 'Q' site.

Photographic evidence would quickly confirm that RAF Sutton Bridge had been far from 'plastered' and the Luftwaffe response was swift but fortunately just as ineffective. Low cloud and drizzle greeted the dawn of the 16th, curtailing flying training until later in the day. By mid-afternoon the cloud base had lifted to 900 feet when, at 3.05 pm, without warning a single Heinkel He 111 appeared out of the murk. It made a half circuit of the airfield, dropping a stick of nine bombs and spraying the area with bursts of machine gun fire, before disappearing back into the cloud as quickly as it came. The whole attack lasted less than two minutes. All bombs fell on open ground, none of which came within a hundred yards of the hangars and there were no casualties.

Evidently the returning crew reported a satisfactory attack, as only one more raid was made on the 'Q' site; two enemy aircraft dropped nine HE bombs just after midnight on 18 February, then there were no more attacks for three months. Since the 'Q' site was clearly very successful and obviously not going to be moved, the local inhabitants decided to make the best of things and submitted another petition to the station, this time to have an air raid warning siren installed!

During the next three months, the aeroplane population of the station almost doubled. At the beginning of May 1941, Sutton Bridge could now muster at least eighty aeroplanes, seventy of which were Hurricanes.

In a momentous weekend, London took its worst hammering of the Blitz on 10/11 May, Rudolf Hess chose that night to fly to Scotland, while during the early hours of Sunday 12 May Sutton Bridge was re-visited by the Luftwaffe as part of a series of country-wide raids directed at airfields and carried out by Luftflotte 3. The raid also coincided with the arrival of a new OTU course intake, at this time numbering eleven officers and twenty-five sergeants. Instead of a quiet training station they would be greeted by the sight of bomb craters and smouldering aeroplanes. That night, between 1.00 am and 2.00 am, three separate attacks, believed by a single enemy aircraft each time, were made on the airfield. Sixteen bombs fell among Hurricanes parked outside the hangars, setting two on fire, seriously damaging seven others and peppering many more with shrapnel. Luckily, apart from bomb splinter damage to roofs and broken windows, few buildings were affected. There was only one casualty; a soldier seriously injured by bomb fragments.

The Luftwaffe did not have things all their own way, however, as post-war research shows. One of the aircraft which attacked Sutton Bridge, Junkers Ju 88A-5, V4+DM, Werk Nr 7170 of 4/KG1, was shot down by AA fire while passing over RAF Watton. Crashing at Scoulton in Norfolk, three crew were killed and the fourth was made a POW. Another 4/KG1 Ju88, detailed to attack Sutton Bridge, failed to return from the sortie and was reported to have crashed into the North Sea, although it is quite possible these two losses may, in fact, refer to the same aeroplane.

This was not the last time RAF Sutton Bridge was raided but later attacks were directed against the Central Gunnery School during 1942 and thus will be covered in a later chapter dealing with that period.

Enemy Air Raids directed at RAF Sutton Bridge & Decoy Site.

Date	Location.
30/31 August 1940	Terrington 'Q' Site
22 September 1940	Terrington 'Q' Site
28 October 1940	Terrington 'Q' Site
14 February 1941	Terrington 'Q' Site
15/16 February 1941	Terrington 'Q' Site
16 February 1941	RAF Sutton Bridge
17/18 February 1941	Terrington 'Q' Site
12 May 1941	RAF Sutton Bridge
24 July 1942	RAF Sutton Bridge

It was a very long time before a 56 OTU pupil actually came anywhere near being able to have a crack at the enemy in this region. During a cross-country flight on 10 March 1942, only a few days before the OTU moved out of Sutton Bridge, Sgt Claude Weaver was tootling along at 12,000 feet, 5 miles north of Spalding, when he spotted an enemy aircraft a little below his level. Identifying it as a Messerschmitt Bf 110, Weaver dived on his target, closed to 300 yards and let fly with two long bursts. No hits were seen and the E/A disappeared into cloud cover so the disappointed Weaver had to return to base empty-handed. Sgt Claude Weaver's personal story brings a stirring finale to that of 6/56 OTU, summing up all the qualities recognisable among all the pilots who passed through its portals while at Sutton Bridge.

Born in Oklahoma City, USA, and always considered a headstrong, wilful young man, he made his own way to Canada where – clutching written permission from his despairing parents – he enlisted in the RCAF on 13 February 1941 at the tender age of 17½ years. Accepted for flying training he made an enthusiastic and able pupil, completing elementary training at 17 Elementary Flying Training School (EFTS) in Nova Scotia on 8 June, followed by a course at 8 Service Flying Training School (SFTS), Moncton, which he completed on 27 July. Several minor discipline infractions did not prevent him being shipped to England to continue his path to becoming a fighter pilot – for which his natural aggression and flying ability seemed admirably suited. A month at the Advanced Flying Unit (AFU) RAF Cranwell, from 6 December 1941 to 5 January 1942, was followed by his arrival at 56 OTU, RAF Sutton Bridge, on 10 February where, as a member of course No.42, he was finally let loose with a Hawker Hurricane. He was 18 years old and it was the beginning of a short but distinguished combat career. With 36 flying hours on the Hurricane and graded 'above average', Claude was posted to 412 Squadron on 15 April 1942 but on 15 July found himself flying a Spitfire off the deck of HMS *Eagle* in the Mediterranean *en route* to 185 Squadron flying operations from Malta. It was from here that Weaver was shot down over Sicily on 9 September 1942 after becoming, while still aged 18, the Allied air forces' youngest fighter ace of the Second World War. When he was shot down he had ten air victories to his name. Having survived the crash landing, he was captured by the Italians. After two failed escape attempts, when the Germans had taken over POW camps from the Italians his third attempt was successful. Heading south through Italy disguised as peasants, Claude and a companion walked 300 miles then rode donkeys through enemy lines to reach safety. Back in England by 18 October 1943, via Malta, Algiers, and a lift in a B-17, newly commissioned Plt Off Weaver soon returned to operations with 403 Squadron. He is credited with two more victories before being shot down on 21 January 1944 during a 'Circus' operation to the Amiens area. Baling out, his parachute canopy snagged on the tail of the aeroplane and Plt Off Claude Weaver III, DFC DFM was dragged to his death. The citation of his DFC said 'his successes are an excellent tribute to his great skill, courage and resolution.'

Despite all these interruptions, life at the OTU carried on apace and next day another batch of thirty-three officers and sergeants – including Sgt Claude Weaver – were posted out to operational fighter squadrons. So, we have heard about life for the pupils at Sutton Bridge but what was it like from an instructor's point of view?

'With effect from 8 November 1940 Fg Off W. H. R. Whitty is posted to 56 OTU for flying instructor duties.' Thus ran the order transferring William Hubert Rigby Whitty from 607 Squadron at RAF Turnhouse, Edinburgh, to RAF Sutton Bridge. Writing from his retirement home in Canada, Bill outlined his RAF service leading up to that posting and he believed it to be typical of many of his contemporaries at the OTU at that time.

Born in 1914 in Litherland, Merseyside, Bill studied engineering at Liverpool University, graduating in 1935. He joined 607 (County of Durham) Squadron of the Royal Auxiliary Air Force in 1937 receiving his flying training to wings standard in Avro 504N, Avro Tutor, Hawker Hart and Demon aircraft. Mobilised initially after the Munich crisis, he was called up for full-time service to 607 Squadron at RAF Acklington in August 1939. Bill had his first taste of combat on 16 October 1939 when he was flying in a section of three Gloster Gladiators that intercepted a Dornier Do 18 flying boat (M7+YK; KuFlGr 806) off the north-east coast and between them shot it down. 607 Squadron moved to Croydon in November 1939 and on 15 November re-located to Merville in France from where, on 10 May 1940, Bill went into action when the balloon went up. Flying Hurricanes on up to four sorties a day, he was credited with shooting down a Heinkel He 111 and a Messerschmitt Bf 109 during the French campaign.

Back in England on 20 May 1940, with just five pilots left, 607 Squadron was sent north to RAF Usworth for re-building and subsequently to play its part in the Battle of Britain. It was here that Bill Whitty had a taste of instructing since it was necessary for a dozen new pilots posted in from OTUs to be brought up to scratch by the five old hands. Bill recalled the squadron was ready just in time to deal with the Luftwaffe's attempted raid on Tyneside from bases in Norway on 15 August. 'The Hun aircraft were off course when they reached the English coast and we were ready for them; it was good training for our new pilots.' He was credited with damaging a couple of Bf 110s during that engagement. 607 moved down to Tangmere on 8 September 1940 from where, after sustaining more losses, it was sent north again, this time to RAF Turnhouse in November 1940. However, promoted to Flt Lt, Bill was posted out to 56 OTU, where he remained as an instructor until March 1942.

Arriving at Sutton Bridge, Bill found himself in the company of many Battles of France and Britain veterans: Flt Lt George Greaves (ex-504 Sqn) was 'A' Flight commander; the 'B' Flight commander was Herbert Hallowes (ex-43); Flt Lt D. P. D. G. Kelly (ex-74) was Chief Flying Instructor (CFI) and the others included the Hon Derek Dowding (ex-74) who was the son of Air Chief Marshal Hugh 'Stuffy' Dowding; Peter Down (ex-56) and Flt Lt Denis Frederic Beardon. Flt Lt George Hugo Formby Plinston, a Battle of France veteran with 1, 607 and 242 Squadrons, was in charge of the target towing flight at that time.

There was a constant turnover of squadron pilots being posted in as instructors for short periods, with several famous names appearing among them. Not least of these was ex-17 Sqn, Battles of France and Britain veteran, Fg Off Harold Bird-Wilson, who would, post-war, become an Air Vice-Marshal with a CBE DSO DFC* and AFC* to his name – but he was a lowly member of 'B' Flight at 56 OTU between 7 November 1940 and 16 January 1941.

List of Flying Instructors on staff of 56 OTU in December 1940.
Sqn Ldr D. P. D. G. Kelly (CFI)
Flt Lt D. F. Beardon.
Flt Lt J. L. Duus.
Flt Lt G. Greaves.
Flt Lt G. Harris.
Flt Lt R. O. Hellyer.
Flt Lt C. D. Palmer.
Flt Lt G. H. F. Plinston.
Flt Lt C. L. C. Roberts.
Flt Lt J. E. J. Sing.
Flt Lt W. A. Toyne.
Flt Lt W. H. R. Whitty.
Fg Off H. A. C. Bird-Wilson.
Fg Off D. H. D. Dowding.
Fg Off P. D. M. Down.
Fg Off K. C. Jackman.

Fg Off R. F. Martin.
Fg Off D. G. Smallwood.
Fg Off W. H. M. Walker.
Plt Off G. R. Bennette.
Plt Off C. N. Birch.
Plt Off F. J. Soper.
Plt Off W. A. Waterton.
WO E. Mayne
Flt Sgt C. A. Deport (French)

On the question of the pilot training programme, Bill Whitty observed:

OTUs did not come under Training Command and we so-called veterans were not trained instructors so ideas about step by step training, with tests two or three times while the pupil was on the course, were generally lacking. You could only watch him while he was in formation with you in the air and talk to him on the ground afterwards.

Numbered flying exercises [see Arthur Lowndes page 150] for each pupil to carry out were first described on the ground then practised in the air, often by the pupil flying alone. These seem to be recorded somewhat haphazardly in their logbooks and I cannot recall what each exercise number referred to. Generally, pupils were given dual on the Harvard or Master then sent off solo on the Hurricane. This might be followed by cross-countrys, formation flights, aerobatics and simulated dog-fights. Occasionally we worked with a nearby Wellington squadron to give their gunners practice in defending against fighter attacks.

Late in the course pupils would be sent over to Flt Lt George Plinston's aerial gunnery flight, for air firing experience but George's aircraft serviceability was poor at Sutton Bridge and Gedney Drove End – where some of the towing aircraft were located. We complained bitterly about this situation as it meant pupils did not get enough – if any – live ammo time. In those days things were not well organised and no-one bothered to check on the effectiveness of one's particular training method. I had my own routine worked out, which basically was to try to ensure all my pupils were happy with their aeroplane when airborne and learned to spend plenty of time practicing watching for Huns – or they wouldn't know what hit them when they went on ops!

In February 1941 I was sent on an instructor's course for a couple of months to Central Flying School (CFS) Upavon and upon my return to Sutton Bridge in April I took command of 'D' Flight. Of all the many pupils I came across in my time at 56 OTU, Plt Off Richard Playne Stevens sticks in my mind most vividly. He was at the OTU in December 1940 and was desperate for a posting to night-fighters, although being over thirty years of age he was rather older than most trainees.

Indeed, Richard Stevens had considerable pre-war flying experience as a commercial pilot and was used to night flying, particularly on the London–Paris route, a skill he put to deadly use in 1941. Richard Stevens achieved his aim on both counts. Becoming a legend as a 'lone wolf' flying night-defence sorties in a Hurricane he rose rapidly to the rank of Sqn Ldr, claiming fourteen air victories at night and earning a DSO and DFC in the short time before he himself was killed in action on an intruder sortie over Belgium in January 1942.

During research, prior to building up a picture of life at this OTU, not only was correspondence exchanged with Bill Whitty but, by an enormous coincidence, on one occasion letters were received simultaneously from Bill in Canada and from one of his former pupils in Sutton Bridge's 'D' Flight who was living in Cornwall.

Fifty years ago, Eric Raybould was a newly qualified Plt Off who found himself attached to 56 OTU in the care of Bill Whitty and who can now put forward an alternative view of life at Sutton Bridge just prior to the period described earlier by Peter Montgomery. By way of contrast, Eric received his basic flying training in England and wrote:

My elementary training was on Tiger Moths at Staverton where I did about fifty hours flying in ten weeks. This was followed by three months at 5 Service Flying Training School (5 SFTS), RAF Tern Hill, mainly flying the Miles Master but I also managed a few trips in a Hurricane, too. SFTS was probably the most perilous period of my RAF service since, out of a complement of forty-two pupils a mere twenty survived the course. I think everyone who survived was given an 'above average' assessment as a consolation!

Even at EFTS I had found aerobatics made me sick. I asked to go onto bombers so what did they do – in true service tradition the opposite happened and I found myself on a fighter SFTS, then was later posted to the fighter OTU at Sutton Bridge. It was

5 June 1941 and with about 140 hours flying time in my log book, including a grand total of two hours at night, I walked the short distance from the station across the Cross Keys swing bridge to the camp. My recollection of the course was that it was short, just five weeks and more than one course ran at the same time. During my time at Sutton Bridge there was only one fatality [Sgt A. M. Duthie killed when L2055 spun in at West Walton on 11 June 1941] but plenty of lesser 'prangs'.

The course content comprised aerobatics, formation flying, simulated dog-fights, gunnery, navigation and ground lectures on tactics and aircraft recognition. It was around this time that I realised I'd sooner be shot down than indulge in prolonged aerobatics – death would be a pleasant relief to the intense nausea I felt. Among my fellow students there was also a general terror of night flying but I found it a positive pleasure compared to aerobatics. Consequently, when nearing the end of the course, I volunteered for night fighters, spending most of the final week practicing night flying on the Hurri.

My compatriots were a mixed bunch that included American, French, Dutch, South African and Norwegian pilots and I recall one of our instructors was the ex-1 Squadron veteran, Fg Off Prosser Hanks DFC. He was introduced to us as our general guide and 'Father Confessor' but thereafter, I don't recall him doing much, although he always seemed to be around, showing a kindly interest – but rarely flying. I do, however, have a strong recollection towards the end of my course, of being allowed to fly an armed Hurricane on a formation Sweep across the North Sea and this was led by Prosser Hanks [later Grp Capt; DSO DFC AFC; thirteen air victories].

Apart from the glorious weather that summer, another vivid memory is of a boxing match against a Midland Area Amateur Boxing Association (ABA) team which made mincemeat of the station team. When the show was over volunteers were called for to participate in exhibition bouts. I was a fairly hefty bloke with no pretensions as a boxer but I resented the behaviour of quite a good middleweight on the ABA team and asked to take him on. It was a helluva fight for an 'exhibition' and although I wasn't knocked about much, I was so utterly exhausted by taking on this chap in my completely unfit condition that I took to my bed for a day to recover.

178

The coincidence mentioned earlier, came to light when close inspection of Eric Raybould's log book showed it to have been signed for that period by none other than Bill Whitty. Furthermore, an entry on 11 June 1941 recorded a 2-hour flight in DH Rapide X7342 with Flt Lt Whitty as pilot and Plt Off Raybould as navigator.

Bill Whitty remembered that trip clearly: 'What a coincidence,' he wrote, 'to hear from Eric Raybould at the same time. I remember that Rapide trip because we landed at RAF Halton first. It was a terrible landing on rough grass, which seemed never to have been rolled for years. Then we went on to RAF Portreath, near Newquay, to drop off some pilots who were going to collect some used Hurricanes for the OTU. It was a lovely flight across England, quiet and peaceful, reminding me of the days when I flew on summer evenings pre-war as an Auxiliary.'

In July 1941, assessed as 'average', Plt Off Eric Raybould got his wish, too, and was posted to a night-fighter unit. However, it was 256 Squadron, which at that time operated the Defiant and a few Hurricanes from Squires Gate, Blackpool. He was not keen on that arrangement and after a few months responded to a call (ever the volunteer!) for volunteers to join new Beaufighter squadrons being formed. He was posted to 68 Squadron (High Ercall, then Coltishall) never having flown a twin-engine aeroplane in his life. 'It didn't seem to matter,' he said, 'as I was given an old Blenheim to play about with first.' After a night-flying career involving postings to North Africa, Tunis, Malta, Sicily, Salerno and Anzio, Eric Raybould finished his operational flying with 600 Squadron in December 1943. He died in 2014.

Bill Whitty left 56 OTU in March 1942 and continued to instruct at 24 EFTS until in 1944 he was posted to Bomber Command to fly the Handley Page (HP) Halifax. Awarded a DFC in 1945, he moved to Transport Command and was de-mobbed in 1946 with the rank of Sqn Ldr. Emigrating to Canada, he made a career as an electrical engineer and died in 2003.

A different side to the life of an instructor can be found in the next story. The flying career of Flt Sgt John Teasdale Craig is a typical example of a pre-war NCO pilot who had to share the burden of the early air battles. Craig joined 111 Sqn. in 1938 and went into action over Dunkirk in May 1940. He fought gallantly in the Battle of Britain until 31 August when he was injured in combat and forced to bale out of his aircraft. Credited with eight enemy aircraft by that time, Craig was awarded the DFM and, after a spell in hospital, he returned to 111 Squadron before a posting to Sutton Bridge on 21 January 1941 as an instructor. Having survived all the enemy could throw at him, on 6 June 1941 Flt Sgt John Craig met a tragic end when his Hurricane W9114 collided with P3162 flown by another ex-Battle of Britain pilot and instructor, Sgt Ivor Bidgood, who also died in the accident. Craig's aircraft fell on Manor Farm at Walpole St Peter, where the site was excavated thoroughly by FAPS in 1978. Bidgood's plane crashed at Terrington St John. While researching among the original Form 1180s in the MoD archive in Old Scotland Yard, London, in 1978, the author discovered both cards for this accident were missing from the filing cabinets – and those were not the only ones!

Two Czech trainees practising combat manoeuvres with cine-guns were involved in the next collision, which occurred near Walpole St Peter on 7 January 1942. Plt Off Jan F. Žerovnicky in Hurricane V7469 misjudged a high-speed approach on W9180 from the rear and ran into it, causing his aircraft to dive into a pear tree orchard on Selby's Farm from 10,000 feet. Sgt František Pokorný, by some stroke of good fortune, managed to crash land W9180, although he sustained severe head injuries in the process. He later flew with 313 Squadron but was posted as MIA on 10 April 1942.

The last collision suffered by 56 OTU before it moved north to RAF Tealing in March 1942 could be said to surpass the others in its seriousness. It occurred on 17 January 1942, when one of its pilots carried out a series of unauthorised mock attacks on a Short Stirling bomber from 7 Squadron based at RAF Oakington that was out on a training sortie of its own. The bomber's sortie had taken it out over The Wash then on that cold January afternoon, it was returning to base following the course of the Bedford rivers. According to the testimony of several eye-witnesses on the ground, Plt Off Derek Malcolm Browne, aged 19, in Hurricane V6865, made several diving passes at Stirling W7467 from the rear, getting a bit closer each time. During these potentially dangerous manoeuvres – probably in a desperate attempt to warn him off – the Stirling captain apparently ordered his gunners to open fire at the Hurricane. Watchers on the ground said they heard the rattle of machine gun fire but Plt Off Browne appeared to ignore this warning and carried on. One pass went too close; the Hurricane was thought to have been caught in the bomber's prop wash and rammed into its fuselage. Both aeroplanes dived into the ground on the flood plain 1½ miles north of Earith Bridge, Cambridgeshire, and all on board were killed.

The Stirling crew was captained by Plt Off Ronald Wilkins Taylor DFM (Aus) – the MoD Form 1180 shows his rank as Flt Sgt – and his crew comprised Plt Off James Douglas Waddell (Navigator (Nav)); Blacklaw (Flight Engineer (FE)); Sgt Francis Joseph Lloyd (WOp); Plt Off Alan John Low (AG); Sgt James McCarley (AG) (MOAS) and Sgt Walter James Mankelow (AG) (MOAS). Another casualty in the Stirling that day was Sqn Ldr John Noel Mahler DFC, who was on board acting as second pilot 'under training'. The site was excavated by the Warplane Wreck Investigation Group in 1984 and wreckage recovered and a memorial was erected by 7 Squadron Association and the Parish Council in 1999. Plt Off Browne is buried in Cambridge City Cemetery. This was the sixth mid-air collision involving pilots from 6/56 OTU while located at RAF Sutton Bridge.

It was not all 'beer and skittles' for the ground crews at Sutton Bridge either. Mention has been made at several points that the aircraft serviceability at 56 OTU fluctuated daily quite considerably. Bearing in mind the size and condition of the airfield, the relatively small number of hangars and the hammering taken by the aeroplanes from heavy-handed trainees, this situation is not surprising. As an example, at random the quantity of serviceable aeroplanes on the station in mid-1941 is shown below. The quantity of aeroplanes actually on charge was not recorded in the Form 540.

Serviceable aircraft at Sutton Bridge mid-1941

Type	Minimum	Maximum
Hurricane	30	67
Master	5	14
Battle TT	3	5
Henley	2	3
Dominie	1	1
Tiger Moth	1	1
Leopard Moth	1	1
Harvard	1	1
Mentor	1	1
Magister	1	1

Always struggling against the elements and aircraft un-serviceability, what was the view like from ground level?

Bill Law from Northampton was a flight mechanic at 6 OTU in 1940. What he remembered most clearly were the times of great camaraderie and the almost constant loss of pilots and aeroplanes in a variety of accidents. One incident of particular sadness for him was when, on 13 October 1940, his pal Aircraftman First Class (AC1) John Richard Leslie Edwards was killed.

> He was my opposite number on the servicing flight; in those days we did twenty-four hours on duty followed by twenty-four hours off. Edwards had just finished his spell of duty and was offered a trip in one of the Masters, N7962, with nineteen-year-old Plt Off Stanley John Thompson. He jumped at the chance but when the pilot made a dummy landing approach out Wisbech way, the aeroplane stalled and dived into the ground killing both men. [Thompson was buried in St Matthew's cemetery and Edwards in his home town of Shrewsbury.]
>
> The Master was not our favourite kite; they had no self-starters fitted to their Kestrel engine. Consequently, we had to use winding handles to start them up and this was a miserable job on a cold and frosty morning.
>
> Almost every day, during my time at 6 OTU, we suffered quite a few accidents, not just to the Hurricanes. These ranged from heavy-handed landings, which made even their sturdy undercarriages collapse, to full blown mid-air collisions or aeroplanes diving in from a great height.

During its two-year stay at Sutton Bridge nearly 300 of 6/56 OTU's Hurricanes met with the variety of accidents referred to by Aircraftman Law. 'At one time there were quite a lot of ex-Canadian Hurricanes among those written off or damaged, distinguishable by their three-digit serial numbers.'

On this latter subject Mr Law is referring to a Hurricane I batch shipped to Canada for use by the RCAF. Produced originally in England for the RAF, these had serials in the 'L' range. When 1 (RCAF) Squadron arrived in England for active service in June 1940, seventeen of this batch came with it. In the same way that OTUs received other RAF 'hand-me-downs' so too did 6 OTU receive some of the RCAF cast-offs as they were gradually replaced by later models – which in this case must have been quite quickly as these serials began to feature in accident reports at Sutton Bridge as early as July 1940. Some seem to have soldiered on at 6 OTU until about April 1941. The table opposite lists the fourteen ex-Canadian Hurricanes which found their way to Sutton Bridge.

Ex-RCAF Hurricanes used at 6 OTU, RAF Sutton Bridge.

Canadian Serial	Original RAF Serial	Notes
310	L1759	15 Nov 1940 tyre burst, u/c collapsed.
313	L1762	10 Feb 1941 u/c collapsed, Plt Off J. Briggs. 26 Feb 1941 heavy landing, Flt Lt D. F. Beardon while testing variable pitch propeller.
314	L1763	19 July 1940 engine failure (e/f), forced landing (f/l) near Sutton Bridge, Fg Off H. C. Mayers (Aus).
315	L1878	7 Nov 1940 forced landing, Sgt H. H. Jennings.
316	L1879	
318	L1881	21 Mar 1941 forced landing, Leiston, Plt Off P. A. Grace.
319	L1882	4 Oct 1940 forced landing, Plt Off P. S. Merritt.
320	L1883	27 Mar 1941, e/f, Fosdyke, Plt Off F. Raw.
321	L1884	
322	L1885	10 Dec 1940, e/f, f/l, Wiggenhall St Mary, Sgt E. H. Burton.
324	L1887	18 Aug 1940 collision with L2082, Mjr K. Niedswieki killed.
325	L1888	
326	L1890	
328	L2022	7 Aug 1940 heavy landing, Flt Sgt R. Grasset (Fr). 21 Aug 1940 heavy landing, Sgt C. Saward.

Another of Mr Law's pals, AC1 Arthur Leslie Watkins earned a place in the annals of RAF Sutton Bridge history by displaying great courage and presence of mind in an emergency. It was 17 December 1940 when, in deteriorating weather conditions, Plt Off J. D. Wright, who had been posted in from 15 FTS on the 10th, was recalled by radio from a pinpointing and homing exercise in Hurricane L1820. On reaching Sutton, Bridge however, the pilot undershot his approach, striking the boundary fence a fearsome blow. Gunning the engine, Plt Off Wright managed to complete a tight circuit with L1820 in a semi-stalled condition before it crashed and burst into flames. It was completely burned out but not before the pilot had been extricated by prompt and selfless action on the part of AC1 Watkins.

For his bravery that day Arthur Watkins received the British Empire Medal (Military Division) for meritorious service, the official citation for which reads:

> In December 1940 an aircraft crashed on an aerodrome and immediately burst into flames. Without hesitation Aircraftman Watkins jumped onto the blazing aeroplane, assisted the pilot clear of the wreckage and put out his burning clothing. The presence of mind and courage of this airman undoubtedly saved the pilot from being severely burned and possibly from being killed. The aircraft contained ammunition which started to explode shortly after the pilot was clear of the wreckage.

Arthur Watkins had the honour of receiving his medal from HM The King at Buckingham Palace on 17 June 1941.

An engineering apprentice before the war, Sgt Albert Norton was 19 years old when he joined up and it was as an armament specialist that he found himself posted to 6 OTU during 1940. On arrival at Sutton Bridge he was billeted in one of the RAF houses on the station boundary and thus had only to walk down his garden path to get to work. He recalled that, during 1940, when it seemed invasion was imminent, the armament staff at the station were ordered to prepare vital installations on the airfield for possible demolition. He said:

> Gun cotton slabs were placed on the water tower directly below the tank and wiring ran down the supports to the ground. On being warned of invasion, our instructions were to climb up the tower, prime the gun cotton slabs, fit delay detonators to the primer, shin down again, connect the wiring to a hand exploder, depress – and run! We put a 250lb HE bomb in the petrol dump, standing upright with a tail fuse and a striker protruding from it. This contraption was even better – the striker was to be hit with a hammer!

The convenience of living virtually on the airfield did not last and when air raids started in 1941, Albert and other SNCOs were moved to civilian billets in the village. Albert lodged with a Mrs Gilbert who he said was 'kindness itself'. Eventually, new RAF accommodation was built for the SNCOs about a mile from the village, where two sergeants were allocated to each room. Of this arrangement Albert said:

> I never did move in because I was so comfortable at Mrs Gilbert's house. I put a few pieces of my personal gear in my new room and I went there occasionally to re-arrange some of it so that the other sergeant would think I was about somewhere. That's how it remained until I was posted away about six months later. I never knew or even saw, my room-mate and he never saw me.

Having witnessed the death of a pilot on the airfield, Albert remembered one particular alarming experience of his own that, even now, remains etched in his mind. It was when, on 17 September 1941, he found himself in the back of a Blenheim being air-tested by the OC 6 OTU Wg Cdr Harold John Maguire.

Blenheims were not on the 6 OTU inventory and the reason for this particular aircraft, a Mark IV V5651, being at Sutton Bridge was that it had been badly shot-up by gunfire and had sought out the airfield for an emergency landing. It was part of an operation by 21 Squadron from RAF Watton making an attack on enemy shipping off the East Frisian Islands on 16 June. The pilot of V5651, Plt Off Reiss, was unable to make it back to Watton and belly-landed it on Sutton Bridge airfield. The crew emerged unscathed and returned to Watton, leaving their beaten-up Blenheim to be repaired. That was a lengthy process undertaken at Sutton Bridge by civilian workers, but by 17 September it was ready for an air test. Wg Cdr Maguire decided to do the job himself and Sgt Albert Norton was told by his officer to go along as crew for the Wing Commander; arm the turret and test it. Albert recalled what happened next.

> We had just become airborne when trouble was indicated by the undercarriage warning going off. The turret was not functioning properly either; its operation was neither smooth nor continuous and soon stopped altogether. The Wingco did a couple of circuits, trying to remedy the trouble but the undercart would not lock. It was also possible we had no flaps because the Blenheim hydraulic system operated the

undercarriage, turret and flaps. Wg Cdr Maguire came in low over the airfield and the duty pilot in the watch hut below fired a red Very flare in our direction. The Wingco gained height, circling the airfield until it was cleared for an emergency landing and then they gave us a green Very flare. As we came in over the boundary I looked out of the turret cupola and saw the ambulance and fire tender were thundering along parallel to us. It was a bumpy old landing. She hit and rose about twice, with bits of equipment floating about inside the fuselage and clouds of dust. Then the undercart collapsed and we slid to a halt. The crash crew had the hatches open very quickly and I was thankful that there was no fire and the kite remained on its belly.

Albert did not know what happened to V5651, but records show that it did not re-join 21 Squadron.

So much for the men, now what about their machines?

From among the thousands of Hawker Hurricanes built – or indeed destroyed – during the war and even among the hundreds which bore the brunt of back-, undercarriage- and engine-breaking duty at establishments like 6/56 OTU, one particular Hurricane epitomises the breed. It made a worthy name for both itself and its pilot and yet even though this aeroplane became just another 'hack' at Sutton Bridge, it surely deserves a special mention.

Built at Hawker's Brooklands factory Hurricane I, L1555 became known unofficially as *State Express* – after a popular brand of cigarettes of the day called *State Express 555* – and was, on 31 January 1938, first issued to 111 Sqn.

The Hurricane represented a vast increase in fighter technology and seemed to be viewed with some trepidation when it reached squadrons. In an effort to promote confidence in this brand-new aeroplane Treble-One's CO, Sqn Ldr John Gillan, undertook on February 20 a high-speed flight from RAF Northolt to RAF Turnhouse (Edinburgh) and the Hurricane he chose to use was L1555.

Encountering strong headwinds on the journey north, he landed at Edinburgh, refuelled and decided to return to Northolt immediately. Sqn Ldr Gillan completed the return leg in a remarkable 48 minutes having covered the 327 miles at an average speed of 408 mph. What was equally impressive was that L1555's engine had been running at full throttle, 2,950 rpm, for the whole trip without any sign of overheating and never missing a beat. It was this flight that did more than any other to convince those pilots that in the Hurricane, they had a potent but utterly reliable machine.

An 80 mph tailwind, a hindrance obviously on the northerly leg, had naturally the opposite effect on the return flight. However, that's how reputations are made and forever afterwards this pilot was known throughout the RAF as 'Downwind' Gillan.

However, even L1555 was to find its way – as did most of its compatriots from 111 Squadron's first batch – to 6 OTU on 7 June 1940. Here her proud past meant little and she simply became one of the many, eventually succumbing just like any other hack to the heavy-handedness of budding tyros. On 2 February 1941, L1555 suffered an undercarriage collapse at the hands of Sgt F. E. Earnshaw when he landed after a cross-country flight. Next Sgt J. N. Yates was briefed on 17 April to carry out an aerobatics exercise in L1555. Burning up fuel prodigiously as he cavorted about the sky, he ran out of petrol and could not make it back to Sutton Bridge. To put the aeroplane down in a reasonable field Yates was obliged to land down-wind with wheels and flaps up and L1555 was extensively damaged. A couple of days later it was shipped off to the Taylorcraft Company for repair but on inspection it was decided the 'old girl' could give no further useful service and L1555 was scrapped in June 1941 – an ignominious end for such a famous aeroplane.

It was now time for 56 OTU to move to more northern climes; to RAF Tealing, near Dundee in Scotland, but things became somewhat rushed in the run-up to that event.

By mid-February 1942 work was already under way for the proposed move to Scotland but pupils were beginning to 'stack up'. Furthermore, the beginning of February had seen significant snowfalls, which further delayed the flying programme. No.41 Course (forty-six pupils), which began on 23 December 1941 was falling behind and so, on 9 February, it was decided to move No.40 Course (20 officers; 29 sergeants, of whom 7 were British, 36 Canadian, 3 American, 2 Czech and 1 Australian) which began on 18 November 1941, together with some Hurricanes and maintenance personnel, out to RAF Wittering (King's Cliffe) in order to finish. Even so, that course was first extended by one week then by a further week soon after. Next No.42 Course (composition not recorded) arrived on 10 February and No.41 Course (14 officers; 32 sergeants) was posted out on 17 March, the same day that No.43 Course (8 officers; 24 sergeants) – the last to begin at Sutton Bridge – arrived.

On 19 February the detachment of aircraft and personnel returned from Kings Cliffe and that very evening an advance party of 2 officers and 124 airmen left by troop train for Scotland. The main ground party departed by train for Tealing on 26 March followed by the air component over the next two days, this latter comprising 33 Hurricanes, 11 Masters, 4 Lysanders (TT), and a small assortment of communications aircraft on 27 March. A further 11 Hurricanes flew to Tealing on 28 March.

We might well ponder about what all those brave men must have thought when they stepped off the train onto the railway station platform in Sutton Bridge. British, American, Australian, Belgian, Canadian, Czech, Danish, Dutch, French, Indian, New Zealander, Norwegian, Polish, South African – all were there, in that remote, wind-swept corner of England. In most cases they had, at least, the companionship of a few of their countrymen as it was customary – and more effective in view of language and culture difficulties – to send each nationality in groups to the OTU. Equally, in view of the multi-racial structure of RAF squadrons during the Second World War – a key factor some regard as underpinning its long-term success – the value of the mixed nationality courses such as those at Sutton Bridge can now be appreciated.

In summary then, the Hurricane OTU at RAF Sutton Bridge began life as 6 OTU in March 1940. As stated earlier, during the summer of 1940 'courses' were difficult to identify but the course numbering system reappeared in the ORB more clearly after The Battle of Britain. Between then and the date 56 OTU moved out to RAF Tealing at the end of March 1942 some forty courses of aspiring fighter pilots had passed through its gates. That first intake for No.5 Course comprised just 17 pilots but it has been noted that later courses fluctuated between 30 and 50 students. The rates at which the intake varied is not known precisely but it is reasonable to consider thirty students as a conservative average course intake over the two years the OTU remained at Sutton Bridge. It can be estimated, therefore, that 6/56 Operational Training Unit, while located at RAF Sutton Bridge, processed well in excess of 1,200 pilots for fighter operations. The most significant statistic, though, is that one arising from the period 6 March to 31 October 1940 when 498 pilots graduated from 6 OTU having learned to fly the Hawker Hurricane and of those, 440 pilots were sent into the Battles of France and Britain at the most crucial period of the air war during the spring and summer of 1940. The fifty-eight other graduates, for one reason or another failed to qualify for the Battle of Britain clasp. As has been indicated above, 6 OTU (renumbered as 56 OTU) continued to turn out graduates of all nationalities at an even greater rate from November 1940 onwards until it left Sutton Bridge in March 1942. In the two years that 6/56 OTU was based at Sutton Bridge, forty-four of its pupil airmen died in training accidents.

Thus, in RAF Sutton Bridge, is found an excellent example of contemporary wartime training for fighter operations. Without doubt the contribution made by 6/56 OTU to the air war was one of the utmost value both to the RAF and to the nation and as such, rightfully deserves a place in recorded history.

8

Sailor's Top Guns

Sqn Ldr Allan Richard Wright DFC* (later AFC) lay prone in the cramped bomb-aimer's compartment of a Hampden bomber. It was 10 March 1942 and far removed from the aeroplane to which he was accustomed. Spitfires were more in his line as he was a veteran, at the age of 22, of air battles over Dunkirk and the south of England, flying with 92 Squadron and being credited with ten enemy aircraft destroyed and three shared.

It was, however, Allan Wright's first trip in a Hampden and he was quite enjoying the ride. His brother, Flt Lt Claude Mandeville Wright was at the controls and knowing he was in capable hands Allan relaxed in the warmth of the sun through the Perspex nose as a panoramic view of the geometric patchwork of fenland fields, criss-crossed by rivers and dykes, unfolded below him. Sqn Ldr Wright had been picked up from RAF Wittering for the short, 25-minute trip to RAF Sutton Bridge to take up his new post as Chief Instructor (CI) of the recently-formed Pilot Gunnery Instructor Training Wing (PGITW) of the Central Gunnery School (CGS).

The River Nene drifted into view and in the distance sunlight reflected on the vast expanse of The Wash. In a few minutes they would be touching down. Suddenly, the nose dropped. Where there had been blue sky and brown fields now an almost vertical view of the river was rushing towards him. With no time to reflect on what was happening, just as suddenly the Hampden flattened out, roaring between those high river banks, skimming just above the surface of the water. Now, a surge of power and noise! He registered a fleeting glimpse of two lattice structures. The nose pointed skyward once more, until the pilot levelled out at a more respectable height for the approach to Sutton Bridge, just coming into view to starboard.

190

Mandeville Wright had decided to show his brother Allan just how competent a pilot he was by flying under the electricity power lines spanning the Nene 4 miles upstream from the airfield. With the lines sagging in the middle, he estimated that clearance for the Hampden was not much more than 10 feet above and below but with a 'generous' 20 feet to spare between the banks on either side.

That was Allan Wright's unusual introduction to RAF Sutton Bridge where he was to spend the next six months as deputy to the legendary Wg Cdr Adolf Gysbert 'Sailor' Malan DSO* DFC*, engaged in the joint, demanding task of getting the Pilot Gunnery Instructors Training Wing off the ground at its new home. Sadly, Allan lost his brother later that year when Mandeville was KIA on a bombing operation over Germany while flying with 115 Squadron.

The philosophy behind the CGS in the Second World War can be summed up quite simply. To be successful at anything requires a continuous process of learning. If learning ceases, failure sets in. In safe occupations, failure may be a slow process but for an air-gunner, especially in war, failure can be sudden and irreversible for him and his crew. If this holds true for the air-gunner in the turret of a bomber, it is equally relevant for the pilot of a fighter aeroplane. All the flying skill of a fighter pilot is of little use if his bullets go wide of the target. A gunner can only retain his expertise by constant practice; by continually getting to grips with new problems resulting from new air tactics, improved aircraft performance or increased armour protection on his opponents. Much of the knowledge necessary to keep standards high comes from the experience of others, who have already proved their ability in these fields. Furthermore, if the first-hand experience passed on is gleaned from a succession of such 'teachers', then that knowledge keeps pace with current developments in the field of combat and at both tactical and command levels.

Recognising this need for continued advanced instruction – championed by AVM Sir Edgar Ludlow-Hewitt, C-in-C Bomber Command (later Inspector General) who was concerned by the perceived poor quality of air gunnery in his command – the RAF, in addition to its ordinary air gunnery training schools, established a Central Gunnery School at which those trained would return to their squadrons to impart their newly acquired knowledge about the latest techniques and tactics to other aircrew colleagues.

Formed on 6 November 1939 under the command of Gp Capt William H. Poole AFC MM, RAF Warmwell was the first home for CGS and although not the only bomber type used – it also had

Hampden, Defiant and Blenheim aircraft on its inventory – the Vickers Wellington bomber eventually became the mainstay of its operations. Originally, CGS efforts were directed solely towards the bomber air-gunner fraternity. Its small nucleus of staff pilots, loaned to the school by Bomber Command, had to develop training methods on their own initiative and aeroplanes were only reluctantly released for this purpose. Just four officers and twelve NCO airmen made up the students of the first CGS course, which ended on 9 December 1939; training concentrated on turret-gunnery techniques. While under the command of Wg Cdr Ian Eustace Brodie OBE, CGS re-located from RAF Warmwell to RAF Castle Kennedy on 1 July 1941, where Wg Cdr Claude Montgomery Champion de Crespigny (later Gp Capt CBE) took over command. This airfield suffered a great deal from waterlogging and from time to time flying was moved to West Freugh so that the courses could keep flowing. This arrangement proved to be both inconvenient and inefficient so CGS was moved yet again, this time to RAF Chelveston on 1 December 1941. On 1 February 1942 Wg Cdr John Mortimer Warfield (later A/Cdre CBE) took over command of CGS when Wg Cdr de Crespigny was posted overseas.

It was on 1 April 1942 that CGS relocated to RAF Sutton Bridge, where it remained for the next two years. The senior officers of the Gunnery Leader (Bomber) Wing at that time were OC Wg Cdr J. M. Warfield; Chief Instructor, Sqn Ldr C. A. Potter; and OC Flying, Sqn Ldr S. H. Potter.

Meanwhile, fighter ace Wg Cdr Adolf Gysbert Malan – universally known as 'Sailor' – had visited Chelveston on 13 January 1942 to discuss his proposal for the formation of a Fighter Wing for CGS. He made several more visits during February and March and, after much lobbying of senior officers, finally received the go-ahead to create a separate Pilot Gunnery Instructor Training Wing (PGITW). This new unit was first established at RAF Wittering on 5 March 1942 where, under the umbrella of CGS it would move to Sutton Bridge on 1 April 1942. It was a logical step to press for the bomber and fighter elements of CGS to be co-located to facilitate co-operation in their practical gunnery exercises and this is why the Spitfire II and Master III aircraft of the PGITW soon joined the Bomber Wing at RAF Sutton Bridge.

When CGS Gunnery Leader Wing (GLW) arrived at Sutton Bridge it was equipped with both the Handley Page Hampden and the Vickers Wellington and although the former was eventually phased out of this role because of its lack of powered turrets, some examples were still

Above: A Gloster Grebe from 32 Squadron, 1926.

Right: Gloster Gamecock J7914, Plt Off Jones with Plt Off Purvis in background in J8406; 23 Squadron 1929.

Fairey Flycatcher N9928 401 Flight FAA over HMS Eagle 1930. (Courtesy Westland Ltd)

Above: Sutton Bridge Armament Training Camp, main entrance, 1929.

Left: Armstrong Whitworth Siskin IIIAs, including J8633, 56 Sqn at Sutton Bridge, late summer 1929. (Courtesy A. R. Richardson)

Flt Lt Harry Broadhurst, centre; Fg Off J. R. Maclacklan, left; Plt Off B. G. Morris, right. 19 Squadron, Duxford 1936. (Courtesy John Barwell)

Above: Hawker Furies of 25 Squadron in front of Sutton Bridge hangars, 1933.

Right: Flt Lt Teddy Donaldson, right, twice the winner of Brooke-Popham Trophy for Air Firing, with, from left: Plt Offs Prosser Hanks, Peter Russell Walker and Rex Boxer. No.1 Squadron Hawker Fury display team, 1937.

Sgt Thomas Dewdney, right, and 87 Squadron 1938 display team: Fg Off G. H. J. Feeney, centre, and Plt Off R. L. Lorimer, with a Gloster Gladiator. (Courtesy Crown)

Hurricane Is of 111 Squadron up from Northolt, in July 1938. The aircraft line-up all flew with No.6 OTU during the Battle of Britain period and includes L1552, L1555 'State Express' and L1548. (Courtesy ww2images.com)

In the foreground, pre-war pilots of 1 Squadron who later served at Sutton Bridge including Soper, Drake, Sqn Ldr Bertram, Palmer, Hanks, Hancock and Walker. Pictured at RAF Wittering with camouflaged Hawker Furies in 1938. (Courtesy 1 Sqn archives)

Right: Wg Cdr P. R. 'Dickie' Barwell DFC, station commander of RAF Sutton Bridge, second left, with King George VI, at RAF Digby, October 1939. (Courtesy John Barwell)

Below: Staff of No.6 OTU in front of the Officers' Mess at RAF Sutton Bridge, 2 June 1940. From left: Flt Lt H. C. V. Jolleff, Flt Lt George Greaves, Fg Off K. C. Jackman, Fg Off A. A. M. Dawbarn, Sqn Ldr Philip Pinkham, Flt Lt P. A. N. Cox, Fg Off H. A. Yeo, Plt Off D. G. Smallwood, Fg Off A. W. A. Bayne. (Courtesy P. N. Saunders)

Above left: Fg Off Peter Ayerst fought with 79 Sqn in the Battle of France before being posted as an instructor to 6 OTU. (Courtesy Battle of Britain International Ltd)

Above right: Plt Off Denis Wissler, 17 Sqn, 1940. (Courtesy B. B. M. London)

After fighting in France, Fg Off John Kilmartin, left, and Fg Off William Stratton were both posted from No.1 Squadron to become instructors at 6 OTU in May 1940. (Courtesy Kelvin Youngs/Aircrew Remembered)

An aerial view of 6 OTU RAF Sutton Bridge in the summer of 1940. (Courtesy Peter Green)

Miles Master I, T8629, two-seat trainer. (Courtesy Peter Green)

Above: Sqn Ldr Kazimierz Niedzswiecki, who died in an air collision at 6 OTU, is seen here, third left, with another 6 OTU graduate, Plt Off Karol Pniak, second right, and pilots of 2nd Av. Regt., Polish Air Force, in 1933. (Courtesy Institute of Aviation, Warsaw)

Left: Sgt Vaclav Jicha, on the first Czech pilot course at 6 OTU, in August 1940. He was in the Battle of Britain with 1 Sqn and later became a Spitfire test pilot at Vickers under Alex Henshaw. Sgt Jicha died in air accident in Scotland in 1945. (Courtesy Tom Dolezal/Free Czech Air Force Assoc)

F/L.Głowacki, S/L.Urbanowicz, W/C.Witorzenc.

A trio of successful Polish pilots from the second Polish course posted from Sutton Bridge on 3 August 1940: Flt Lt Glowacki, Sqn Ldr Urbanowitz and Wg Cdr Witorzenc. (Courtesy ww2images.com)

PILOT, PUPIL OR PASSENGER	DUTY (Including Results and Remarks)	SINGLE-ENGINE AIRCRAFT				MULTI-ENGINE AIRCRAFT						PASSENGER	INSTR./CLOUD FLYING [Incl. in cols. (1) to (10)]	
		DAY		NIGHT		DAY			NIGHT					
		DUAL	PILOT	DUAL	PILOT	DUAL	1ST PILOT	2ND PILOT	DUAL	1ST PILOT	2ND PILOT		DUAL	PILOT
		(1)	(2)	(3)	(4)	(5)	(6)	(7)	(8)	(9)	(10)	(11)	(12)	(13)
	TOTALS BROUGHT FORWARD	1·00	14·20											
For 30th July – 9th August 1940	1. TIGER MOTH.	0"40	10"45											
3 of A.C. aircraft	2. HECTOR.	0"20	4"05											
·40 Types	3. ——													
R. Mouchotte	4. ——													
SELF	DUAL ON TYPE.	1·00												
& TRAGUE	LANDINGS.		1·00											
SELF	EXPERIENCE ON TYPE.		1·10											
——	LOCAL FLYING PRACTICE.		1·00											
——	FIRING GUNS.		0,45											
——	MAP READING AND PIN POINTING PRACTICE		1·00											
——	TARGET.		0,50											
——	CLOUDS FLYING.		1·00											
——			0,55											
——	DOG FIGHTING		1,20											
——	FIRING GUNS AND LOW FLYING		1·15											
——	FORCED LANDINGS AND DOG FIGHTING		1·00											
——			1·00											
——	D/F HOMING		1,25											
24 August – 11 August 1940	1. HARVARD	1·00	1·50											
Nt 6	2. HURRICANE		11·50											
·40														
	TOTALS CARRIED FORWARD	2,00	28,00											

A page from the flying log book of French Plt Off Rene Mouchotte, showing his first week at 6 OTU and his drawing of a Hurricane. (Courtesy Yorkshire Air Museum)

Lt Noel Castelaine, who trained at Sutton Bridge in August 1940, is seen here on the right, with Lt Joe Risso (left) and Lt Raymond Derville (centre). They are standing in front of a Yakolev Yak-1b of the French Normandie-Nieman Fighter Group, in Russia in 1943.

Above left: Norwegian pilot Marius Eriksen, who trained at Sutton Bridge in 1941. (Courtesy Tor Idar Larsen, Norwegian Spitfire Foundation).

Above right: South African Fg Off J. J. 'Chris' le Roux, in 1941. (Courtesy South African Military History Society)

Canadian ace Flt Lt Hugh Godefroy. (Courtesy Hugh Godefroy)

The first batch of American pilots in the RAF, outside the officers' mess at Sutton Bridge, March 1941. Back row from left: Plt Offs Fenlaw, Reed, Pendleton, Davis, Durham, Olson, Hall, Wallace, McColpin. Front row, from left: Plt Offs Ward, Hill, Mize, Scudday, Laughlin, Coen, McGerty. Not in photo: Plt Off Eddie Miluck and Sgt Bert Stewart. (Courtesy Collier Mize via Jim Gray, Eagle Squadron Association)

Fg Off Richard Fuller Patterson, a former pupil at 6 OTU, seen here with 121 (Eagle) Squadron Spitfire Vb, W3711, AV-H, on 28 November 1941, just nine days before he was killed in action. (Courtesy Aircrew Remembered/ Kelvin T Youngs)

Sgt Hubert 'Bert' Stewart was part of the first American batch at Sutton Bridge; he is seen here as a USAAF Lieutenant in a Spitfire of 334FS, 4FG in 1942. (Courtesy 4th Fighter Group Association)

Rene Mouchotte, second left, with Jack Charles, left, 'Sailor' Malan and 'Al' Deere at RAF Biggin Hill in 1942. (Courtesy ww2images.com)

Above: An Indian pilot,
Flt Lt Mahinder Pujji, is seen
here in his Hurricane, named
'Amrit' after his wife.
Note the shell-hole
damage below windscreen.
(Courtesy Mahinder Pujji)

Right: A Danish pilot, Jorgen
Thalbitzer, is seen here on the
wing of a presentation Spitfire
named 'Niels Ebbessen',
which was frequently flown in
combat by his friend Jens Ipsen.
(Courtesy Museum of Danish
Resistance 1940–1945, via
Mikkel Planthinn)

Sutton Bridge 'old boys'* as No.1 Squadron pilots at the end of the Battle of Britain. Top from left: Flt Lt Arthur 'Darkie' Clowes; Sgts Zavoral (Cz)*; Prihoda (Cz)*; Plt Off Elkington. Middle: Plt Off 'Moses' Demozay (Fr); Sgts Kuttelwascher (Cz); Novak (Cz); Stefan (Cz)*. Bottom: Plt Off N. P. W. Hancock*; Flt Lt Mark 'Hilly' Brown (Can); Plt Off Chetham*; Sgt Plasil (Cz)*. (Courtesy 1 Squadron archive)

Sqn Ldr Allan Wright, left, with Wg Cdr Adolf 'Sailor' Malan, outside the Pilot Gunnery Instructor Training Wing (PGITW) office at Central Gunnery School (CGS) Sutton Bridge, 1942. (Courtesy Allan Wright)

Senior staff of PGITW of CGS 1943, from left: Sqn Ldr Bob Dafforn, Chief Instructor; Gp Capt Charles Beamish, CGS & Station Commander; Wg Cdr Peter Walker, Officer Commanding (OC) PGITW; Fg Off George Beurling, instructor.

A CGS Spitfire breaks away after a simulated attack on a Wellington bomber. (Courtesy Crown)

CGS PGITW pupils in January 1943, back row from left: Flt Sgt L. M. Meijers (Dutch), Unknown, Flt Lt Dafforn, Fg Off Gossland, Plt Off Frost; seated from left: Flt Lt MacMillen, Flt Lt Chamberlain, Sqn Ldr Killian, Wg Cdr Daniel Albert Raymond Georges le Roy du Vivier (Belgian), Flt Lt Brown, Flt Lt Moody. (Courtesy Pieter Meijers via Geoff Taylor, South Holland Heritage)

CGS Gunnery Leaders Wing staff at Sutton Bridge, from left: Flt Sgt V. I. Jones, WO R. C. Hillebrandt, Fg Off W. W. Cumber, Flt Sgt H. A. Matthews, Sgt R. F. Crabb, Flt Sgt E. Saunders, Gp Capt C. E. St J. Beamish, Wg Cdr J. C. Claydon, Sqn Ldr K. M. Bastin, Flt Lt W. E. Nicholas, Flt Lt M. C. Cleary, Flt Lt V. W. C. Taylor, Flt Lt A. J. Savage, Plt Off R. L. A. Woolgar, Flt Lt H. S. Griffiths, Plt Off E. J. Law, WO E. J. Saunders. (Courtesy Tom Williams)

Reviewing officers at the passing out parade of No.6 (French) Course at 7 Service Flying Training School (SFTS) RAF Peterborough (Westwood), 6 Nov 1945, from right: Air Cdre Duncan West VC; Gp Capt James Addams, OC 7 SFTS; Air Cdre J. G. Hawtrey, ADC to AOC; Air Marshal Sir Arthur Coningham, AOC 21 Group; General De Vitrolles, head of French AF training. (Courtesy J Baxter)

Cross Keys Bridge and the memorial to all those who trained at RAF Sutton Bridge. The plinth is topped with a propeller blade, recovered by the Fenland & West Norfolk Aircraft Preservation Society, from 6/56 OTU Hurricane, L2529, that crashed at Tilney St Lawrence on 21 March 1941.

on charge as late as November 1942. At least one Lockheed Hudson has also been noted; usually employed for training Coastal Command personnel. The Spitfire IIs were often augmented by other types brought in by pupils, such as Mustang I and Spitfire V.

To illustrate the overlapping nature of the one-month duration courses No.34 Gunnery Leader (GL) course was the first one to begin at Sutton Bridge on 16 April 1942 and it graduated on 13 May. The first Pilot Gunnery Instructor (PGI) course to actually begin at Sutton Bridge was No.2 PGI on 28 April 1942. No.33 GL course had started at Chelveston but graduated at Sutton Bridge and No.1 PGI course, which had begun at Wittering, graduated from Sutton Bridge on 15 April 1942.

It was the opinion of Wg Cdr Alan Christopher ('Al') Deere DSO DFC* (later Air Commodore OBE), another of the leading fighter pilots of the day, that the foresight of Malan in pressing for a fighter gunnery wing to be established was one of the most productive steps in fighter pilot training during the Second World War. He also considered it was to the credit of Air Marshal Trafford Leigh-Mallory, the then Air Officer Commanding (AOC) 11 Group, that he backed Malan's idea even though Malan had disagreed strongly with the former's favourite 'big-wing' concept. South African 'Sailor' Malan had proved himself an excellent shot, as his tally of at least thirty-two enemy aircraft testifies, so he knew what he was talking about. His list of 'Ten Golden Rules of Air Fighting', written while based at RAF Kirton-in-Lindsey, were pinned to many a squadron and Operational Training Unit notice board.

When 56 OTU departed for northern climes there was a significant change at the top with the arrival, on 7 May, of Gp Capt Claud Hilton Keith as Station Commander. This post at Sutton Bridge had recently been upgraded to a Group Captain appointment and Keith brought with him a fearsome reputation as an experienced bomber operations and gunnery training specialist.

It was as a result of the latter that he had been posted to Picton Air Base as OC of the only RAF Air Gunnery & Bombing School in Canada. Recalled to England in April 1942 he was, according to his autobiography (*I Hold My Aim*, Allen & Unwin, 1946; the title of which was taken from the motto of CGS), unable to ascertain why. As a result, he was 'going begging with no immediate job', when the AOC 25 (Armament) Group sent him to command CGS. The AOC told him his new command was 'dirty, unhappy and inefficient'. Gp Capt Keith recalled: 'I flew to Sutton Bridge and confirmed the truth of this!'

It is essential to remember that training at CGS was run on much different lines to that encountered at the basic Air Gunnery schools and Gp Capt Keith clarified this difference.

CGS provided post-operational training for air gunners and fighter pilots. Its pupils were those with experience on active operations and who had shown themselves sufficiently successful to justify their being given an advanced course in air gunnery, lasting a period of one month. Each course catered for ten fighter pilots and thirty-two air gunners and with a 50% overlap, there were always twice those numbers of airmen on the station. It was intended that the school was the last word in everything to do with air gunnery. Although instruction was never as complete as I would have liked it to have been, undoubtedly pupils did benefit considerably and went back to operational stations to preach their added knowledge to others with confidence. People like 'Sailor' Malan knew exactly what to do in an air scrap and at CGS they passed on this knowledge first hand.

According to Gp Capt Keith:

[Malan] was a first-class exponent of air gunnery and lived up to it but he was not ever very interested in what the air gunners of bombers did. These latter were trained by the Bomber Wing, commanded by Wg Cdr John Mortimer Warfield [later CBE and ironically, an ex-Malta campaign fighter pilot] but he was succeeded on 25 June by an old hand on bombers, Wg Cdr J. J. Sutton.

It was intensive training with air-gunners manning the turrets of a Wellington bomber while being attacked by fighter pupils in Spitfire IIa aircraft. Instructors in the bomber watched what was being done and taught such things as the concept of 'fire-control' for example, where one gunner – positioned either in one of the turrets or in the astrodome – would act to co-ordinate and direct via the intercom all gunfire in the bomber against a potential attacker. Miles of cine film were exposed, by air gunners using camera guns fitted to their turrets and by fighter pilots alike, with exhaustive viewing and evaluation sessions after each sortie. Ground training also included the theory of ballistics, discussion of tactics, aircraft recognition and later on, clay pigeon shooting, – this latter was ideal for deflection training. Some 'stand-alone' turrets, mounted and fully manoeuvrable were also specially modified for clay shooting, being armed with one 12-bore shotgun barrel. This device was first introduced into the training scheme back in April 1940 and even now there were plans to introduce free-standing clay-pigeon shooting to the curriculum to reinforce the need to master the art of deflection shooting.

All of this was supported by the use of towed targets, courtesy of the Henley and Lysander aeroplanes of 1489 Target Towing Flight, formerly known as station flight, who were kept very busy. Station flight was re-designated 1489 Flight in September 1941 but the cadre of this unit subsequently moved out to RAF Matlaske in April 1942 when CGS arrived at Sutton Bridge and began to operate its own integral Target Towing Flight. Among the workhorses of the School have been identified: Henleys L3267, L3273, L3310, L3320, L3335 and L3375; Lysanders: T1429, T1459, T1618, V9496, V9813 and W6955. Holbeach range continued to provide the air space and ground targets for air-to-air, air-to-ground and low-level strafing practice.

On the subject of ground attack exercises, Allan Wright remembered they included a 'minimum exposure' run-in and get-away. The run-in was usually at a very low level across the marsh, then a quick climb and dive on the target. One day after making such an attack one of the trainees, an American, called up on his radio to say his engine was running roughly and losing power and he was returning to the airfield. He made a good landing and taxied to the parking area. On switching off the engine, to everyone's surprise, most of all the pilot, his propeller was only two-thirds of its proper size. The end of each blade was splintered and its length reduced. No damage was found to the engine nor elsewhere on the Spitfire. The pilot had simply flown that bit too low on his run-in, scrubbed off the ends of the prop on the ground but got clean away with it.

It is worth listing here the duties and responsibilities that were expected of a newly qualified Bomber Gunnery Leader when he returned to his unit:

1) To serve as an air gunner in the air and personally maintain a high standard of marksmanship.
2) To know and understand his air gunners, to stimulate their interest, improve their operational efficiency and maintain their morale; and to ensure their physical fitness.

3) To initiate and control training in gunnery and aircraft recognition.
4) To check, but not technically supervise, gun and turret maintenance and the harmonisation of sights.
5) To advise air gunners and other members of the squadron on gunnery equipment and its uses.
6) To help Squadron and Flight Commanders in administration and disciplinary matters affecting air gunners.
7) To discuss, collate and explain all facts and principles relating to air fighting tactics.

From February 1942 graduates of GLW courses were graded:

A: Distinguished pass as Gunnery Leader.
B: Pass as Gunnery Leader.
C: Not categorised as Gunnery Leader but passed course insofar as it is an advanced gunnery course; lacks qualities of leadership. If the pupil is considered suitable he may be recommended for an Air Gunner Instructor course.
D: Fail.

To get a feel for what it was like for the staff of the Bomber Wing, we can refer to the reminiscences of Wg Cdr Kenneth Montague Bastin DFC. As a Sqn Ldr, Ken Bastin was Chief Instructor (CI) of the Bomber Wing from 4 August 1942 to 25 June 1943. Ken had been a pupil on the very first course that the CGS ran at RAF Warmwell, way back in 1939, and after a successful operational tour, he was back at CGS as deputy to Wg Cdr Sutton.

Aerial combat exercises were a vital part of the syllabus for both Wings and whether it was planning these with 'Sailor' Malan or his successors, Ken Bastin needed to prepare them very carefully because of the dangers involved. Ken himself or his deputy managed the exercise until the bomber took off; then the instructor in the bomber controlled it. These exercises were carried out in the wide skies over the surrounding fenland and the ranges in The Wash. Both aircraft used cine guns for taking films of their combat for later analysis – there was a Photographic Section on the station where WAAFs developed miles of cine film. But the risks of combat conditions could not be eliminated if the exercises were to be anything like realistic. Mistakes were almost inevitable and the threat of a mid-air collision was ever-present.

These aerial combat exercises covered two aspects of Ken's syllabus. Firstly, air practice for the gunners in the turrets and secondly for the fire controller gunner who stood in the astrodome controlling and directing the aircraft's gunnery defences as well as giving orders to the pilot for evasive action. The instructor taking the exercise would be in the second pilot's seat observing and listening on the intercom. The bomber pilots would not stint in throwing their aircraft around in response to evasion instructions. So violent were these manoeuvres that often the Wellington was pulling two or three 'G' of gravity, such that the crew would be pinned down and it was hard for them even to lift an arm. On 12 June, during an air exercise one of Ken's pupils, Flt Lt A. H. Draper, lost his footing while acting as the fighting controller in Wellington N2874. The pilot threw it into such a violent corkscrew away from a fighter attack that Draper sustained a broken left leg and minor injuries to his face. This training was for real!

Sqn Ldr Ken Bastin left CGS in June 1943 and during his time at Sutton Bridge he reckoned 550 airmen had passed through his Gunnery Leaders Wing. He was posted as Chief Instructor with the rank of Wing Commander to 1 Air Gunners School at RAF Pembrey but returned once more to CGS as OC Gunnery Leaders Wing when the School moved to RAF Catfoss.

It was the constant quest to bring quality and experience to the pool of instructors that saw the arrival of Flt Lt Richard Algernon Dacre Trevor-Roper DFC DFM at the Gunnery Leader Wing on 24 August 1943. Flt Lt Trevor-Roper leapt to fame as the rear gunner in Wg Cdr Guy Gibson's crew on the Dams Raid just three months prior to this posting – but this is not to suggest that CGS equated fame with ability. In Trevor-Roper's case, he had already completed one tour with 50 Squadron for which he was awarded a DFM and commissioned shortly after. After a 'rest' spell at a training station, he was posted back to 50 Squadron and had almost completed his second tour when he was posted as Gunnery Leader to 617 Squadron for the Dams Operation – for which he received his DFC. Acknowledged among aircrew as one of the best of the experienced air gunners in Bomber Command – he must have been, to meet with the approval of Gibson, who was only interested having in the best men for the job. His hefty physical stature, matched a boisterous, outgoing nature to make him an invaluable asset to any crew and indeed in any mess. CGS ORB does not state when he was posted away from Sutton Bridge but it is known Trevor-Roper was serving with 97 Squadron when he died on the night of 30/31 March 1944 as one of the many losses during the infamous Nuremberg raid.

The Vickers Wellington was the workhorse for these combined fighter/bomber exercises and was well suited to it. There were standing instructions for these aerial combat sessions. Each session lasted about an hour and the bomber would have four pupils aboard. The initial exercises would be on range estimation followed by quarter attacks, then varied attacks. The latter would include attacks from quarter, half-roll from above and from below, then all angles and head-on. The later stages of the course would involve full evasive action of the bomber and all the variety of fighter attacks. Normally these exercises would take place at about 3,000 feet altitude, but attacks on low flying bombers were practised too. Of all these, the head-on exercises were the most dangerous because of the high closing speed. The initiative for these attacks lay with the fighter pilot who had to work out his approach thoroughly and most importantly, his breakaway options. At the end of the course the fighter pilots would have the chance to take a trip in a bomber and try out the turrets, to give them an idea of the air gunner's point of view. These combat exercises sparked a great deal of friendly rivalry between the two Wings – the air gunners having the opportunity to test themselves against highly experienced staff fighter pilots and the most able pilots from operational fighter squadrons. This all led to an exciting – and sometimes 'hairy' – atmosphere for those involved.

One of the big gripes from Bomber Wing pupils concerned the Browning .303 machine guns in their turrets. Instructors at the School found themselves regularly emphasising that there was nothing wrong with this .303 machine gun if used properly. Often, they had to correct a widespread perception among the ranks of air gunners that the maximum range of the .303 was 600 yards; probably a misunderstanding arising from actual suggestions that 600 yards might be regarded as a range at which to open fire.

Even if recommended to attend, acceptance on a GLW course was by no means automatic. Since candidates of dubious ability were being encountered (some being described as having 'disgracefully low ability') and places usually over-subscribed, in August 1942 CGS GLW implemented a stringent initial competency test to weed out those not really up to the job. This test was based on the passing-out standard expected of gunners who qualified under the 'war syllabus for training air gunners' at an Air Gunners School. The standard was set out in a signal from AOC HQ 25 Group to AOCs of Bomber, Coastal, Army Co-op and Flying Training Commands as follows.

Central Gunnery School is intended to be the university of gunnery instruction and has a right to expect entrants have attained a certain standard of knowledge. Any gunner who does not keep himself up to this standard in a squadron is not fit to be a gunnery leader. Commands are to be advised that entrants must be up to this standard upon arrival. In particular they must be proficient in the following:

- Sighting as laid down in AP1388D, June 1942.
- Browning gun; general description, performance and names of essential parts, stripping down and assembly. Mechanism, loading, unloading, safety devices. Breeching up, changing feed, fitting link chutes. Stoppages and their clearance.
- Aircraft recognition; the appearance of allied and enemy aircraft in flight, their span and dimensions. NB, this test will be carried out on reasonable and fair lines. Current and well-known types being used on the Hunt range or shadowgraph
- It is recommended that the fact that failures will be returned to their units is given wide publicity.

By way of example: five RAF GLW candidates were rejected for No.68 course on 3 October 1943, all of whom scored below 30 per cent on guns and below 25 per cent on aircraft recognition in the initial test – with one actually scoring –1 per cent for aircraft recognition – which is a bit worrying! Grasp of the English language was also important and on 26 February 1943 Plt Off Miroslav Čtvrtlík, a Czech air gunner, was deemed to have insufficient grasp of speaking or understanding English to warrant him remaining on his course. Serving with 311 (Czech) Squadron since late 1940 Miroslav had flown on ops – including the first two 1,000-bomber raids – but presumably had little need to speak anything other than his native tongue to his compatriots.

It should not be overlooked that fighter pilots and 'free-gunners' from the USAAF and US Naval Air Corps (USNAC) in the UK also attended or were nominated to attend CGS courses. Usually just one or two places were allowed for US personnel on each course – at the expense of places for RAF Commands – and there is good evidence of Americans in PGITW and GLW course photographs. For example, on GLW course No.45 held in September 1942 – which was attended by Grp Capt Beamish – two USAAF gunners, Sgts Champion and Eichel, can be seen in the end-of-course photo. Correspondence was often exchanged with the US military on the vexed subject of 'suitability' and not all US air gunners and other assorted US personnel that were nominated were accepted, mainly on the basis that the courses were not run for basic tuition purposes – a condition that was not fully appreciated within USAAF, USNAC (or even in some RAF circles). On 18 December 1942, for example, the Air Ministry wrote to HQ 8th Air Force as follows.

> The Chief Instructor at CGS informs me that the personnel you are sending to the School are not quite the right material. With three notable exceptions, most of the candidates are nearly all armourers and not air crew. The Gunnery Leaders Course is not an armament course but a course to develop a sense of leadership and authority among air gunners and to prepare them for the duties of a Gunnery Leader. These duties as a general rule include taking an active part in operational flying. The vacancies on the CGS course are not plentiful and it is most essential that only air gunners employed on operations.... should be sent on the courses. The Chief Instructor suggests you send a suitable Staff Officer from your HQ to visit CGS to clarify the position of Gunnery Leaders as employed in the USAAF.

After due consideration, Lieutenant General (Lt Gen) Ira Eaker, Commanding General of the United States 8th Air Force, sent a signal to CGS (copied to Minister of State for Air) on 2 March 1943.

> It has been found that the Gunnery Leaders Course does not provide training which is suitable for the type of operations in which USAAF personnel are participating. Your co-operation in providing training facilities for our personnel on the GL courses is appreciated. Since the qualifications of US personnel does not seem to fit them for attendance at the flexible GL course it is confirmed that vacancies are no longer required for our flexible gunners at this course.

Absence of US personnel from subsequent course photos seems to confirm that decision.

Elsewhere in May 1942, momentous events in the operational arena were to filter down even to training unit level. Much has been written and debated about the three 'Thousand Bomber' raids, including the motley collection of tired old aircraft and green crews drawn from the second line units that helped to achieve the magical number – and CGS played a small part in this major event.

'Area Bombing' was a new RAF strategic policy adopted early in 1942 after acceptance of the limited ability of RAF bombers to find and destroy individual targets at night. This new policy marked a major turning point in Bomber Command operations when much larger geographic areas of German industrial towns would become a target instead of pinpoint installations such as specific factories or railway yards. No longer would there be any concession for residential or cultural areas under the Area Bombing concept; all would be legitimate targets now, and most of a raiding force, sent out as a cohesive stream of aeroplanes, could be expected to hit some part of such a large target.

Initially the new bombing policy was put into practice with a large raid on Lübeck in March and repeated attacks on Rostock in April 1942. Although post-war analysis of raids on these two targets suggests they were not as successful as the public was led to believe at the time, they did successfully test Sir Arthur Harris's Area Bombing concept and allowed him to push forward with his revolutionary idea for a massive 1,000-strong bomber attack on either Cologne or Hamburg. In the event it was weather conditions which finally persuaded Harris to select Cologne for this first 'Thousand Raid' on the night of 30/31 May 1942.

How, then, did Central Gunnery School come to be involved in this attack?

In order to achieve the magic 1,000-aeroplane figure, Harris had to pull in men and machines from every unit in Bomber Command, right down to the Command's own OTUs. When Coastal Command, which originally agreed to contribute 250 bombers, was ordered out of the first raid by the Admiralty – the result of a long-running political argument between the two Services – Flying Training Command, of which CGS was a part, was also scoured for suitable aircraft. Just four Wellingtons were contributed by Training Command, largely because most of that Command's bombers were inadequately equipped for night bombing operations or so 'tired' they were incapable of making a long journey.

This is where CGS made its small contribution to the momentous Operation *Millennium*. The small quantity was indeed because by the time a Wellington reached CGS it was usually in a 'war weary' condition, having come off ops and often lacked fully functional instruments and equipment. One such example was Wellington Ia, N2894. Delivered to the RAF in November 1939, this aircraft was one of 149 Squadron's contingent despatched on 18 December 1939 to attack Wilhelmshaven during what became known as the Battle of Heligoland Bight. It was one of two aircraft that turned back from that raid due to technical problems and was, therefore, fortunate to survive the subsequent loss of half of that attacking force.

At CGS these hand-me-down Wellingtons were serviced in a manner that kept them airworthy for their diet of low-risk, short-duration, short-distance sorties, trundling around relatively friendly airspace above The Wash and dealing with mock attacks by reasonably friendly Spitfires or firing at towed targets. When Harris's clarion call for aircraft came, only three CGS bombers could be repaired and serviced – with some cannibalised parts – in time to bring them up to a standard that would enable them to have a chance of staying in the air long enough to get to Cologne and back; to be able to communicate and also to defend themselves on the way.

Thus, on 26 May, three Wellingtons from CGS, including N2894 and L7785 (the third CGS aircraft has not been identified), were detached to the nearby operational station at RAF Feltwell, according to CGS ORB: 'for special operational co-operation with Bomber Command'. Staff pilots, wireless operators (from the WOp/AGs), air-gunners and complete ground crews were supplied by CGS on detachment for the few days around the raid date. Four out of the six in each crew were provided by CGS and the other two were 'spare bods' from 75 Squadron. When the attack began in the late hours of 30 May 1942, it is known that the two above-mentioned CGS Wellingtons took off from Feltwell as part of the 23-strong force launched by 75 Squadron together with one aircraft from 1 Air Armament School (1 AAS), a Training Command unit normally based at RAF Manby.

Forty-one aircraft were lost that night from a total of 1,047 despatched and RAF Sutton Bridge took its share of those casualties too.

Wellington Ia, N2894, of CGS was reported missing. It was the last bomber to take off from Feltwell, at 23.57 hours on 30 May and was not heard from again. Four of the crew of six were members of CGS staff and there was a mood of sadness on the station for the loss of Plt Off David Johnson, who went along as aircraft captain; Flt Sgt Josiah Connor, WOp/AG; Flt Sgt John McLean, air gunner; and Flt Sgt Gordon Waddington-Allwright, rear gunner. Acting as second pilot for the trip was WO Oldřich Jambor, a Czech pilot who had flown 34 ops in his first tour with 311 Squadron – including 18 as aircraft captain.

Having only recently finished a four-month spell of instructing, Jambor was posted back to ops with 75 Squadron at Feltwell, arriving just before the end of May. Not yet crewed-up, as a 'spare bod' he therefore found himself in this ropey old CGS Wellington for the 'big show', along with spare navigator Flt Lt Hector Batten also from 75 Squadron. After the war it was discovered that, having successfully bombed Cologne, N2894 was shot down over Klarenbeek, near Apeldoorn, Holland, by a Messerschmitt Bf 110 night-fighter flown by the ace Oblt Helmut Woltersdorf of 7/NJG 1. This was one of his last victims as he himself died on 2 June as the result of crash landing his battle-damaged Bf 110.

With the exception of rear gunner Flt Sgt Waddington-Allwright, who baled out and was made a POW, the remainder of the crew of N2894 died and are all buried in Ugchelan-Heidof cemetery.

The second identified CGS Wellington, L7785, was manned by Flt Sgt Geale, pilot/captain; Sgt Metoděj Šebela (Czech; 75 Sqn, later DFC), 2nd pilot from 75 Sqn; Sqn Ldr C. A. Potter (CGS GLW CI), observer/navigator; Flt Lt William Joseph Winter, WOp; Flt Sgt Smith (NZ), front gunner; Plt Off Ronald John Andrews, rear gunner. Take-off time was 23.51 hours; landed back at 04.45 hours. The third CGS aircraft has not been identified and after careful examination of 75 Squadron ORB, it seems possible that, although it was recorded by CGS Sutton Bridge as being detached to Feltwell for the raid, it may have gone unserviceable (u/s) and thus did not actually take part in the operation. CGS did not contribute any more aircraft or crews to the subsequent two 1,000-raids.

With training activity now beginning to settle down, it was not long before the inevitable procession of accidents began too.

The dubious distinction of having the first mishap with a CGS aeroplane from Sutton Bridge fell to Canadian Flt Sgt David Robert Morrison DFM (later Plt Off, DFC) on 13 April 1942. Trying to find his way back to Sutton Bridge in Spitfire II, P8279, he encountered hazy weather. While attempting to climb above it he became lost and only regained his bearings when he reached the Humber Estuary – roughly 100 miles north of the station! Setting course south once more, unfortunately he ran out of fuel before reaching the airfield and crash landed at Wyberton near Boston but emerged unhurt. Already an accomplished fighter pilot, he was detached from 401 Squadron for a CGS course from 28 March, returning to operations on 4 May. It was as a result of his many operational sweeps over France that he was commissioned and awarded a DFC, but after accumulating four kills plus three shared and four probables, he was shot down on 8 November 1942 during a fighter sweep over Lille. With his aircraft on fire and severely wounded in a leg and an arm during that combat, he managed to crash land and was made a POW. German surgeons amputated his left leg above the knee and after recovery he was sent to Stalag Luft 3. Morrison spent about three months in the prison camp before the severity of his injury qualified him for repatriation to England in November 1943.

There were many and varied reasons for these crashes; engine failure, burst tyres and undercarriage collapses were among the most common, although one Wellington managed to hit a tree and still stagger back to base without crashing. This was P9209, flown by WO David John North-Bomford, a somewhat accident-prone staff pilot and certainly one of the most colourful characters to serve at CGS. Son of Irish landed gentry from County Meath, according to former member of the Sergeants' Mess staff, Vic Goodman, 'Bomber' – as he was nicknamed – was 'noted for his natty line in richly lined uniforms, sporting a large ginger handlebar moustache and with a penchant for wearing exotic headgear such as a wide-brimmed Stetson or even a jockey hat while on duty!' North-Bomford first joined the RAF as a pilot on a short-service commission in 1934, resigned his commission in 1937, then re-enlisted on the outbreak of war as a non-commissioned pilot. He flew with 17, 111 and 601 Squadrons during the Battle of Britain, then with 7 OTU as an instructor before the end of the Battle. He left the RAF in 1947 and took his own life at the family property in Ireland in 1949.

Further confirmation of the gestation and subsequent activities of CGS comes from ground crew mechanic, Aircraftman Douglas Broom, a native of Crowland in Lincolnshire. As a keen 20-year-old airman in 1941, Douglas began his service as an engine fitter with 651 Army Observation Post Squadron at Old Sarum, working on Taylorcraft Austers. He returned to home territory on 6 March 1942 when his diary records a posting to RAF Wittering.

On 6 March [1942] I was posted to the Central Gunnery School at RAF Wittering. On the way I stop off at nearby Peterborough to see my wife, then arrive at Wittering only to find my billet is in Burghley Park, about a mile from the camp. The next couple of days were quiet so at night I thumbed a lift home and borrowed a bike to get back to camp. I did the same the next night but the bike went for a Burton on the way back. These were the first of several unofficial jaunts home – well it was too good an opportunity to miss!

On 12 March some of our Spitfires began to arrive and I was put on P7818, a Mark IIa, with AC1 Hebson and Cpl Durkin. I was quite proud when this kite flew off to Blackpool, piloted by none other than the OC CGS Fighter Wing, Wg Cdr 'Sailor' Malan.

We were on the move again on 27 March when CGS moved from Wittering to RAF Sutton Bridge and I went with it. Sutton Bridge was a deadly place with terrible food – an important yardstick for us blokes in those days.

On my first day there I did a daily inspection (DI) on a Lysander Target tug and watched all our Spitfires and Masters arrive. A couple of days later a Blenheim IV, Z5494, from 17 OTU at Upwood, crashed in a field close to the camp. It had engine trouble and although the pilot, Sgt Heagety, tried to get into Sutton Bridge, he undershot and flew into the raised bank at the perimeter. It was a write-off job but the pilot got away with it.

At the end of the month I was put onto the Servicing Flight with Abe, Tich and Sgt Milton. It was a good scrounge but I sailed a bit close to the wind on 4 April when I left work at 1.00 pm to cycle home. The sergeant asked for me a few times but each time the lads covered for me by saying I was in the lavatory. Had a great time at home and stayed overnight. In April I was moved yet again, this time onto 'D' Flight. This was the Fighter Combat Flight and I began to come into contact with heaps of highly decorated pilots passing through the courses. I was also getting settled into the daily servicing routine and now felt no qualms in carrying out forty-hour inspections on our Spitfires.

By comparison with the famous pilots arriving at Sutton Bridge, the arrival of yet one more anonymous Spitfire IIa among so many would hardly turn anyone's head at CGS. Spitfire P7350, however, was destined to lead a life far more exotic than any of her stable-mates and of a length undreamed-of in those hectic days of war.

Built at Vickers Castle Bromwich factory, she is believed to have been only the fourteenth Spitfire off its production line. Issued first to 266 Squadron on 6 September 1940, P7350 saw Battle of Britain service with 266 and 603 Squadrons before being damaged in combat during October and forced to crash land. Repaired over the winter of 1940 this Spitfire was then re-issued to 616 Squadron in March 1941, then 64 Sqn in April 1941 before being sent to various third-line units until April 1942. On 27 April 1942, P7350 was flown to RAF Sutton Bridge where she spent the next ten months in the service of CGS, chasing Wellingtons and her contemporaries rather than Bf 109s and He 111s.

What is it that makes this particular Spitfire so worthy of comment? Well, P7350 has managed to survive to this day as the oldest airworthy Spitfire in the world and is currently operated by the RAF Battle of Britain Memorial Flight. Furthermore, not only does she thrill modern-day air show crowds more than 50 years after she first took to the air but being based at RAF Coningsby in Lincolnshire, P7350 is still a frequent sight and sound in that very fenland sky in which she spent the longest period of service with any wartime unit.

Douglas Broom had a great treat about a week after the big 1,000-bomber raid.

> I had a flip in one of the CGS Masters. We had a great time doing rolls and loops above the wide-open fens around Wisbech and March. After half an hour of stunting though, I started to feel a bit queasy and was pleased to get down again. June was a pretty good month, with lots of daily inspections and a forty-hour inspection to keep me busy. This reflected the constant flying programme run by CGS to keep up the flow of aircrew cramming our little station. Occasionally we had unusual visitors at Sutton Bridge, often to undertake trials work down at the firing range on nearby Holbeach Marsh, at the edge of the Wash. One such visitor was a Hurricane which flew in on 1 July, carrying what looked like three bombs under each wing. A terrible disaster struck this aeroplane, flown by a Wing Commander, on the way to the range. Just as it passed over the town, the port main-plane ripped off and it crashed behind the cookhouse of the camp extension on the edge of town. The pilot was killed instantly. I learned later that those 'bombs' were actually rocket projectiles and this was the first installation trials aircraft up from Farnborough for live firing tests.

Douglas' version of this story naturally only deals with the accident itself. It was, however, an illustration of the wider role which RAF Sutton Bridge and Holbeach range played, as a venue for experimental aero-armament tests, in addition to its more conventional gunnery training role. As mentioned in an earlier chapter, in the latter stages of the Battle of Britain for example, 20 mm cannon armament for fighter aircraft was tested over the Holbeach range.

Back in mid-1941, British military mission representatives in Moscow witnessed a demonstration by the Soviet Air Force of a rocket projectile (RP) that was fired directly forwards from beneath the wings of an aircraft. It was said to be able to be used against air, ground and sea targets. The British were agreeably surprised by the consistency of this weapon's trajectory and arranged for a Russian aircraft, equipped with this device, to be sent to England in October that year. In the event, the Russians backed out and nothing materialised. There had already been a little work on this subject undertaken in this country by the Directorate of Armament Development, specifically for the evaluation of its anti-tank potential. When the Russian report materialised, this project was immediately given high priority.

While the Aircraft & Armament Experimental Establishment (A&AEE) Boscombe Down undertook development of a 3-inch solid-head projectile, RAE Farnborough set about testing first the vulnerability of the underside of a Hurricane wing to flames from the RP propellant when it was fired, then to design and construct suitable carrier rails for a Hurricane. The specification was for three rails underneath each wing. Trials installations were to be complete by 24 October 1941 when A&AEE would begin air-sighting tests to settle the harmonisation of the RP and gunsight and to give the test pilots experience of the weapon.

By December flight trials over ranges near Exeter and Bridgewater had proved the viability of the weapon and the lack of flame effect on the carrier's wings. However, these ranges were not as well-equipped or convenient as the Holbeach Marsh/Sutton Bridge combination.

Testing progressed slowly until mid-1942. Wg Cdr Albert Frank Rueben (Robin) Bennett was on the Special Duty List attached to Farnborough specifically for the RP trials. Two Hurricanes were allotted for these trials, Z2415 and Z4993, and Bennett's team comprised two other pilots: Flt Lts Letts and Martin, operating under the banner of Instrument, Armament & Defence Flight, RAF Farnborough. Previously Hurricane Z2415 had been used for terminal velocity trials and high-altitude research and its main wing spar was specially strengthened for those projects. Because of this, it was deemed a suitable testbed for the wing-mounted RP trials.

Bennett flew Z2415 to RAF Sutton Bridge in the late afternoon of 30 June where, making the most of the light evenings, he immediately put in more than 2 hours of trial firings at Holbeach range.

1 July dawned fine again and Z2415 was loaded with six RP for more trials. Wg Cdr Bennett took off and headed towards the range. The aeroplane had just cleared the village when the air was rent by an explosion and bright flash. When the smoke cleared the Hurricane was found to have crashed on Bridge Farm, off New Road, Sutton Bridge, littering wreckage over a wide area. Bennett died in the crash and two civilian women were seriously injured by flying debris.

In such circumstances life must go on and the next day Flt Lt Martin flew Z4993 to Sutton Bridge, did a 30-minute sortie to the range then returned to Farnborough. After the accident, trials of airborne RP increased considerably until, by August 1942, in addition to Z4993, other Hurricanes were allocated to the task: Z2457, Z2320, Z2895, Z3564 and Z2961.However, for reasons probably due to the contention with CGS for range airspace the increased testing would bring, the venue for firing tests was moved to RAF Warmwell. This sad incident closed with the removal of Wg Cdr Bennett's body by train from Sutton Bridge railway station *en route* for burial in Brookwood cemetery.

It was a bad time for 'prangs', for on the evening of the very next day, 2 July, another Spitfire, P8583, was lost. Sgt Charles Ian Scott, a CGS pupil from RAF Matlaske, died when his aircraft collided with a Hampden from 14 OTU, a few miles south of Spalding. Around this time several CGS Wellingtons and Hampdens also suffered mishaps in the air and on the ground, which was inevitable considering what constant work they had to do at the school. Sgt Scott was born in Chile of British parents. His Spitfire crashed on Holmes Farm, Cloot Drove, Crowland and he is buried in St Matthew's cemetery. The Hampden lost an engine but remained airborne. It was not over yet, for on the 4th, Fg Off N. S. Dunkerton was chauffeuring trainees to Holbeach range in Wellington IA, N2893, when hydraulic failure cut short the sortie. He had to use the emergency system to lower the undercarriage but landing without flaps and with the undercart unlocked, he pulled off a creditable landing in which only the tail wheel suffered total collapse.

There was another narrow squeak for the youngsters of Dawsmere School the very next day, 5 July. Returning from a target-towing sortie in Lysander T1618, staff pilot Sgt W. M. L. Penny narrowly missed hitting the school when he had to force-land due to running out of petrol. Then, on the 6th, WO North-Bomford, with a crew of air-gunner trainees on board, got into difficulty in Wellington L7774, a real 'oldie', while on their way to the range. Failure of a piston caused oil pressure to drop in the port engine and it caught fire. Unable to maintain height, North-Bomford could not make it back to the airfield so he force-landed at Basses Farm, Wingland. He and the crew, some of whom were slightly injured, scrambled clear before the Wellington went up in flames and was completely burned out. The first CGS Hampden recorded as having a mishap was P2084 on 21 June 1942, when it suffered hydraulic failure, leaving the undercarriage and flaps useless. Flt Sgt E. H. Noxon managed to pump down the flaps with the emergency system and bring the aeroplane down on the airfield for a 'repairable' belly-landing.

Douglas Broom noted at this point that 'Jerry' had started to stooge around the area by day and night.

> Some of our fighter chaps jumped at the chance to go up and see if they could catch one but they had no luck. However, there came a rude awakening when, at 00.40 on 24 July 1942, a Dornier 217 dropped four 500-lb bombs on the camp. One of these hit the armoury and sent loads of bullets and cannon shells whizzing all over the place. Part of a bullet even landed – smoking – on my bed and there was bags of panic, with people crashing round in pyjamas and steel helmets. The small fire was put out within minutes but there was not much sleep afterwards, though. In our billet we had to sleep three chaps in two beds because McIntyre's bed was saturated by the fire extinguishers. The war came jolly close that night!

Next morning everyone was up early to view the damage. One Hampden and several Spitfires and Masters, eight aircraft in all, had been damaged by four 500-lb HE bombs. In addition to completely demolishing the armoury, its entire contents – many hundreds of thousands of ammo rounds – went sky high in a huge pyrotechnic display. PGITW office, including lecture and cinema rooms were badly damaged as were numerous technical buildings, including two hangars, a decontamination centre and the Clerk of Works' store.

As a result of the raid one airman, Aircraftman Second Class (AC2) R. S. Resoli, suffered severe shock following his temporary burial when one explosion sent a huge cascade of earth into his gun-post. AC2 A. Gibbs was injured by flying glass that wounded him in the stomach while he slept in his bed. AC2 L. C. Malling sustained slight burns to one foot and Sgt Davison suffered severe bruising when debris fell on his leg. Next day it was all hands to the pumps to get the mess cleaned up. Sqn Ldr Allan Wright and his boss Wg Cdr Malan, were both living off the station with their families at this time; Alan being only recently married and in temporary accommodation in the village of Terrington St. Clements. A grim sight greeted them when they arrived for work to find the Fighter Wing office and lecture rooms totally demolished and much of their cine equipment destroyed.

Eighteen-year-old Aircraftman Norman 'Taff' Warren recalled there was some concern for the safety of the duty armourer who should have been in the armoury at the time of the attack. Fortunately for him he was not at his post as he had skived off for a cup of tea, but it is not known if he was put on a charge or whether, in the circumstances, a blind eye was turned to the matter. Two hangars, a decontamination centre and the orderly room were also damaged.

Midst all this gloom it could not have passed unnoticed to the airmen of the station that the population rose substantially with the arrival on 11 May of no less than 2 officers and 181 other ranks of the Women's Auxiliary Air Force (WAAF). It was recorded in the Station Form 540 that on 3 July, Section Officer S. Ottaway was posted in to command the WAAF detachment. Among that first WAAF contingent was Corporal (W) Olive Moule (now Mrs Olive Denis) who has memories, both fond and sad, of RAF Sutton Bridge during her service there in 1942/3.

At first Olive worked in the photographic section, helping to process those 'miles of cine-gun film' before transferring to the Bomber Wing with its Wellingtons and air-gunners. There Olive was the corporal in charge of a gun turret – one which remained indoors and firmly fixed to the ground – an early example of a simulator. Air-gunners sat in this turret while Cpl Moule moved it with random operation of a set of levers and cams. While counter-acting the motion of the turret, gunners 'fired' at a screen displaying cine-film images of attacking fighters. Of this turret, Olive said, 'I recall it was necessary for quite a bit of climbing on and off this apparatus and a monkey couldn't have done it better than me after a while.'

Located in the village across the river, close to the small dock, was the 'WAAF-ery', a group of Nissen huts. They were so close to the river that when the Nene carried a really high tide they were prone to flooding. Other WAAF accommodation was situated on open ground near New Road in the village centre.

Amenities for us WAAFs were so basic', said Olive, 'that we had to have a rota for baths. They were the old-fashioned "hip"-type, where either your feet stuck out over one end or you just stood upright in them. We were allowed one a week and it was all very communal. I was a bit shy of bathing with so many other girls so I used to slide my bath to the back part of the bath house. One day, when my turn came around, the other girls waited for me to sit down in the regulation 3 inches of water then a group of them rushed up, picked up the bath with me in it and dumped me in the yard outside. That certainly knocked the shyness out of me! Thereafter I made certain I bathed in the middle with the rest.'

Olive Moule also knew sadness at Sutton Bridge. She met and married a young air-gunner while at CGS. Their wedding was on 10 April 1943 but one week later her husband was killed over Germany on what would have been his last op before being posted as an instructor. Olive left CGS after a while, having made up her mind as she put it 'to get my own back' and in July 1943 she re-mustered as a radar operator.

While the author was seeking corroboration of the 1930 incident, mentioned in an earlier chapter, Olive brought to light a second 'who flew under the Bridge' story. Olive responded with an eye-witness account not of the 1930 incident but of another during 1943. She wrote: 'I think it was a Canadian pilot. Several of us watched him do it, with sheer horror, as we stood somewhere near the old railway station or at the WVS, both of which were by the side of the River Nene and close to the bridge. The reason for us being there was probably because we went to the WVS around mid-day to avoid the awful cookhouse food!' On the latter emotive subject, the CGS '540' had recorded that on 10 October 1942 'a new cookhouse was opened on No.2 Site and the old one at the camp closed down. It is a great success, being much brighter and more efficient.' Evidently that seems to have been a matter of opinion!

Olive was quite adamant she saw an aeroplane fly beneath the bridge but sadly she was unable to say what type of aeroplane it was or who the dare-devil might have been. Is it just possible that it was that most rebellious of Canadian pilots George 'Screwball' Beurling, who was actually serving as an instructor at CGS Sutton Bridge between April and July 1943? We shall probably never know.

'Taff' Warren was among many airmen who found himself moved out of the station and billeted in the village. He was not sure whether this was a safety measure as a direct result of the bombing raids or the result of the influx of the WAAF – but more likely the latter.

He had the pleasure of staying with Mrs Sage in Custom House Street, about half-a-mile from the camp. Widow of the former railway stationmaster, Mrs Sage had Taff and one other airman under her roof, receiving the sum of six shillings (30p) per week from the RAF for doing so. Inevitably the airmen and WAAFs quickly got on good terms and Taff Warren was no exception. He worked as a fitter on 'C' Flight with Lysander target tugs and he met his future wife at the station where she worked as an armourer, the station armoury being located adjacent to 'C' Flight dispersal.

Douglas Broome again:

On 2 August 'Jerry' was still active and yet more Red warnings were issued during the day and night. That same afternoon Spalding was bombed pretty badly. I went on leave on the 3rd after three warnings had gone off that morning. Just as I reached Peterborough, blow me, if there was yet another to greet me. Back from leave and I was on duty crew in the early hours of 11 August. A Lancaster landed at 2.00 am after a mine-laying raid on Kiel. One engine was dead, the bomb doors had been shot away and there was much other *flak* damage. The pilot and crew were all safe but he had only enough fuel for another five minutes flying and was dead lucky to drop into Sutton Bridge – just in time for the inevitable air-raid warning!

We lost another Hampden, P1163, on 17 August together with the pilot, Flt Sgt S. L. Vinton, a New Zealander. He was on his first solo on the type, in the local area when he hit some trees and a house before finishing up in flames at Wingland, a few miles from the camp. The occupants of the house, a woman and her child, were slightly hurt.

The 'liberty' bus to Peterborough was cancelled on 28th so I caught another bus to Spalding, fourteen miles, then walked another eight miles to Crowland where I phoned for my father to come and pick me up for the last eight miles. Good old dad came in his car (running on paraffin!) and I was able to stay the night. I missed the train back to camp and had to walk to Thorney, eight miles, then hitched a lift to Wisbech and thence to Sutton Bridge. I arrived back way overdue and the work parade had long since passed, so I went sick and luckily got away with it.

On the subject of 'going sick' there was a scare at the station in August when an airman was diagnosed with typhoid fever. He had recently been posted in from RAF Henlow where there had been several cases of the disease. He was quickly despatched to Boston isolation hospital and a mass fumigation and disinfection carried out in his wake, while his contacts were subjected to rigorous daily monitoring. Fortunately, no further cases were reported.

To mark the passing of the third year of the war, on 3 September a special open-air service of prayer was held at the camp, with Gp Capt Keith taking charge as his last official duty. On 5 September 1942, Gp Capt Charles Eric St John Beamish DFC took over command of CGS, while shortly afterwards the Fighter Wing was commanded by Wg Cdr Peter Russell Walker DSO DFC (later OBE), who would have memories of Sutton Bridge before the war when he visited for summer camps during the 1930s. The original CGS team was moving on, having seen their new 'baby' begin to grow. Wg Cdr 'Sailor' Malan was now posted to command RAF Biggin Hill, while Sqn Ldr Allan Wright joined three other highly experienced RAF fighter pilots on a tour of the US to instruct American fighter pilots in combat tactics suitable for European skies. 'Sailor's' final duty at Sutton Bridge was to lead the local parade on 20 September, marking the anniversary of the Battle of Britain.

A career airman, Peter Walker – one of the many Walkers in the service who came to be known as 'Johnnie' – joined the RAF in 1935. Posted to 1 Squadron as a fighter pilot, Walker did not take long to make his mark as an excellent flyer. In 1937 he was a member of the squadron's Hawker Fury aerobatic team led by the ebullient Flt Lt Edward 'Teddy' Donaldson, twice winner of the Brooke-Popham Air Firing Trophy at Sutton Bridge. Flt Lt Peter Walker went to France with 1 Squadron in September 1939 and in March 1940, is reputed to have shot down the first Messerschmitt Bf 110 to fall to the RAF. By the end of the campaign in France, Walker was credited with three enemy aircraft destroyed; two shared destroyed and two unconfirmed destroyed and was awarded a DFC. Upon his return to England he was posted as an instructor to 5 OTU at Aston Down. This posted lasted until November 1940 and he therefore took no active part in the Battle of Britain. In 1941 he commanded 253 Squadron and in 1942 was leader of the Tangmere Wing during the Dieppe Operation, for which he was awarded a DSO. Flying a desk at HQ 11 Group for a year during 1943, he then became OC PGITW at CGS Sutton Bridge, initially from September to December 1942, then again from June to October 1943. Peter Walker rose to the rank of Group Captain, remaining in the RAF after the war until his retirement from his final post as Station Commander of RAF Fassberg in Germany in the late-1950s. He was appointed a CBE in 1958.

As mentioned earlier, when Sqn Ldr Alan Wright relinquished his post as CGS Fighter Wing CI, he was posted with three others to tour the USA. This mission returned to England on 23 November 1942 and shortly afterwards one of its members, also a former CGS instructor, Wg Cdr James Rankin DSO DFC, was posted to command the Fighter Wing at Sutton Bridge. On his return, Allan Wright did a conversion course to night fighters, joined 29 Squadron and added one more 'kill' to his tally.

Life on the base was still hectic for ground crew such as Douglas Broom and Taff Warren and 16 September was probably one of their busiest days so far.

> We had thirty-seven aircraft to service, including Blenheims, Whitleys, Wellingtons, troop carriers and some Yankee P-38 Lightnings. Three American Lightning pilots joined a CGS course on 18th and their machines were much admired and said to be very fast. The pilots showed them off to us after dinner. When pilots were posted to Sutton Bridge for the fighter gunnery courses, they often brought their own aircraft with them, which is why we occasionally had Yank types and others such as Mustang Mk Is from some of the Army Co-Operation units.

There were still regular 'prangs' to lighten the daily routine, too. Spitfire P7851, Plt Off Chandler, landed with the wheels up on 20th and on 25th. Hampden P5341, Sgt Vern, swung so violently during take-off that the undercarriage collapsed. Both pilots were unhurt. Also, on 25th in Spitfire P8087, Fg Off Thwaites got a bit too low over the perimeter ridge and the undercarriage was neatly torn off. He pulled off a belly-landing and was unscathed. Next day, 26 September, Master DL684 spun in and crashed on a road at Harold's Bridge near Wisbech. The control column had seized up but the pilot, Fg Off Henry Lardner-Burke DFC and his pupil, Flt Lt George St Clair Boyd Reid managed to bale out safely at about 6,000 feet altitude.

Lardner-Burke was a veteran of the Malta air battles and had earned his DFC in combat over the island. George Reid is an interesting character, too. After his CGS course he saw service with 91 Squadron and died when his Spitfire MK453 crashed at Maldegam in Belgium on 28 October 1944. He was flying an operation escorting 250 Lancasters on a daylight raid to Cologne when his aircraft was seen to dive out of a thick low-level cloud bank and crash. At the time, what was believed to be his body was recovered from an aeroplane wreck and buried in Slipje cemetery. In 1996 however, Sqn Ldr Reid's Spitfire was discovered in a field about 30 miles from where he was originally thought to have crashed. When the wreckage was brought to the surface, human remains were found inside and it was established beyond doubt that the remains were those of George Reid. He now rests in Adegen Canadian War cemetery and grave of the body buried in Slipje has been re-marked as that of 'an unknown airman.'

Douglas Broom noted in his diary:

> Yankee formations were impressive to watch as they wheeled over The Wash area during assembly before setting off on their raids. Another B-17 made quite an arrival when it landed unexpectedly at Sutton Bridge. It was one of twenty aircraft which set out to bomb shipyards at Lorient. The mission was aborted due to bad weather and they headed back for The Wash to get rid of their bombs. This aeroplane had to get down quickly when a survival dinghy blew out of its housing during flight and fouled the elevator. It landed safely and we chatted to the crew while they waited for a transport to collect them. They were a friendly bunch and shared some of the emergency rations from the wayward dinghy with us. On the morning the pilots were due to take off from our little field, word had spread and hundreds of villagers lined the perimeter road to watch the spectacle. With its roaring engines run up to full throttle and the noise shaking camp buildings and nearby houses, it sprang forward off the brakes, thundered down the longest grass-run and leaped into the air amid cheers from the watching crowd. [This aeroplane was B-17F, 41-24460; 423BS, 306BG].

Sutton Bridge represented a welcome haven for returning 'lame ducks' of both air forces; for example, on 14 October Halifax W1102 of 35 Squadron dropped in for a forced landing on the way home from a night op to Kiel.

As CGS was the temporary home of several American pilots drawing on the experience of the RAF, it also became a target for VIP visits. An example of this occurred on 22 October, when a Douglas C 47 Skytrain landed, bringing with it Brigadier-General

James Doolittle (he of Tokyo Raid fame) and an entourage of American brass-hats, including Colonels Turner and Vandenberg. There was no formal parade as they were there to look at training methods at CGS and fit in some air firing experience for themselves in Spitfires.

The weather turned so unseasonably cold during October that the station MO had to seek permission from the station commander to light fires in the sick quarters on four days during the month. In November the level of flying activity slackened off with the arrival of the first thick fenland fogs, which led to all aircraft being grounded on the 12th. This cold weather was partly to blame for an MO's inspection of accommodation for the station's Direction Finding (DF) apparatus. The three DF stations (receivers at Walpole Marsh and Wrights Lane in Sutton Bridge and the transmitter at Westmere also in Sutton Bridge) – which were manned as self-contained units – were pretty primitive outposts and living conditions were badly in need of immediate improvement, particularly to cope better with the weather and because it was intended that they were to be manned entirely by WAAFs in the future.

After the fogs came the hard frosts of December, but no let-up in the monotonously frequent crashes at Sutton Bridge, as evidenced by the demise of Hudson N7405 on 7 December. Hudsons were used to train Coastal Command crews at CGS and this pilot was under instruction on the type when the aircraft swung on take-off. Things got dicey when the starboard leg collapsed and punctured the petrol tank. The aircraft caught fire and in a very short time it was a burned-out wreck but fortunately the crew escaped in time. Apparently, this was a common result in such circumstances due to the design of the Hudson having a 'wet' wing fuel tank immediately above the oleo leg and near the hot engine – very dodgy in a crash! The crew was Sgt Molyneaux and Flt Lt C. T. Boxall.

This was followed on 17th by the pilot of Lysander V9496, Sgt Giles, making a rough landing which caused the undercarriage to collapse and, shortly afterwards the undercart of Master W9056, with an American and a Belgian on board, refused to lower. The 'Lizzie' collapsed in a heap and the Master bellied in, with both crews getting away with cuts and bruises. These latter were Lt McKelvey USAAF, who was a pupil at CGS, and Flt Lt Giovanni Ernest Fernand Dieu, one of the PGITW instructors. Dieu was a pre-war pilot in the Belgian Air Force who escaped to France when the Germans invaded his country. After serving with the French Air Force he escaped by ship to England when France capitulated. Joining the RAF, he fought in and survived the Battle of Britain with 236 Squadron and later flew operations with 609 and 245 Squadrons before being posted to RAF Sutton Bridge to pass on his experience at the CGS. Promoted to Sqn Ldr, he moved away to take up a staff post and flew a desk for the rest of the war. Awarded an OBE and AFC in 1945 he returned to Belgium, retiring from the Belgian Air Force in 1954. He died in 1978.

'I drew night guard duty regularly throughout that freezing cold December,' said Douglas, 'and I latched onto the wheeze of sleeping in a Spitfire. Very cosy! Christmas rolled round again and on the 24th I caught an evening train home to Peterborough and stayed (unofficially) overnight. Christmas dinner was grand and we even had chicken. Good old Dad drove me back to camp in good time for work parade. The festivities were rounded off that night with a trip into Wisbech with the boys. We all got pretty merry.'

While Douglas enjoyed home-cooked fare those back at camp celebrated Christmas dinner in the traditional Service manner with meals being served by the Station Commander, Gp Capt Beamish, his officers and senior NCOs.

I was on duty ground crew for the next two days but it started to snow and apart from one P-38 Lightning, which called at the watch office, there were no visitors at all and by 31 December about four inches of snow had fallen. The weather improved a little on 3 January 1943. I was on duty crew again with plenty of visiting aircraft to attend to. It snowed hard again, however, on the 6th and my mates and I were called out from 8.30 pm to midnight to picket down the kites out on the airfield. The howling wind and driving snow mixed with rain was horrendous and I was dog-tired and soaked to the skin when I finally turned in. Next morning, being slightly late on duty, the lovely Sgt Stafford put me on a charge. I was up before Wg Cdr Fletcher and got four days Confined-to-Camp. My pals 'Titch' Hebson, Taylor and 'Jelly', were all on charges and received 'jankers' too. We had the bind of reporting in full kit to the guard room at 6.30 am, 1.00 pm, 6.30 pm and 10.00 pm each day for our sins. What a bind! The weather turned foul again in mid-January. After hail, snow and rain, for good measure, there was thick fog too. Out on the airfield it became waterlogged and we had to push all the kites into hangers for protection. Ice covered the puddles on the airfield and it was declared serviceable for Masters only, because the Spitfire undercarts and flaps were liable to be damaged. The station commander even visited Marham and Downham Market to discuss the possibility of doing some flying from either of those airfields. The weather improved and on 18 January there was the first flying for a fortnight. The 'drome, however, was still badly waterlogged and on 23rd all our Spitfires went u/s on their first trips. This was due to water damaging their flaps as they landed back and hit the great puddles out on the field. Flying activity gathered pace once more after the spell of bad weather. Then it started to rain heavily on 29 January and the wind was very rough, so that by the beginning of February the 'drome was waterlogged and rendered u/s again. Our kites were heavily used but with the relatively small size of the maintenance facilities available for such a large number of aeroplanes, aircraft serviceability was always a problem. On the 9th, for example, even working flat out all day, we could still only get twenty aircraft serviceable out of sixty on the 'drome.

Yankee Thunderbolts seem to like 'buzzing' Sutton Bridge and the habit is becoming very regular! There were heaps of Thunderbolts over on 16 February [escorts for a US raid on St Nazaire] and two of this type landed at Sutton Bridge on 18th. They are 'tubby' but very powerful-looking aircraft compared to our dainty Spitfires. More of them came over on 26th, this time together with some Mitchell bombers. As duty crew that night I had to wait up late for one of our pupils, a Yankee pilot, who lost his bearings and ended up way down on the South Coast. I took a dim view of this! I was quite pleased to get away on seven days leave but when I returned to Sutton Bridge, it was business as usual. A white 'Wimpy', LB230, of 3 Coastal Command OTU Cranwell, lay out on the field badly smashed up. The accident happened on 14th, as the aeroplane dropped in over the threshold. It had hit a pillbox and having lost the port wheel, Fg Off Hollinson belly-flopped the Wellington onto the airfield, where it ground-looped ripping off the starboard leg before finally careering to a halt.

Two days later, on 22nd one of our CGS Wellingtons, N2876, crashed at Terrington Marsh, near King's Lynn, when first the starboard then the port engine cut out. In the ensuing crash one of the air gunners, Flt Sgt Edgar John Davis, an air gunner pupil was killed and the rest of the crew slightly injured. This was followed on 24th by Master, W8969, which had its undercarriage collapse on landing causing the prop to go for a 'Burton'. A Spitfire, with 2/Lt. Cole USAAF on board caused a lot of panic just after take-off. The pilot thought one of his tyres had a possible puncture and perhaps a damaged u/c leg. He was ordered to do a circuit, which confirmed his suspicions but he pulled off a great landing in spite of one flat tyre. All this excitement certainly kept us ground crew on top line trying to put the pieces together again.

Our Wellington crews did their bit for the Wings for Victory Week efforts in the local area by laying on a low-level formation flypast over the town of Wisbech on 28 March. Gp Capt Beamish took the salute at a parade through the town.

Similar events were held over the next few months in Spalding and Holbeach, each attended by at least one of the famous instructor pilots from CGS, such as Jamie Rankin and George Beurling. On 1 April the 25th anniversary of the birth of the RAF was celebrated at Sutton Bridge when a party for 100 ATC cadets from Spalding and Holbeach squadrons toured the station in the afternoon and were guests at a special tea party. Work for all sections on the station ceased at 4.30 pm and there was a gala dance from 8.00 pm at which officers and wives from local ATC squadrons were entertained as special guests.

It was bad enough that pilots should have to live with the possibility of an aero-accident but on one occasion an American trainee had a very narrow escape from death in the icy waters of The Wash. LAC (Armourer) Eric Joyce recalled the day he and this American met out on the bleak Wash marshes.

One sunny February afternoon in 1943, I biked round the perimeter road heading for 'B' Flight dispersal. I was going to work on the front turret of a Wellington; the rotating service joint of which was leaking. As I propped up my bike the Tannoy blared out my name – and others – to report immediately to the orderly room. Fearing the worst, I did as ordered and was relieved to find I was detailed to go to an aircraft which had force-landed on the sand off the out-marsh at a place called Fosdyke about ten miles from Sutton Bridge. The panic was due to the fact that the tide would cover the aircraft at 5.00 pm. This would not do the aeroplane any good!

One man from each trade, including me as armourer, was instructed to get as much off the aircraft as possible in the time available. Grabbing some tools at random, off we raced in a lorry, being met by some civvies near the village church, two of whom were to act as guides for the dangerous trek out onto the marsh. That was a god-forsaken place. Miles from anywhere, shifting sands, mud, deep sometimes hidden creeks, leading out to flat sands as far as the eye could see, with the sea way out beyond that. The danger was from the tide which raced in and crept up the creeks behind you but this all passed over my head at the time.

Two miles out onto the marsh and there was our aeroplane, perched on a narrow strip of shining sand. It was a Spitfire and bearing a single white American star on the fuselage. The young American pilot, Lt Wallace, a pupil at CGS on attachment from the USAAF, stood alongside dressed only in a thin shirt and slacks. Airborne over the range for gunnery practice in Spitfire Vb W3133, his engine packed up and he force-landed on the firm sand at low tide. The aeroplane seemed quite undamaged but we all set about our tasks at once. Even if the other fellows helped, with the few tools at my disposal there was no possibility of removing the two 20 mm cannon – I was a Wellington fitter, I had no Spitfire spanners! After an hour of concentrated effort, I had coaxed the machine guns to drop from their mountings onto the sand – that is all except the fourth gun. I noticed it dropped with a splash. When I looked up, to my horror the sand had gone. Nothing but water as far as the eye could see! On the skyline in the direction of Fosdyke was the sea bank and the small figures in the distance legging it for all they were worth were my so-called comrades. Completely oblivious to my surroundings I had not heard my mates shout that they were off and neither had the Yank. The tide was racing in by the minute; too deep even now to risk falling in a creek if we set off for the bank.

Only three hours ago I had a cushy little job to do on a Wimpy and could pan it out until the NAAFI wagon came but now there was just me and a Yank, marooned in The Wash with this damned Spitfire. As the water rose, we sat side-by-side astride the cockpit canopy and waited. Nonchalantly, Lt Wallace produced a couple of 'ceegars' and offered me one but I didn't smoke and didn't feel like starting either. As the light faded, the wind picked up and grey water crept upwards, first covering the star then lapping at the tops of my gumboots. Wallace must have been half-frozen because, even with my oilskin on, I was miserable and getting numb with cold and fear.

Suddenly a voice came out of the gloom, "Hold yew on hard, bor, we'll soon git yew out of it!" There was a boat, not more than 20 feet away, with two men in it. Rowing right up to the cockpit, all we had to do was slide off and into the sanctuary of the dinghy. Talk about relief. I had had the foresight to stow the four machine guns inside the cockpit and I wasn't about to let them go now, so these were retrieved, together with the small red canister with a pull-tape, known as a Bomb, Aircraft Destroying, which I stuffed in my mac pocket. We reached a type of tug vessel which turned out to be the River Nene Catchment Board boat, used to inspect banks and navigation channels. Its snug wardroom and mugs of hot cocoa made it seem like heaven. The skipper, however, was not amused when the bomb fell from my coat pocket and rolled about the deck. In no uncertain terms he told me, Air Force property or not, to 'get rid of that ... infernal thing in the sea!'

Tying up at Fosdyke Bridge quay, the American and I were taken to a nearby pub for a wash and a meal. We were being regally entertained by the locals and well-oiled when the door burst open and in walked my mates – with a load of excuses for their unseemly departure. They had had to hoof it back over the mud and looked a sorry mob. Well, mates can't fall out so we had a few more beers all round before the lorry from Sutton Bridge arrived to take us back to reality.

Douglas Broom recalled:

On 1 April, two Thunderbolts puzzled us by making about six circuits of the airfield. They evidently decided they could actually land on our little pocket handkerchief and the first one touched down without difficulty. The second, however, also touched down but believing he would overshoot, the pilot slammed on his brakes. That great windmill of a prop dug into the turf as the tail shot upwards and the pilot was lucky it did not turn over. [He was 1/Lt. Calvin Webb from 82 FS,78 FG at Goxhill in P-47C 16389]. That might have been considered an amusing enough April Fool's day event but imagine my panic when later that day I received a telegram asking me to go home urgently. It was from my family and rushing round like a madman I managed to get ten days compassionate leave. I arrived home to find I was the father of a bonny baby boy! Then, as if to top even this, I received yet another telegram on 3 April, ordering me to return to Sutton Bridge at once. I rang the station to establish just what the flap was all about only to find that I was posted. The good news was that I was allowed to finish out my leave.

Back at the station, my time there drew to a sad close, with two very bad crashes. In the first on the 9 April 1943, Spitfire, P7678, dived straight into the ground at Basses Farm, Tholomas Drove, near Wisbech at 11.50 am. The pilot was a New Zealander, Fg Off [Gordon Griffith] Thomas, from 486 Squadron who was briefed to practise stern attacks and evasions on a CGS 'Wimpy'. I was one of the recovery detail sent to the site. We dug down in the running silt soil to a depth of about 18 feet but the machine was smashed beyond recognition and very little of the pilot's body was found. It was thought he may have blacked out, poor fellow. Salvage efforts were abandoned on the 12th because the wreckage was just being sucked down and down into the soft silt. This tragedy was followed next day when another one of our Spitfires – coincidentally P7677 – made a dummy attack on a 'Wimpy' [N2865] failed to pull out of his dive in time and ran into the Wellington, which crashed killing all on board. Both aeroplanes came down at Abbots Ripton in Cambridgeshire. The Spitfire pilot, Flt Lt Ernest Hamilton Griffith (Aus) managed to bale out but injured his face and was hospitalised in Ely. [Having survived this incident, Flt Lt Griffith died in an air accident on 29 September 1943 while flying a Mosquito with 456 Squadron]. The Wellington crew was Flt Lt Terence Cathcart Stanbury; Flt Sgt Eric Cooke (Instructor); Pupils: Plt Off Reginald Ross Hely (Aus); Plt Off John Alfred Town (Can); Sgt Clifford Harrison; Sgt Charles Ronald Archer, all of whom died. This dismal period closed with us parading on 13 April for the burials of Fg Off Thomas and Flt Lt Stanbury in St Matthew's Churchyard. It was on this sad day, after just over a year at the CGS, that I received my clearance chitty, signed ready for my posting the following day.

From among the many famous names to pass through the gates of RAF Sutton Bridge, one in particular stands out in 1943. Fg Off George Beurling's name became synonymous with the air battles over Malta – indeed his autobiography is entitled *Malta Spitfire*. Although many other pilots achieved prominence in the defence of the island,

Beurling became by far the leading scorer with twenty-four enemy aircraft claimed as destroyed. This, with his two earlier claims over France, earned him a commission, a DSO, a DFC and two DFMs.

According to his contemporaries, among them top 'ace' John Edgar 'Johnnie' Johnson, the key to Beurling's success was his combination of personal attributes such as excellent eyesight, phenomenal shooting skill – particularly in the art of 'deflection' – and an aggressiveness that drove him to engage the enemy whatever the odds. Over Malta in 1942 the RAF was almost always at a disadvantage from numerical and tactical viewpoints and this imbalance could only be made up by men displaying just such attributes as Beurling's, often forced to fight alone, on their own initiative. Such conditions suited a loner like Beurling, but returning to England in October 1942 he found the teamwork and discipline necessary under European theatre tactical conditions hard to adapt to. After a spell of leave in his native Canada and having raised his score to thirty-one enemy aircraft destroyed he now enters the narrative of CGS.

Arriving at RAF Sutton Bridge for instructor duties on 27 May 1943, George Beurling, known to some as 'Buzz' and others as 'Screwball', in his brief six-week stay made his mark in the minds of young and old on the station and in the locality. He is generally portrayed as a tough, hard-living, unruly and undisciplined individual. In the circumstances in which he carved out his reputation perhaps such an attitude was appropriate, although it was often disdained, it is said, by other flyers. In any event, he was a very effective fighter pilot at a time when results counted. There is no evidence from his time at CGS to suggest he thought himself special; on the contrary, for a supposed loner he seems to have been approachable and appears to have joined in local activities as the 'quiet' celebrity. More than five years later upon his untimely death in an air crash in Italy in 1948, the *Lincolnshire Free Press* was moved to say of him:

He was a familiar and popular figure in the Sutton Bridge district. Fg Off Beurling is particularly remembered for his attendance at the Wings for Victory Week events [during 1943] and only a day after baling out of a blazing Spitfire he still found time to judge an aero-modelling competition in the Corn Exchange, Spalding, and visit cadets of 1406 (Spalding) Air Training Corps Squadron.

There are even some airmen and airwomen who served at CGS who claimed Beurling was 'the crazy Canadian pilot who flew under the Bridge', a story which is still repeated among the locals. With his combat background and the view of life generally credited to him, a routine training job might very easily become boring to him. Undoubtedly, he had the nerve to try such an escapade and eyewitness accounts, such as that of WAAF Olive Moule mentioned earlier in the chapter, match the time Beurling was at CGS. In a Spitfire is stretching imagination but a Master or Magister, both of which were available on the station, is feasible.

Could an attempt on the bridge, coupled with him removing three Spitfires from the RAF inventory in the space of six weeks, have been too much for the top brass to tolerate even from a national hero?

Those six weeks also brought 'Buzz' three more brushes with the grim reaper. Taking off after lunch on 8 June, Beurling intended to carry out what was described officially as a 'tactical evasion exercise' in company with fellow Canadian and Malta ace, Flt Lt Robert Buckham DFC. Less than an hour later he was floating to earth beneath his parachute and Spitfire II, P7913 had buried itself deep into fenland subsoil on a farm in Middle Drove near Wisbech. Landing safely, George was given a cup of tea at a nearby house while the incident was reported to CGS and transport arranged to collect him. Myths relating to Beurling are many and varied; it is said locally for example that, during the walk to the cottage, Beurling said something to the effect that 'that Spitfire was going to claim someone's life as it was all but worn out and to prevent this happening [he] buried it!' His official report, however, claims he abandoned the aircraft when the engine caught fire due to a glycol leak.

There is even a third version of this incident. Sometime later, after his friend Buckham had been lost in action, Beurling is said to have claimed that the 'real' cause of his bale-out was because he was shot down when Buckham accidentally fired a burst of gunfire as he caught Beurling in his gun-sight during their mock dogfight. The glycol tank was ruptured and its contents burst into flame over the hot engine. Whether this is true or just another 'Beurling myth' is hard to say but in 1985 some evidence came into the light of day – although it did little to really clarify the matter.

After a long search, members of the Fenland and West Norfolk Aircraft Preservation Society (FAWNAPS) found the site of Beurling's crashed Spitfire and mounted a recovery dig. In the course of the dig, in addition to copious amounts of twisted fuselage and wing material, items such as rudder pedals, compass, pilot seat, control column, gun sight and even the 'Form 700' with other documentation – still readable – emerged as the excavator went ever deeper. At a depth of 26 feet the most significant find emerged from the all-embracing blue fenland clay – the virtually intact Merlin XII engine. Close inspection, however, suggested to the FAWNAPS enthusiasts that there was little or no sign of fire damage to either the engine or the cockpit area. In fact, so complete and in good condition was the engine that the Society was able to restore it to pristine display standard for their museum in Wisbech, where it is much admired by the public and a credit to the ingenuity of this reputable group of aviation archaeologists.

George was back in the air very quickly but two weeks later, on 24 June, up-ended Spitfire II, P7496, when the undercarriage locking pin seized and cracked its housing, so that the wheels would not lock down. On touch down at Sutton Bridge the undercarriage collapsed and pitched the aeroplane onto its nose but Beurling emerged unhurt.

His third mishap was to write off Spitfire, P8010, when its engine seized up after loss of oil pressure. This time he was flying out over The Wash but, fortunate that the tide was out, he managed to glide to a crash landing on Pandora Sand – where presumably the Spitfire still remains. On that day Fg Off George Beurling was posted out from CGS, to 61 OTU at RAF Rednal, but he certainly made an impact while he was there and will never be forgotten.

Another Malta 'old boy' and both a former instructor at 56 OTU and a pupil at CGS, Sqn Ldr Robert Chippindall 'Bob' Dafforn DFC arrived once more at Sutton Bridge at about the same time as George Beurling. Awarded a DFC during the Battle of Britain, he was a flight commander in 501 Squadron when he was posted on 22 October 1941 for flying instructor duties at 56 OTU Sutton Bridge. During January 1942 he was posted overseas to the Middle East theatre and then to 229 Squadron in to Malta where he was shot down, wounded and caught undulant fever, being invalided home in August 1942. He returned to flying duties in November of that year.

Standing 6 feet 6 inches tall – a tight squeeze in a Spitfire – Old Harrovian Bob was next posted to CGS Sutton Bridge as a pupil on one of the Fighter Wing courses in December 1942. Being a highly experienced fighter pilot with more than 1,000 flying hours and eight air victories to his credit, he was posted back again on 23 June 1943 to replace Sqn Ldr Thomas 'Tommy' Balmforth DFC as Chief Instructor of CGS PGITW.

Educating fighter gunnery pupils was a task involving both ground and air duties and it was essential for the CI to keep his own hand in as well as co-operating with pupils during tactical exercises in the air. It was one such training sortie that was to cost Sqn Ldr Dafforn his life. Sadly, there would be occasions when vast experience and having survived all the enemy could throw at a pilot would be to no avail. Tiredness perhaps, or a momentary lapse of concentration, or both, was all it needed. On 9 September 1943 Bob Dafforn had just completed an air-to-air firing sortie over Holbeach range in Spitfire V, P7289. He was seen very low down between the range and the village of Long Sutton, in a steeply banked turn, during which the port wing touched the ground. An eyewitness was local Home Guard member Tom Simpson, who recalled that the pilot seemed to be having a bit of fun 'buzzing' some farm labourers working in a field. Coming in for another very low pass, the Spitfire seemed to stagger momentarily in the air, then the left wingtip hit the ground. P7289 cart-wheeled into the ground in a welter of earth and debris on land in Green Dyke road, between Gedney Dyke and Lutton, that belonged to Redhouse Farm, killing its pilot. It emerged later that, in this unauthorised exhibition of low flying, the aeroplane had struck high-tension power lines during that last pass. Next day Gp Capt John Leacroft MC*, an old Sutton Bridge hand from pre-war days (1927), arrived to conduct an inquiry into the accident and, the day after that, Sqn Ldr Dafforn's coffin was conveyed to the railway station from whence it travelled to Maidenhead for a private burial.

Replacing Bob Dafforn would not be easy but Sqn Ldr Archie Winskill was an excellent choice. Destined, post-war, to rise to command the Queen's Flight, he reached Air Commodore rank and became a Knight into the bargain. One month later, the command of CGS Fighter wing changed again and Sqn Ldr Winskill found himself deputy to one of the foremost fighter pilots in the RAF at that time: Wg Cdr Alan Christopher Deere.

Among the many pilots noted in the ORB as being posted in for a spell as instructor at PGITW are:

Flt Lt J. M. Beard
Plt Off G. Conway
2/Lt M. F. De Bordas (Free French)
Fg Off G. E. F. Dieu
Flt Lt A. G. A. Fisher

Plt Off W. E. Grant
Flt Lt H. S. Griffiths
Fg Off A. S. Harker
Fg Off W. L. Johnston
Plt Off D. E. Jones
Fg Off H. P. Lardner-Burke
A/Sqn Ldr E. Mayne
Flt Lt R. Morant
Plt Off I. J. McNeill
Sqn Ldr M. E. Reid
Fg Off G. G. R. Thomas
Plt Off W. de Wolff.

Of his term of office as the last CO of CGS Fighter Wing in its days at RAF Sutton Bridge, Wing Commander (later Air Commodore OBE) Alan Christopher Deere DSO DFC* recalled:

I first heard of my appointment to CGS from Gp Capt Sailor Malan who was, at that time, commanding RAF Biggin Hill. It was great news as, having been the 'Biggin Wing' Leader for the previous nine months, I expected a posting to a desk job, a prospect which held no appeal for me whatsoever. RAF Sutton Bridge was a station known to me already, having landed there for air-firing practice on a number of occasions pre-war, while flying Gloster Gladiators with 54 Squadron. How it had grown in the intervening years.

Holding a training post was a new experience for me but I knew my recent operational record would carry some weight with the student intake. It was comforting, though, to have the support of two excellent deputies, Sqn Ldr Roy Morant in charge of ground training and Sqn Ldr (later Air Commodore Sir) Archie Winskill as CI.

Gp Capt Charles Beamish, the station commander, was an old friend from pre-war RAF rugby football circles. In modern parlance, Charles was very laid-back but very much on the ball too; he never interfered but was always there to encourage and advise when needed.

In fact, as a trained fighter pilot, one of Gp Capt Beamish's first acts on taking command had been to join Gunnery Leaders Course No.45 when it commenced on 19 September 1942 to see for himself just how the Bomber Wing operated.

We had a pretty intensive training schedule, tied in of course with the Bomber Wing, whose pupils would benefit enormously from having to handle fighter attacks by staff pilots with formidable records and pupils with great potential. At this time the Bomber wing was commanded by Wg Cdr Lofty Lowe, a pre-war NCO with a distinguished operational record. Lofty in size and nick-name, he was a real go-er.

Competition for places on the Fighter Course was intense and such was the calibre of pilot that there were few, if any, failures. In my opinion, there is no doubt that our training scheme gave those pilots a greater awareness of the art of air gunnery and an edge when it came to applying that training in subsequent combats.

Quite a lot of these fellows succeeded and one example in particular springs to mind from my period in command. He was a young American, from the 8th Air Force (we took pilots from all the Allies) who expressed an outspoken determination to become the best shot in his squadron. He achieved that ambition with something like twenty confirmed victories. His name escapes me now but I remember he was known as Willie and he spoke in one of those Deep-Southern American drawls. I met him a few times after the war, although I lost track of him in the 1960s. In our conversations he always gave the credit for his success to the training he received at CGS.

They were happy months for me at Sutton Bridge, staying in post long enough to move the School to RAF Catfoss, 12 miles NE of Hull, in Yorkshire. I am unsure why we had to move but I suspect it was because, with the gradual build-up of the US 8th and 9th Air Forces, the sky over East Anglia became a bit too congested and the relatively clearer sky over Yorkshire offered safer areas for daytime training. After the move was completed I was posted to a staff job at HQ No11 Group.

After several visits by Sutton Bridge station commander Gp Capt Michael Harrington Dwyer (later AVM, CB CBE) to finalise details, the move to RAF Catfoss took effect from 21 February 1944 when the advance party left Sutton Bridge. On 24 February the main party moved out en masse by air, rail and road and CGS was up and running and continuing its good work at Catfoss next day. Commencing on 17 February 1944, No.43 PGITW and No.76 GLW were the last CGS courses to start at Sutton Bridge.

Suddenly, once more RAF Sutton Bridge reverted to a Care & Maintenance basis for a period until a new role could be found. This was not long in coming and training would still be the order of the day. While the sound of foreign tongues, however, was destined to be heard again in the village, this time the aircrew would not be the cream of the fighter profession but instead include the fledglings of what was to become the nucleus of the post-war French Air Force.

9

Vive La France and Au Revoir

Making his first public appearance since being appointed AOC RAF Flying Training Command, Air Marshal Sir Arthur Coningham KCB DSO MC DFC AFC, reviewed the passing out parade of No.6 (French) Course at RAF Peterborough. Accompanying AM Coningham on that chilly morning of 6 November 1945 was his contemporary from the French Air Force, the splendidly named General-de-Division Aérienne, René Marie Yves Louis d'Arnaud de Vitrolles GCLd'H, chief of the French Air Force flying schools, who flew in from Le Bourget with his entourage. This parade was the culmination of three months of RAF-style flying training for twenty-seven young French Naval and Air Force pilots. Now they were ready to join others of their similarly trained countrymen in laying the foundations of the post-war French Air Force.

By mid-1944 RAF Sutton Bridge had become a satellite airfield to RAF Peterborough (Westwood) but it by no means took a back seat when it came to flying training. Courses specifically handling the training of French pilots began at Peterborough in September 1944 and between that date and November 1945 – including No.6 Course – 198 French airmen had passed through both stations to reach RAF Wings standard.

But what had been happening at Sutton Bridge in the intervening period?

From the end of 1943 it is reasonable to consider fenland sky as largely the domain of the bomber. However, with The Wash range and local air activity being conducted at the intensity required by Central Gunnery School, it became obvious that this could not continue without serious interference to the American Eighth Air Force (8th

AF) bomber training programme – and a hazard to both parties. With such numbers of aircraft milling around in that piece of sky it was just asking for trouble.

Central Gunnery School, therefore, was moved north to RAF Catfoss in Yorkshire and for a short time RAF Sutton Bridge came under the temporary control of RAF Peterborough before being revived as a satellite initially for RAF Newton then, in August 1944, for RAF Peterborough once again. Flying activity in this new role, however, was far less intensive than during the old CGS days, it being composed mainly of night flying training. Later on in 1944, the role of Sutton Bridge was further extended to become the base for 7 Service Flying Training School (7 SFTS), which became known as the 'French Air Force SFTS' and it also continued to operate as a base for the Holbeach range air weapons facility.

At this point it is relevant to note that USAAF operational bombing and air gunnery standards up to the end of 1943 were judged by 8th AF high command to be in need of much improvement. As the celebrated aviation historian Roger Freeman put it (*Mighty Eighth War Manual*, Janes, pp 125/6):

Several [RAF] ranges were offered for American use. An immediate problem [though] was safety. The high altitude at which [their] bombing and gunnery would be carried out increased the possibility of error and danger to civilians and property in the vicinity of these ranges. As 8th AF grew in strength so did the problem of acquiring suitable ranges. Only Brest Sand, located in The Wash off King's Lynn, was acceptable to become the first range used by B-17s in 1942/43. Later in 1943, as more ranges were created elsewhere, Brest Sand was allotted specifically to Bomb Groups of the First Air Division. For air-to-air gunnery practice, the Americans set up their first range at Snettisham beach, on the eastern shore of The Wash. Other ranges, established elsewhere in the UK, were a long way from USAAF bases in East Anglia; involving long transit times and complicating practice-mission logistics. Bombing and gunnery ranges in The Wash area, on the other hand, proved ideal both in terms of environment and convenience thus accounting for the high level of US activity in this area.

Congestion, though, was always a problem, even in an area with 500 square miles of air space to offer. Before very long, Snettisham range became over-subscribed and in 1943 another range – which had to co-exist with Snettisham, Brest Sand and Holbeach Marsh – was established for the USAAF over on the west shore at Wainfleet Sands (between Boston and Skegness). Wainfleet Sands itself had been in use as an RAF bombing range since 1938. During the Second World War it was regularly used by 5 Group and notably, had been used by 617 (Dambusters) Squadron at various times. It seems likely that by late-1943, Wainfleet fulfilled an air-to-air and other US-fighter general gunnery training need, while Snettisham, designated as 1 Combat Crew Gunnery School (1 CCGS), specialised in ground-to-air firing practice for US bomber gunners (Freeman states specifically: B-17 gunners). With 'traffic' in The Wash at its current level and rising, it was now impractical to carry out this latter activity as an entirely airborne operation. Brest Sand continued to soak up both inert US practice bombs and discarded live loads, while Holbeach Marsh, as described in the previous chapter, served CGS – which itself included some USAAF fighter pilots and air gunners among its pupils – and other RAF needs.

Having decided to do something to improve its air gunnery, the 8th AF found it had neither targets nor target-towing aircraft with which to achieve it. Turning to the RAF for assistance, a US target-towing organisation soon became operational from mid-1943, using mainly Westland Lysanders and a few Miles Masters transferred from RAF towing units. They even acquired at least a couple of venerable Defiant TT4s, which are believed to have seen service over Snettisham range at some time.

Of the three US target-towing units originally established, 2nd and 3rd Gunnery & Tow Target Flights (2 & 3 G&TTF) were activated at RAF Goxhill on the Lincolnshire coast north of Grimsby and regularly flew target-towing sorties over The Wash. The third unit, 1 G&TTF, began life in Wales in August 1943 but from May to November 1944, took up residence at RAF Sutton Bridge when CGS had moved out and from where it co-operated with 1 CCGS at Snettisham.

It was during this period that American-built Vultee A-35B Vengeance aeroplanes were assigned to Tow Flights as the standard replacement for their ageing Lysander and Master tugs. Originally designed as a two-seat dive-bomber, the Vengeance was supplied by the USA to the RAF early in the war, serving principally in the Far East. It was mainly the later Mark IV (RAF) version which, being surplus to requirements, was converted for target-towing duties. Some Vengeance aircraft were transferred to the USAAF while still retaining their RAF roundels, including those which served with 1 G&TTF at

Sutton Bridge. Evidence of the latter is provided by a photograph of Vengeance A-35B 41-31384 (formerly RAF Mk IV, FD195) taken on 12 June 1944 near Castle Rising. Engine failure *en route* Sutton Bridge to Snettisham forced 2/Lt Maurice J. Harper to crash land 41-31384 at Knights Hill, fortunately with only minor injuries to himself and his winch operator, Cpl Theo Brand.

When, in late April 1944, Central Gunnery School moved north it left RAF Sutton Bridge facing an uncertain future for the first time in a number of years. Such was the scale of air war operations in the area around The Wash that coupled with other factors such as the physical constraints of the grass airfield, and the long-term demand for aircrew slowing down, a major review of its role became inevitable. However, RAF Sutton Bridge had, as has been shown, performed its wartime duty with an enviable vitality and was, despite its limited size, functioning as a well-oiled establishment. This latter situation was due in no small part to the succession of exceedingly able and energetic Station and Unit Commanders.

In fact, the future of RAF Sutton Bridge was assured for a few years yet but would now become largely dependent upon its neighbour, RAF Peterborough.

Home to 7 (Pilot) Advanced Flying Unit (7 (P) AFU), with about 130 Miles Masters, 15 Hurricanes and more than 200 pilots to cope with, resources at Peterborough, too, were really stretched to the limit at this time. (P) AFU flying training programmes were designed to bring the basic flying skills of pilots trained under the Empire Air Training Scheme up to European theatre standards. In effect, overseas-trained pilots were shown in about four weeks how to (try to) cope with operating in poor weather, at night in the blackout and to navigate under wartime conditions.

In January 1944 discussions had already taken place between RAF Peterborough and RAF College SFTS, one of Cranwell's resident units, with a view to doing a swop of location to try to relieve the pressure. It was decided, however, that this move was not a practical proposition. Furthermore, on 4 February 1944, word came down from on high that 7 (P) AFU would have to undertake the duties of parent unit for a Care and Maintenance party which was to take over RAF Sutton Bridge when CGS moved out. In true military style, before C&M was implemented the brass hats changed their minds! Sutton Bridge was now allotted as satellite station to 16 (Polish) SFTS based at RAF Newton (Nottingham) but only for the duration of repair work to the latter's airfield surface.

Despite this somewhat confused situation, at least it meant flying training would continue at Sutton Bridge, but the harsh realities of the profession were never far away. 'Rookie' pilots hadn't changed much over the years and within a month all three of the above-mentioned units (7 (P) AFU; RAFC SFTS and 16 (P) SFTS) had sustained casualties, some fatal, within the region.

While associated with 16 (P) SFTS several Miles Masters and a Polish pilot course were transferred from Newton to Sutton Bridge. It was not long before it was quite like the old days of 6 OTU with the Poles 'dropping in' again on local farmland. Eight crashes, including one fatal, were recorded by this Polish unit while based at Sutton Bridge between 13 March and 16 May. Even averaging one mishap per week was, sadly, not at all excessive by contemporary flying training standards. About one month after the fatal accident – when on 16 May 1944 LAC Zbigniew Modest Czaplicki in Master II DK857 spun in at Long Sutton – the detachments from RAF Newton ended. LAC Czaplicki was buried in the Polish War cemetery in Newark, Nottingham.

Yet another change of system on 21 June saw night flying training for 7 (P) AFU – previously conducted from Peterborough airfield – with occasional use of Sibson and Wittering – also being transferred to RAF Sutton Bridge. This was only a temporary relief arrangement for Peterborough as shortly afterwards Sutton Bridge actually went onto a Care & Maintenance basis under the command of Flt Lt W. F. Carson, pending yet another re-assessment of its future. This inactivity, however, did not stop Sutton Bridge becoming a haven of refuge for B-17 43-37799 after it had suffered battle damage and crash-landed on the airfield on 8 July.

It was the demise of Peterborough's current satellite, RAF Sibson, which finally brought this C&M period to a close in August 1944 and with it brought a modicum of stability for a further couple of years. Two main factors were responsible for this change. First, on 4 July, in order to speed up throughput of aircrew, the basis of flying training at 7 (P) AFU Peterborough changed to a 'course-based' system. This meant that each 'Flight' at Peterborough was made responsible for both day and night training of a complete 'course' of (at that time) about thirty-seven pilots for a four-week period. Various administrative changes were also proposed, all with the aim of using main and satellite airfields more effectively, particularly in respect of accommodation issues. Second, at the end of July, Sibson airfield's grass surface, having taken a lot of wear and tear, was declared unfit for use and in need of re-seeding. This was a lengthy, time-consuming process so Flying Training Command took the easier option by giving up Sibson and declaring that Sutton Bridge, being immediately available, would take on the role of satellite airfield for RAF Peterborough. This decision was implemented on 8 August 1944 although Sibson actually still remained designated as a relief landing ground (RLG).

It was on that day (8 August) that Gp Capt James Ramage (Jimmy) Addams AFC, OC RAF Peterborough, had the misfortune to become one of his own accident statistics. Taking off in Hurricane AG284, after visiting his new satellite station, the engine cut out at 50 feet and he had to force-land just outside the airfield perimeter with the wheels up. Between July and September, mishaps involving Masters from 7 (P)AFU flying from both Peterborough and Sutton Bridge continued to occur at regular intervals. Of the seven recorded, three had fatal consequences.

Activity at the (P) AFU peaked by mid-1944 after which output from the overseas schools began to reduce. Such was the optimism about the outcome of the war that by the end of 1944 the Empire Air Training scheme was virtually at an end. With fewer conversion students to cater for, the specific task of 7 (P) AFU itself also drew to a close. Pilot training continued, of course, but at Peterborough it now took on a more general and extended nature than before.

In September 1944 there was yet another change for Sutton Bridge. Ever destined to be associated with foreign pilot training, RAF Sutton Bridge's final lease of life was now as home to part of the intake for No.1 Course of what became known as the 'French SFTS'.

Fifteen new instructors were posted in from RAF Newton on 13 September for the specific purpose of training French pilots at Sutton Bridge. Airspeed Oxford twin-engine trainer aeroplanes would be transferred to the airfield although, at least initially, servicing work on them would have to be carried out at Peterborough. By mid-November there were sufficient aeroplanes located at Sutton Bridge to equip three Oxford Flights, plus a few specialist Oxfords for bombing and beam-approach duties and some Masters for gunnery training. Over at Peterborough another three Flights had also been established, equipped with the Miles Master III.

At this point a final major organisational change occurred when 7 (P) AFU was re-titled 7 SFTS and the term 'French SFTS' disappeared. By the time No.1 Course of thirty-two pilots passed out in February 1945, the pattern of training for the French pilots had evolved into single-engine students (equal to one-third of the course complement) based at Peterborough and twin-engine students (equal to two-thirds) at Sutton Bridge. Miles Masters were gradually phased out, up to June 1945, being replaced by the North American Harvard trainer.

Ken Taylor, a former Air Training Corps (ATC) cadet with 1406 Squadron ATC, Holbeach Detached Flight, remembered this period as a very happy time. 'RAF Sutton Bridge was an open house to us cadets,' he said.

> We used to bike to the airfield most Sundays, show our '3822' cadet identity book and went up in anything that was going. I had been in the ATC since the days of 56 OTU and CGS and had loads of trips in Maggies [Magisters], Tiger Moths, Battle and Lysander target tugs, Hampdens and Wellingtons. On one or two sorties in the latter I had a chance to sit in the rear turret and watch the Spits beat us up. Great times!

Ken also recalled one particular trip in a 7 SFTS Oxford with a French pupil and an English instructor. The instructors spoke little or no French and vice versa, so, with his schoolboy French, Ken found himself acting as interpreter on more than one occasion. One quite unnerving experience occurred while Ken sat on the main spar watching the pupil bringing the Oxford in for a landing.

> If the undercart was not down as the aircraft dropped below 100 feet, then a klaxon hooter would sound off as a warning. This student was concentrating so intensely that he either just didn't hear or simply ignored the klaxon wailing. In the end the instructor knocked the pupil's hands away from the controls and aborted the landing and I had to explain to the distraught Frenchman what was going on!

While epitomising this period of Sutton Bridge history, one fatal air accident in particular also played its part in forging a permanent bond between the community and the French nation. Among over sixty military headstones arranged in their neat rows in the village churchyard, stands a cross bearing the inscription:

MOITESSIER C. G.
MATELOT. FRENCH AIR FORCE
MORT POUR LA FRANCE
LE 13.8.1945

The war was over but No.6 (French) Course of 7 SFTS was well into its stride. From Sutton Bridge on 13 August 1945, Oxford PH414 took off, with Caporal-chef Vincent Maestracci and Matelot Charles Georges Moitessier aboard. Briefed for a routine dual sortie of 45-minutes duration in the local area, they were to land at the end of that time and change places, prior to making another sortie. It was quite usual for competent pupils to be briefed to fly as a crew without the presence of an instructor and Maestracci had already been under training for at least ten weeks.

This exercise was destined never to be completed. Nearing the village of Clenchwarton, PH414 was last seen emerging from low cloud in a spin from which it did not recover. Hitting the ground on East Anglian Farm at speed, it was completely destroyed and both Frenchmen died instantly. Despite speculation, as on so many occasions, no real cause for the accident could be established. Maestracci's body was returned to his home on Corsica for burial while Moitessier, whose family home was in Morocco, was buried with full military honours in St Matthew's churchyard.

In the immediate post-war years, in common with towns and villages across the nation, monuments to the fallen were being erected. Particularly with its connections to the RAF airfield, Sutton Bridge was no exception and the churchyard of St Matthew, last resting place of so many brave young men from all parts of the world, was honoured with a Commonwealth War Grave Memorial Cross. At a ceremony in 1947, this memorial was unveiled and consecrated. Making the long journey from his home in Casablanca to be present on that emotional occasion was Monsieur Henri Moitessier, father of the young pilot killed two years earlier.

Returning now to that chilly morning at RAF Peterborough in November 1945, it was to a stirring rendition of *La Marseillaise*, played by 21 Group HQ Band, that the review programme began in the more comfortable climate of one of the hangars.

Gp Capt J. R. Addams AFC, OC 7 SFTS, opened proceedings with his course report. Providing a useful insight to the organisation of the SFTS at that time, he referred to courses being divided into two Squadrons: 1 Squadron, stationed at Peterborough, trained with single-engine Harvards, while 2 Squadron, based at Sutton Bridge, used twin-engine Oxford aeroplanes. Nine pupils, he said, had passed on Harvards and eighteen on Oxfords. Names of these graduates and the senior officers present at the ceremony, are listed in the accompanying table (*see* below).

General De Vitrolles then presented Wings and certificates and addressed his fellow countrymen. AM Coningham, in his own speech, said it gave him particular pleasure, on this his first engagement in his new post, to be among Frenchmen once again. He reminded his audience that he had had French squadrons under his command in North Africa and after the invasion, with 2TAF in Europe. General De Vitrolles took the salute at the march-past of all units present and the afternoon closed with VIPs being entertained to tea in the Sergeants' Mess.

No.6 (French) Course, RAF Peterborough, 6 November 1945. Passing Out Parade Reviewing Officers:
Air Marshal Sir Arthur Coningham, AOC Flying Training Command, RAF.
General-de-Brigade De Vitrolles, AOC Training, French AF.
Air Commodore J. G. Hawtry, AOC 21 Group RAF.
Air Commodore J. West VC, Director Allied & Foreign Liason RAF.
Colonel Coustie, C-in-C French AF in England.

Senior Staff of 7 SFTS RAF Peterborough and RAF Sutton Bridge:
Group Captain J. R. Addams, Station Commander RAF Peterborough and OC 7 SFTS.
Commandant Feuvrier, OC French Personnel at 7 SFTS.
Wing Commander J. H. M. Smith, Chief Flying Instructor.
Wing Commander D. Kinnear, OC RAF Sutton Bridge.
Wing Commander F. Stevens, Chief Technical Officer.
Squadron Leader C. J. Rose, Chief Ground Instructor.
Squadron Leader B. Ruffell, OC 1 Sqn 7 SFTS (RAF Peterborough).
Squadron Leader L. S. Holman, OC 2 Sqn 7 SFTS (RAF Sutton Bridge). [Note: This is the same Leslie Stephen Holman who, when a Sergeant, rescued a small boy from the River Nene way back in 1931].

Graduates of 7 SFTS, No.6 (French) Course. 6 November 1945.

1 Sqn (Harvard) Peterborough	2 Sqn (Oxford) Sutton Bridge.
Sous/Lt J. Regnier	Sous/Lt M. Carreras
Sgt G. Desseaux	Sgt P. L. Bex
Sgt J. Cave	Sgt M. Biskup
Sgt P. J. Cazaty	Sgt P. G. V. Bousquet
Sgt P. Chaucard	Sgt G. J. Combes
Sgt P. Guilland	Sgt C. A. Debono

Sgt J. J. P. Guilhemdebat
Sgt E. Mestre
Sgt J. Picard
Sgt R. L. B. Saint-Martin

Sgt L. M. Giguelay
Sgt R. L. V. Jourdain
Sgt M. F. Pedespan
Sgt J. M. E. Souillard
S/M H. Bartolomei
S/M P. G. Y. Bouchet
S/M R. L. M. Cadoux
S/M M. J. D. Caron
S/M Y. Guillou
S/M H. P. E. Hostachy
S/M A. M. Rolin

The value of flying training undertaken by both RAF Sutton Bridge and Peterborough at this period cannot be overstated, since from aircrew trained at these two airfields was born the nucleus of post-war French military aviation.

In April 1946, as military exigencies shrank, RAF Sutton Bridge and RAF Peterborough were required to perform their sterling service no longer. Both stations were stood down from active flying duties when 7 SFTS moved north to occupy RAF Kirton Lindsey.

In the case of RAF Sutton Bridge, the airfield at the heart of this story, twenty years of flying history had come to a close. After the flying units ceased to use the airfield, the station drifted in the doldrums on an RAF C&M basis for many years, the premises at one time being utilised by the British Army as Northern Command Signals HQ, while some of the buildings were used as a furniture and equipment store for Bomber Command.

A modicum of aviation-related life returned during 1954 with Sutton Bridge becoming home to 58 Maintenance Unit (58 MU) from 20 July 1954, when an advance party of 50 RAF personnel arrived under the command of Wg Cdr William Cunliffe OBE. He was replaced during April 1956 by Wg Cdr Frederick John Walters MBE, who appears to be the final station commander of RAF Sutton Bridge.

Occupying the station until 31 October 1957, this last RAF unit, 58 MU, was mainly occupied as a repair and salvage unit, which had a Rolls Royce Derwent Engine Field Servicing section operating from the hangars while out on the airfield surplus aeroplanes were broken up by the sledge-hammer-wielding airmen of the Salvage & Recovery section.

They not only went out to recover crashed aircraft in the east of England between the Thames and the Humber but also broke up some of the last unwanted Lancaster bombers for scrap to be carted off by lorries to civilian scrap-metal dealers.

Vacated again, the aerodrome property remained in Air Ministry hands until 1962 when the 289-acre site was sold to the Ministry of Agriculture and then gradually rented out for various farming and industrial uses. In 2019, what became known as the Wingland Enterprise Park continues to flourish and even with the huge power station next to it, still has plenty of room for expansion. Meanwhile, Holbeach range continued to operate as an air weapons range and, under the control of RAF Marham, indeed it remains fully operational in its RAF and NATO capacity to the present day. It is true to say that since the end of the Second World War the sky over the district has never lost its affinity with aviation, both through its attractiveness as a flying training area and through its proximity to The Wash range.

Although Sutton Bridge and Peterborough had been closed for flying operations, there was no let-up in the post-war RAF pilot training programme throughout the region and in many ways, events of subsequent years brought with them constant reminders of days gone by. For example, back in 1926, until the airfield at Sutton Bridge had got into its stride, aircraft using Holbeach range originally operated directly from their home bases. This was how it would be in the future, with range visitors coming not only from airfields all over the UK but also from mainland Europe. Other reminders of past eras came with Canadian and American pilots returning to use airspace around The Wash, as did pilots from RAF squadrons that have featured earlier in this story. To complete that sense of change and continuity, the range itself, now designated RAF Holbeach and encompassing an area of 16 square miles including a small domestic site – still located in Durham's Lane near the sea bank – and observation towers, is an RAF station in its own right, run by a government department under the title of Defence Infrastructure Organisation, Holbeach Air Weapons Range. It is one of five air weapons ranges currently operating in the UK.

Although Harvard aircraft had left Sutton Bridge and Peterborough, their distinctive 'buzz-saw' drone could still be heard across the Fens for the remainder of the 1940s. Harvard IIb were operated by 3 FTS at RAF Feltwell to the east, 7 FTS at RAF Cottesmore to the west and by the RAF College at Cranwell to the north, so fenland skies were, as ever, an aerial playground for student pilots. The Wash region in the 1950s was a veritable spotter's paradise, too. Growling Rolls-Royce Merlin and Griffon engines gave way to the *whoosh* of RR Derwent or De Havilland Goblin and Ghost jet engines as the propeller age changed to the jet age. Still encircled by active airfields in the early 1950s, for a while, props would remain in evidence at the Flying Training Schools. Harvards, for example, gave way to the Percival Prentice T1 at RAF Feltwell, Boulton Paul Balliol T2s entered service with both 7 FTS and CFS at RAF West Raynham and RAF College Cranwell, while the latter also operated DH Chipmunk and Percival Provost trainers, all of which graced fenland skies day after day.

On the other hand, Meteor F4 and T7 jets were filtering through to Advanced Flying Schools such as 206 AFS at RAF Oakington, several of whose aircraft were lost in accidents around The Wash in the early 1950s. Later in that decade, the arrival of De Havilland's Vampire T11 and FB5, at RAF Swinderby, Cranwell and Oakington, extended jet training across the region. Meteor F8 day fighters were in front-line service, for example, with 56 Squadron at RAF Waterbeach and 92 Squadron at RAF Coningsby, while night fighter Vampire NF10s of 253 Squadron at Waterbeach and Venom NF2 aircraft from 23 Squadron at Coltishall, were regular sights even in daytime. It is not surprising, therefore, that air activity around The Wash was as intense as ever.

Of course, the political climate, too, played its part in deciding which aircraft could be seen in the region. In the early 1950s, for example, the Korean War occupied the attention and resources of both Britain and the US. In order to strengthen NATO aircraft guarding Europe at this volatile time, the RCAF was called upon to deploy a number of squadrons to England and, in February 1952, 1 Fighter Wing RCAF took up residence at RAF North Luffenham, Rutland. Thus, in addition to the usual RAF inventory, an exciting new shape in the form of the swept-wing Canadair Sabre Mk 2 – US North American F-86 Sabres built under licence – could be seen frequently traversing the fens and The Wash, often at 40,000-plus feet altitude. The Canadians remained at Luffenham for almost three years, during which there was the inevitable crop of accidents before the Wing re-deployed to France and Germany at the end of 1954.

Although US bombers had been based in England since the early 1950s, it was not until about 1957 that the enforced removal of foreign aircraft from French soil meant US fighter types would once again grace Fenland skies. Thereafter the Wash ranges witnessed a procession of USAF fast jets, beginning, for example, with Republic F-84F Thunderstreaks of 81 Fighter Bomber Wing (FBW) from Shepherds Grove. The catalogue of Holbeach range users continues through the 1960s with F-100D Super Sabres, principally those from 20 Tactical Fighter Wing (TFW) Wethersfield and 48 TFW Lakenheath, together with F-101C Voodoos from 81 TFW Bentwaters. Each of these units suffered losses due to air accidents in The Wash area during the 1960s. By 1965, 10 Tactical Reconnaissance Wing (TRW), operating from Alconbury airbase, had traded in its RB-66s for the ubiquitous F-4 Phantom and its RF-4C models became a regular sight and sound for the next fifteen years as they smoked down the Rivers Welland and Nene, day and night, heading for Holbeach and Wainfleet ranges. In contrast, many other US types could be observed at higher altitudes tracking north to south or vice versa, heading into or climbing out of the massive USAF base at RAF Mildenhall on the southern edge of the fens. Among those most frequently seen were Boeing KC-135 tankers, C-141 Starlifter and Lockheed C-5 Galaxy, but in recent years of the 21st century these are no longer seen and have been largely replaced by occasional views of McDonnell-Douglas C-17 Globemaster III, the ubiquitous Lockheed C-130 Hercules transport and the exotic-looking Bell-Boeing V-22 Osprey.

It is a pity that misfortune has had to be one of the routes by which some of the course of this story is charted, for such incidents are often sensationalised by the media in a way that misrepresents those involved and distorts the wider picture. This story has shown that the human price of defending the sky in such a professional way is high, but Trenchard's legacy – that 'quality in men, machines, training and organisation' – mentioned at the very outset of this story, has stood the test of time and should not be forgotten.

As for the village of Sutton Bridge, it no longer echoes with the foreign voices of airmen in uniforms of different hues, seen strolling down that long main street or in the bars of local pubs. There are, though, in 2019 still plenty of foreign tongues to be heard all over the district – a legacy of Britain's membership of the EU. This is an emotive issue in these parts, but one that should prompt us at least to remember the debt we owe to the previous generation of Continental Europeans who passed this way all those years ago.

Apart from the remnants of old buildings – such as that first rigid hangar, both Married Officers Quarters houses, squash court and air raid shelters and one of the two Bellman hangars – signs of the airfield itself are slowly fading away under industrial development, not least of which is the massive gas-fired power station. The sound of aeroplanes, such as RAF Typhoon and USAF F-15 jets and soon perhaps the new Lockheed F-35 Lightning II, still crackles above the old airfield, their crews following the river down to the range just as their predecessors did more than ninety years ago, when they were aiming to be Top Guns.

On 1 September 1993 a memorial dedicated to all those who served at RAF Sutton Bridge was unveiled on a grassed area by the side of the Cross Keys Bridge, just a stone's throw from the old airfield. In glorious sunshine, without a cloud in the sky, the memorial was blessed by the Padre of RAF Marham. Then Ernest Mottram, the first airman to arrive at RAF Sutton Bridge all those years ago in 1926, together with Martin Cowley, at age 13 the youngest ATC cadet from 272 (Wisbech) Squadron, drew back a pale blue sheet to reveal the memorial. It is a brick plinth surmounted by a slightly bent metal propeller blade, the product of a recovery dig by FAWNAPS, from 56 OTU Hurricane, L2529, which crashed on 21 March 1941. Its pilot, Sgt R. W. 'Dick' Read, survived the mishap by baling out before his aeroplane crashed at Tilney St Lawrence.

Now all heads turned skywards as the unmistakable growl of a Merlin grew ever louder, until a lone Spitfire (a Mk V, AB910 of the BBMF) swooped low over the crowd, the pilot making two passes over Cross Keys Bridge and the former airfield so familiar to his forebears. Finally, Jack Flint, another Sutton Bridge 'old boy', read the Act of Homage before a bugler played *Last Post* and *Reveille*.

Station & Unit Commanders at Sutton Bridge

Armament Practice Camp

1926   Flt Lt Andrew Ronald Mackenzie.
1927   Sqn Ldr Anthony Rex Arnold DSC DFC.
1928   Sqn Ldr William Sowrey DFC AFC.
1929   Sqn Ldr Cyril Bertram Cooke.
1930   Wg Cdr Dermott Lang Allen AFC.
1931   Wg Cdr Kenneth Caron Buss OBE.

No.3 Armament Training Camp

1932 & 1933   Wg Cdr William Sowrey DFC AFC.
1934   Wg Cdr Frederick Sowrey DSO MC AFC.
1935 to 25 Aug   Sqn Ldr Charles Ley King MC DFC.
1935 from 26 Aug
  to 30 Nov 1937   Wg Cdr Harry Augustus Smith MC.

No.3 Armament Training School

Dec 1937 to Feb 1938   Wg Cdr Harry Augustus Smith MC.
Mar 1938 to Jul 1939   Wg Cdr Frank Ormond Soden DFC.
Aug 1939 to 2 Sep 1939 Wg Cdr John Melbourne Mason
                          DSC DFC.

RAF Sutton Bridge

2–9 Sept 1939   Flt Lt R. P. Smillie   Care &
                                                Maintenance.

10 Sep 1939 to   Flt Lt H. N. Hawker   No.3 Recruit
  31 Oct 1939   Training Pool.

1 Nov 1939 to Jun 1940	Wg Cdr Philip Reginald Barwell DFC	254/264/266 Sqns & 6 OTU.
Jun 1940 to 20 Aug 1940	Gp Capt Henry Dunboyne O'Neill AFC	6 OTU.
20 Aug 1940 to 10 Jun 1941	Gp Capt Bruce Bernard Caswell	6/56 OTU.
10 Jun 1941 to 24 Sep 1941	Gp Capt Frank Ormond Soden DFC	56 OTU.
25 Sep 1941 to Apr 1942	Gp Capt Ian A. Bertram	56 OTU/CGS.
7 May 1942 to 5 Sep 1942	Gp Capt Claud Hilton Keith	CGS.
5 Sep 1942 to 26 Nov 1943	Gp Capt Charles St John Beamish DFC	CGS.
26 Nov 1943 to March 1944(?)	Gp Capt Michael Harrington Dwyer CB CBE	CGS.
March 1944 to August 1944	Flt Lt W. F. Carson	C & M.
Aug 1944 to April 1946	Wg Cdr David Kinnear AFC AFM	7 SFTS.
May 1946 to July 1954	Care & Maintenance.	
20 July 1954 to March 1956	Wg Cdr William Cunliffe OBE	58 MU.
April 1956 to 31 October 1957	Wg Cdr Frederick John Walters MBE	58 MU.

Officers Commanding 6 OTU at RAF Sutton Bridge

(22 Jan 1940 St Athan) to

9 June 1940	Sqn Ldr Philip Campbell Pinkham.
9 June 1940 to 27 April 1941	Wg Cdr John Humphrey Edwardes-Jones.
27 April 1941 to 8 Dec 1941	Wg Cdr Harold John Maguire.

8 Dec 1941 to 23 Feb 1942	Wg Cdr George Desmond Garvin.
23 Feb 1942 to (27 March 1942 to Tealing)	Sqn Ldr John Morton Littler.

Officers Commanding, Pilot Gunnery Instructor (Fighter) Training Wing, CGS

Mar 1942 (Wittering) to Sep 1942	Wg Cdr Adolf Gysbert Malan.
Sep 1942 to Dec 1942	Wg Cdr Peter Russell Walker.
Dec 1942 to Jun 1943	Wg Cdr James Rankin.
Jun 1943 to Oct 1943	Wg Cdr Peter Russell Walker.
Oct 1943 to (Feb 1944 to Catfoss)	Wg Cdr Alan Christopher Deere.

Chief Instructors, Pilot Gunnery Instructor (Fighter) Training Wing, CGS

Feb 1942 (Wittering) to Sep 1942	Sqn Ldr Allan Richard Wright.
Oct 1942 to Feb 1943	Sqn Ldr Peter William LeFevre.
Feb 1943 to Jun 1943	Sqn Ldr Thomas Balmforth.
Jun 1943 to Sep 1943	Sqn Ldr Robert Chippindall Dafforn (Killed).
Sep 1943 to (Feb 1944)	Sqn Ldr Archibald Winskill.

Officers Commanding, Gunnery Leader (Bomber) Wing, CGS

Feb 1942 (Chelveston) to Jun 1942	Wg Cdr John Mortimer Warfield.
Jun 1942 to Jun 1943	Wg Cdr J. J. Sutton.
Jun 1943 to Dec 1943	Wg Cdr John Churchill Claydon.
Dec 1943 to (Feb 1944)	Wg Cdr Arthur Ernest Lowe.

Chief Instructors, Gunnery Leader (Bomber) Wing CGS

Feb 1942 (Chelveston) to Aug 1942	Sqn Ldr C. A. Potter.
Aug 1942 to June 1943	Sqn Ldr Kenneth Montague Bastin.
Jun 1943 to (Feb 1944)	Sqn Ldr W. E. Nicholas.

Postings of Pilots from No. 6 OTU Sutton Bridge between 6 March and 31 October 1940

*= In from 11 Group Pool, St Athan, out from 6 OTU Sutton Bridge.
F = fought in Battle of France; B = fought in Battle of Britain; X = Neither.
Spellings of names and Squadrons/Units shown are as recorded in 6 OTU ORB at date of posting.
The year is 1940, except where shown.

Name	Date IN	Date OUT	To Sqn Number	Battles
F/L M. L. Robinson*	30 Jan 39	16 March 40	87	FB.
P/O D. S. Scott*	1 Feb	16 March	73	FB.
P/O J. B. Ashton*	1 Feb	21 March	85	FB.
P/O P. V. Boot*	1 Feb	23 March	1	FB.
F/O C. F. G. Adye*	2 Oct 39	25 April 40	213	F.
P/O O. E. Lamb*	? March	13 April	1 AAS	B.
Sgt G. Tock*	? March	25 April	7 B&GS	X.
P/O R. H. Dibnah*	11 March	26 April	1	FB.
P/O G. E. Goodman*	11 March	26 April	1	FB.
P/O C. M. Stavart*	11 March	26 April	1	FB.
P/O H. W. Eliot*	11 March	26 April	73	FB.
P/O A. McFadden*	11 March	26 April	73	FB.

Name	Date IN	Date OUT	To Sqn Number	Battles
P/O V. D. M. Roe*	11 March	26 April	73	F.
P/O R. D. Rutter*	11 March	26 April	73	FB.
Sgt L. Y. T. Friend*	11 March	26 April	73	F.
P/O D. H. Wissler*	11 March	26 April	85	FB.
P/O P. L. Jarvis*	11 March	26 April	87	F.
P/O A. E. LeBreuilly*	11 March	26 April	87	F.
Sgt E. J. K. Penikett*	11 March	26 April	?	X.
Sgt K. N. V. Townsend*	11 March	26 April	607	F.
Sgt H. D. B. Jones*	? Feb	1 May	504	B.
Fg Off F. R. Carey	2 May	10 May	3	FB.
P/O B. P. Legge*	28 Feb	11 May	73	FB.
P/O J. J. Le Roux	?	17 May	85	F.
Sgt J. Wright	11 March	6 July	79	B.
Sgt L. F. Ralls	? April	7 May	607	FB.
Sgt J. H. Terras	?	9 May	1	X.
P/O C. A. McGaw	28 April	11 May	73	FB.
P/O J. E. P. Thompson	28 April	11 May	73	F.
P/O F. Sydenham	28 April	11 May	73	F.
P/O N. C. Langham-Hobart	28 April	11 May	73	FB.
P/O A. E. Scott	28 April	11 May	73	FB.
Sgt A. E. Marshall	?	11 May	73	FB.
F/O W. G. New	4–8 April	12 May	17	F.
P/O G. C. T. Carthew	4–8 April	12 May	17	B.
P/O P. O. D. Alcock	28 April	12 May	17	B.
P/O H. G. Hardman	29 April	15 May	111	B.
P/O N. N. Campbell	4–8 April	15 May	32	FB.
P/O A. R. M. Campbell	28 April	15 May	54	B.
P/O W. P. Hopkin	28 April	15 May	54	B.
P/O A. J. Smith	28 April	15 May	74	B.
P/O D. Hastings	28 April	15 May	74	B.

Name	Date IN	Date OUT	To Sqn Number	Battles
P/O M. Rook	28 April	15 May	504	FB.
P/O A. L. B. Raven	28 April	15 May	610	X.
P/O J. D. Smith	13 May	15 May	73	FB.
P/O J. H. R. Young	28 April	15 May	74	B.
P/O I. A. H. Stewart	28 April	15 May	?	X.
P/O J. Brewster	28 April	15 May	615	B.
P/O L. H. Casson	28 April	15 May	501	FB.
P/O T. B Murray	28 April	15 May	79	FB.
Sgt D. F. Corfe	28 April	15 May	73	FB.
Sgt H. H. Chandler	28 April	15 May	501	FB.
Sgt P. O'Byrne	28 April	15 May	73	FB.
Sgt W. A. Wilkinson	28 April	15 May	501	FB.
Sgt G. W. Brimble	28 April	15 May	242	FB.
P/O J. Lockhart	14 May	24 May	85	B.
P/O H. J. Walsh	28 April	15 May	?	X.
P/O P. L. Gossage	14 May	24 May	85	X.
P/O J. L. Bickerdyke	14 May	24 May	85	B.
P/O W. H. Hodgson	14 May	24 May	85	B.
Sgt J. H. M. Ellis	18 May	24 May	85	B.
Sgt E. R. Webster	18 May	24 May	85	B.
P/O C. E. English	18 May	25 May	85	B.
Sgt W. R. Evans	18 May	25 May	85	FB.
P/O D. C. Leary	18 May	25 May	17	FB.
P/O J. K. Ross	18 May	25 May	17	FB.
Sgt D. Fopp	18 May	25 May	17	FB.
Sgt G. Griffiths	18 May	25 May	17	FB.
P/O H. W. Cottam	18 May	25 May	213	B.
P/O J. E. P. Laricheliere	18 May	25 May	213	B.
Sgt G. D. Bushell	18 May	25 May	213	B.
Sgt I. K. J. Bidgood	18 May	25 May	213	B.
Sgt E. G. Snowden	18 May	25 May	213	B.

Name	Date IN	Date OUT	To Sqn Number	Battles
Sgt H. S. Newton	18 May	25 May	111	B.
Sgt R. A. Spyer	18 May	25 May	111	B.
S/L N. C. Odbert	23 May	31 May	64	B.
S/L P. Pinkham	17 Jan 39	9 June	19	B.
F/L G. D. M. Blackwood	20 May	5 June	213	B.
F/L W. W. Loxton	20 May	5 June	25	B.
S/L P. H. Smith	22 May	5 June	213	X.
F/L P. A. N. Cox	17 Jan 39	6 June 40	501	FB.
P/O C. A. C. Chetham	27 May	6 June	1	B.
P/O E. G. Parkin	27 May	6 June	501	FB.
P/O R. S. Don	26 May	6 June	501	FB.
Sgt E. Richardson	28 May	6 June	242	FB.
Sgt A. D. Meredith	26 May	6 June	1	FB.
F/Sgt R. V. Ellis	27 May	6 June	73	FB.
Sgt J. A. Porter	27 May	6 June	1	FB.
Sgt H. G. Webster	27 May	6 June	73	FB.
Sgt F. J. P. Dixon	26 May	6 June	501	FB.
P/O D. N. W. L. Anthony	28 May	6 June	73	F.
F/O R. E. Drake	1 June	6 June	BAFF via Hendon	F.
F/L A. W. A. Bayne	27 June 39	8 June 40	17	B.
S/L J. W. McGuire	1 June	8 June	A&AEE	X.
P/O J. W. Hamill	28 May	8 June	229	B.
P/O D. B. H. McHardy	28 May	8 June	229	B.
Sgt G. N. Wilkes	26 May	8 June	213	B.
Sgt R. D. Dunscombe	26 May	8 June	213	B.
Sgt J. H. Dickinson	27 May	8 June	253	B.
Sgt E. H. C. Kee	27 May	8 June	253	B.
Sgt J. Metham	28 May	8 June	253	B.
P/O W. G. Dickie	27 May	8 June	601	B.
Sgt F. J. Cullen	26 May	9 June	145	X.

Name	Date IN	Date OUT	To Sqn Number	Battles
Sgt J. P. Mills	26 May	9 June	43	B.
Sgt G. C. Brunner	2 June	9 June	43	B.
Sgt A. H. D. Pond	27 May	9 June	601	B.
P/O D. J. Gorrie	27 May	9 June	43	B.
P/O J. Cruttenden	28 May	9 June	43	B.
F/O T. Grier	28 May	9 June	601	B.
S/L H. A. V. Hogan	6 June	15 June	501	B.
S/L T. G. Lovell-Gregg	27 May	15 June	87	B.
F/L T. F. D. Morgan	4 June	15 June	43	B.
P/O C. O. J. Pegge	27 May	15 June	610	B.
P/O F. T. Gardiner	1 June	15 June	610	B.
F/L A. C. Rabagliati	28 May	15 June	46	B.
Sgt C. A. Parsons	27 May	15 June	610	B.
S/L H. C. Sawyer	27 May	15 June	7 OTU	B.
P/O B. V. Rees	28 May	16 June	610	B.
P/O W. H. Millington	1 June	17 June	79	B.
P/O A. G. Osmand	1 June	17 June	213	B.
P/O C. D. Francis	2 June	17 June	253	B.
P/O L. W. Stevens	8 June	17 June	17	B.
P/O G. H. E. Welford	1 June	17 June	607	B.
Sgt R. J. Ommaney	2 June	17 June	229	B.
F/L A. D. Murray	1 June	17 June	46	B.
F/O W. H. Stratton	28 May	17 June	to S Rhodesia	F.
Sgt W. C. Wills	3 June	23 June	3	B.
P/O P. G. Thornton-Brown	3 June	23 June	263	X.
F/O J. R. Tobin	3 June	23 June	263	X.
P/O A. O. Moffett	3 June	23 June	263	X.
P/O R. F. Ferdinand	3 June	23 June	263	B.
P/O H. N. Hunt	3 June	23 June	263	B.
F/L A. R. Putt	2 June	24 June	501	B.

Name	Date IN	Date OUT	To Sqn Number	Battles
Sgt C. F. Cotton	2 June	25 June	KOAS	X.
F/L G. S. Powell-Shedden	15 June	30 June	242	B.
P/O A. J. Haggar	2 June	1 July	Sch of Air Nav	X.
P/O P. V. Ayerst	14 June	3 July	7 OTU instr	F.
S/L W. F. C. Hobson	4 June	4 July	64	B.
P/O P. W. Dunning-White	28 June	4 July	145	B.
P/O R. A. de Mancha	8 June	6 July	43	B.
P/O F. N. Cawse	8 June	6 July	238	B.
P/O R. W. Foster	3 June	6 July	605	B.
P/O C. J. Batho	4 June	6 July	605	X.
P/O D. H. Hone	3 June	6 July	615	B.
P/O O. V. Tracey	? June	6 July	79	B.
S/L H. Harkness	8 June	6 July	257	B.
S/L I. Kirkpatrick	6 June	6 July	RAF Aldergrove	X.
S/L H. Eeles	24 June	6 July	263	B.
Sgt L. A. Parr	8 June	6 July	79	B.
Sgt J. Wright	11 March	6 July	79	B.
Sgt R. B. Sim	26 May	6 July	111	B.
Sgt J. L. Crisp	2 June	6 July	43	B.
Sgt P. R. C. MacIntosh	3 June	6 July	151	B.
Sgt J. A. C. Chomley	8 June	6 July	257	B.
Sgt E. W. Wright	2 June	13 July	238	B.
F/L W. Pankratz	23 June	16 July	145	B.
F/O A. Ostowitz	23 June	16 July	145	B.
P/O S. Lapka	23 June	16 July	302	B.
P/O E. R Pilch	23 June	16 July	302	B.
P/O W. M. C. Samolinski	23 June	16 July	253	B.
P/O T. Nowak	23 June	16 July	253	B.

Name	Date IN	Date OUT	To Sqn Number	Battles
F/S L. Ward	12 July	17 July	500	X.
Sgt L. Pidd	26 May	17 July	238	B.
Sgt P. B. Nicholson	3 June	17 July	232	B.
Sgt J. K. Pollard	3 June	17 July	232	B.
P/O K. M. Carver	16 July	18 July	229	B.
P/O N. D. Solomon	16 July	18 July & 10 Aug	17	B.
Sgt R. F. Bumstead	16 July	18 July	111	B.
S/L A. R. Collins	18 June	18 July	72	B.
P/O G. E. Ellis	19 May	20 July	64	B.
P/O G. J. D. Andrae	22 June	20 July	64	B.
S/L H. M. Starr	1 July	20 July	245	B.
F/L G. H. F. Plinston	30 June	20 July	607	B.
P/O L. L. Pyman	22 June	20 July	65	B.
F/O W. H. Nelson	24 June	20 July	74	B.
F/O D. N. E. Smith	22 June	20 July	74	B.
F/O C. D. Whittingham	22 June	20 July	151	B.
P/O P. A. Worrel	22 June	20 July	85	B.
P/O J. C. L. D. Bailey	22 June	20 July	46	B.
P/O J. M. F. Dewar	22 June	20 July	229	B.
P/O A. A. G. Trueman	24 June	20 July	258	B.
P/O A. M. W. Scott	22 June	20 July	3	B.
P/O H. Bandinell	22 June	20 July	3	B.
P/O P. R. F. Burton	22 June	20 July	249	B.
P/O G. H. Nelson-Edwards	22 June	20 July	79	B.
LAC Z. Urbancyk	14 July	22 July	18 OTU	X.
F/L G. E. B. Stoney	? July	27 July	257	B.
S/L A. L. Holland	8 July	1 Aug	501	B.
F/O E. C. Lenton	5 July	3 Aug	56	B.

Name	Date IN	Date OUT	To Sqn Number	Battles
P/O I. B. Westmacott	6 July	3 Aug	56	B.
P/O E. B. Rogers	6 July	3 Aug	615	B.
P/O C. K. Gray	6 July	3 Aug	43	B.
Sgt A. L. M. Deller	6 July	3 Aug	43	B.
Sgt D. Noble	6 July	3 Aug	43	B.
Sgt H. F. Montgomery	6 July	3 Aug	43	B.
P/O R. E. N. E. Wynn	6 July	3 Aug	249	B.
Sgt W. L. Davis	6 July	3 Aug	249	B.
P/O A. R. H. Barton	6 July	3 Aug	32	B.
P/O K. Pniak	14 July	3 Aug	32	B.
P/O J. P. Pfeiffer	14 July	3 Aug	32	B.
P/O B. Wlasnowolski	14 July	3 Aug	32	B.
P/O K. C. Gundry	6 July	3 Aug	257	B.
Sgt P. T. Robinson	12 July	3 Aug	257	B.
P/O E. J. Watson	6 July	3 Aug	605	B.
P/O J. Fleming	6 July	3 Aug	605	B.
P/O G. M. Forrester	6 July	3 Aug	605	B.
Sgt D. F. Imbush	6 July	3 Aug	605	X.
F/O J. Gillan	6 July	3 Aug	601	B.
F/O H. C. Meyers	8 July	3 Aug	601	B.
Sgt N. Taylor	6 July	3 Aug	601	B.
F/O D. P. Hughes	11 July	3 Aug	238	B.
P/O M. Steborowski	14 July	3 Aug	238	B.
Sgt G. Gledhill	6 July	3 Aug	238	B.
Sgt M. B. Domagala	14 July	3 Aug	238	B.
F/L T. Chlopik	14 July	3 Aug	302	Battle.
P/O S. Skalski	14 July	3 Aug	302	B.
F/O S. Witorzenc	14 July	3 Aug	501	B.
Sgt A. Glowacki	14 July	3 Aug	501	B.
F/O W. Urbanowicz	14 July	3 Aug	145	B.
F/Sgt J. Kwiecinski	14 July	3 Aug	145	B.

Postings of Pilots from No. 6 OTU Sutton Bridge

Name	Date IN	Date OUT	To Sqn Number	Battles
F/L A. S. Forbes	8 July	3 Aug	303	B.
Sgt M. M. Shanahan	6 July	3 Aug	1	B.
F/O F. R. Carey	2 May	6 Aug	Hawkinge ops room	B.
F/O C. J. Mount	21 July	8 Aug	602	B.
W/O A. Littolf	20 July	10 Aug	Odiham	F.
W/O G. Grasset	20 July	10 Aug	Odiham	X.
W/O J. Denis	20 July	10 Aug	Odiham	X.
W/O R. Speich	20 July	10 Aug	Odiham	X.
W/O L. Ferrant	20 July	10 Aug	Odiham	X.
F/Sgt A. Moulenes	20 July	10 Aug	Odiham	F.
F/Sgt R. Grasset	20 July	10 Aug	Odiham	X.
Sgt R. Guedon	20 July	10 Aug	Odiham	X.
Sgt C. A. D. Deport	20 July	10 Aug	Odiham	X.
Sgt X. A. M. E. de Scitivaux	20 July	10 Aug	Odiham	X.
Sgt N. Castelain	20 July	10 Aug	Odiham	X.
Sgt J. Joire	20 July	10 Aug	Odiham	F.
F/L M. V. Blake	11 Aug	15 Aug	238	B.
P/O H. T. Gilbert	3 Aug	16 Aug	601	B.
F/L C. L. Page	3 Aug	16 Aug	145	B.
F/O M. Duryasz	18 July	17 Aug	213	B.
Sgt A. Wojcicki	18 July	17 Aug	213	B.
P/O W. Rozycki	18 July	17 Aug	238	B.
P/O S. Surma	18 July	17 Aug	151	B.
Sgt F. Gmur	18 July	17 Aug	151	B.
P/O K. Olewinski	18 July	29 July	KOAS	X.
Sgt F. A. Sibley	29 July	17 Aug	238	B.
Sgt P. Thorpe	22 July	17 Aug	145	B.
Sgt D. B. Sykes	22 July	17 Aug	145	B.
P/O A. R. I. G. Jottard	30 July	17 Aug	145	B.

Name	Date IN	Date OUT	To Sqn Number	Battles
P/O B. M. G. De Hemptinne	30 July	17 Aug	145	B.
P/O J. H. M. Offenberg	30 July	17 Aug	145	B.
Sgt F. A. Silk	25 July	17 Aug	111	B.
Sgt R. F. Sellars	25 July	17 Aug	111	B.
F/O J. Topolnicki	1 Aug	17 Aug	601	B.
F/O J. Jankiewicz	1 Aug	17 Aug	601	B.
P/O W. Towers-Perkins	3 Aug	20 Aug	238	B.
Sgt S. A. H. Whitehouse	3 Aug	21 Aug	32	B.
F/L D. S. McDonald	15 Aug	23 Aug	213	B.
Sgt L. J. Tweed	3 Aug	24 Aug	111	B.
Sgt C. J. Saward	3 Aug	24 Aug	615	B.
Sgt R. J. K. Gent	3 Aug	24 Aug	32	B.
Sgt T. G. Pickering	3 Aug	24 Aug	32	B.
Sgt G. W. Jefferys	3 Aug	24 Aug	43	B.
Sgt H. J. R. Barrow	3 Aug	24 Aug	43	B.
P/O A. J. Mackie	27 May	24 Aug	1 AAS	X.
P/O K. M. Scanders	2 Aug	26 Aug	242	B.
P/O J. D. Crossman	3 Aug	26 Aug	32	B.
Sgt S. Duszynski	1 Aug	31 Aug	238	B.
Sgt J. Jeka	1 Aug	31 Aug	238	B.
F/O Z. Kustrzynski	1 Aug	31 Aug	111	B.
P/O J. Macinski	1 Aug	31 Aug	111	B.
F/O P. Niemiec	1 Aug	31 Aug	17	B.
P/O T. L. Kumiega	1 Aug	31 Aug	17	B.
P/O M. Chelmecki	1 Aug	31 Aug	56	B.
P/O Z. Nosowiz	1 Aug	31 Aug	56	B.
S/L K. Niedzwiecki	1 Aug	18 Aug	KOAS	X.
P/O R. A. Kings	7 Aug	31 Aug	238	B.
Sgt O. W. Porter	3 Aug	31 Aug	111	B.
Sgt C. C. Palliser	3 Aug	31 Aug	17	B.

Name	Date IN	Date OUT	To Sqn Number	Battles
Sgt J. P. Morrison	3 Aug	31 Aug	17	B.
Sgt R. D. Hogg	3 Aug	31 Aug	56	B.
Sgt C. V. Meeson	3 Aug	31 Aug	56	B.
Sgt G. Stevens	3 Aug	31 Aug	151	B.
P/O G. North	3 Aug	31 Aug	85	B.
Sgt A. D. Page	3 Aug	31 Aug	111	B.
Sgt T. C. E. Berkeley	3 Aug	31 Aug	85	B.
P/O D. M. P. McGee	3 Aug	18 Aug	KOAS	X.
Sgt R. J. Skuse	25 July	16 Aug	1 OTU	X.
P/O S. Fejfar	17 Aug	7 Sept	310	B.
S/L J. Ambrus	17 Aug	9 Sept	312	B.
P/O R. Rohacek	17 Aug	11 Sept	601	B.
P/O K. J. Vykokal	17 Aug	11 Sept	111	B.
P/O F. Kordula	17 Aug	11 Sept	1	B.
P/O F. Fajtl	17 Aug	11 Sept	1	B.
P/O K. Mrazek	17 Aug	11 Sept	43	B.
P/O F. Weber	17 Aug	11 Sept	145	B.
P/O J. Machacek	17 Aug	11 Sept	145	B.
P/O J. Himr	17 Aug	11 Sept	79	B.
Sgt V. Jicha	17 Aug	11 Sept	238	B.
Sgt J. V. Kucera	17 Aug	11 Sept	238	B.
Sgt V. A. Kopecky	17 Aug	11 Sept	111	B.
Sgt V. Cukr	17 Aug	11 Sept	43	FB.
Sgt J. Hlavac	17 Aug	11 Sept	79	B.
Sgt K. Stibor	17 Aug	3 Sept	KOAS	X.
Sgt F. J. Howarth	17 Aug	3 Sept	KOAS	X.
S/L G. C. Tomlinson	?	5 Sept	307	X.
P/O R. C. Graves	18 Aug	7 Sept	253	B.
P/O J. V. Marshall	?	11 Sept	232	B.
P/O D. B. Ogilvie	17 Aug	11 Sept	601	B.

Name	Date IN	Date OUT	To Sqn Number	Battles
P/O A. J. M. Aldwinckle	17 Aug	11 Sept	601	B.
P/O J. K. Kay	17 Aug	11 Sept	111	B.
P/O D. S. Harrison	17 Aug	11 Sept	238	B.
P/O M. C. Adderley	18 Aug	11 Sept	PAU St Athan	X.
Sgt R. Beamish	17 Aug	11 Sept	601	B.
Sgt E. L. Hetherington	17 Aug	11 Sept	601	B.
Sgt H. W. Coussens	18 Aug	11 Sept	601	B.
Sgt T. A. McCann	21 Aug	11 Sept	601	B.
Sgt F. A. Bernard	17 Aug	11 Sept	601	B.
Sgt G. V. Hoyle	17 Aug	11 Sept	232	B.
Sgt G. A. Walker	18 Aug	11 Sept	232	B.
Sgt C. G. Hodson	17 Aug	11 Sept	238	B.
Sgt J. McConnell	18 Aug	11 Sept	145	B.
Sgt J. K. Haire	18 Aug	11 Sept	145	B.
Sgt M. P. C. Choron	19 Aug	11 Sept	242	B.
Sgt X. de C. de Montbron	19 Aug	11 Sept	242	B.
Sgt H. C. Lafont	19 Aug	11 Sept	245	B.
Sgt R. G. O. J. Mouchotte	19 Aug	11 Sept	245	B.
Sgt G. C. Perrin	19 Aug	11 Sept	245	B.
Sgt J. R. Farrow	17 Aug	11 Sept	229	B.
Sgt J. W. McLaughlin	17 Aug	12 Sept	238	B.
Sgt V. Horsky	17 Aug	12 Sept	238	B.
P/O D. Stein	5 Sept	13 Sept	263	B.
Sgt C. P. Rudland	5 Sept	13 Sept	263	B.
P/O J. C. Garland	?	17 Sept	92	X.
Sgt G. Hardie	17 Aug	20 Sept	232	B.
P/O A. Kershaw	4 Sept	21 Sept	1	B.
P/O G. J. A. Millard	4 Sept	21 Sept	1	B.
Sgt J. Weber	31 Aug	21 Sept	1	B.

Name	Date IN	Date OUT	To Sqn Number	Battles
Sgt S. Warren	31 Aug	21 Sept	1	B.
P/O J. H. Rothwell	3 Sept	21 Sept	32	B.
P/O R. R. Hutley	4 Sept	21 Sept	32	B.
P/O J. L. Ward	31 Aug	21 Sept	32	B.
P/O L. N. Landels	4 Sept	21 Sept	32	B.
P/O P. D. Thompson	4 Sept	21 Sept	32	B.
Sgt H. F. W. Shead	31 Aug	21 Sept	32	B.
Sgt D. T. Hick	31 Aug	21 Sept	32	B.
Sgt S. E. Lucas	31 Aug	21 Sept	32	B.
Sgt N. Frychal	1 Sept	21 Sept	32	B.
Sgt W. Sasak	1 Sept	21 Sept	32	B.
P/O E. W. Jereczek	1 Sept	21 Sept	43	B.
P/O J. Gil	1 Sept	21 Sept	43	B.
P/O B. Bernas	1 Sept	21 Sept	302	B.
P/O S. Kleczkowski	1 Sept	21 Sept	302	B.
Sgt J. Zaluski	1 Sept	21 Sept	302	B.
Sgt Z. Kleniewski	1 Sept	21 Sept	302	B.
P/O K. W. Mackenzie	31 Aug	21 Sept	43	B.
P/O G. H. Westlake	31 Aug	21 Sept	43	B.
Sgt F. J. Twitchett	31 Aug	21 Sept	43	B.
F/O I. B. Difford	11 Sept	21 Sept	85	B.
Sgt T. M. Calderwood	31 Aug	21 Sept	85	B.
P/O M. S. Marcinkowski	1 Sept	21 Sept	151	B.
P/O J. K. Haviland	4 Sept	21 Sept	151	B.
P/O R. L. Goord	5 Sept	21 Sept	151	B.
Sgt W. B. Holroyd	31 Aug	21 Sept	151	B.
Sgt A. D. Wagner	31 Aug	21 Sept	151	B.
P/O J. McGibbon	31 Aug	21 Sept	615	B.
P/O D. G. A. Stewart	5 Sept	21 Sept	615	B.
P/O J. J. Walsh	5 Sept	21 Sept	615	B.
P/O N. D. Edmond	5 Sept	21 Sept	615	B.

Name	Date IN	Date OUT	To Sqn Number	Battles
Sgt N. F. Finch	17 Aug	21 Sept	615	X.
P/O A. J. Rippon	9 Sept	26 Sept	601	B.
P/O B. G. Collyns	10 Sept	28 Sept	238	B.
Sgt D. C. Deuntzer	7 Sept	28 Sept	79	B.
Sgt P. Pearson	?	28 Sept	238	B.
P/O J. C. Carver	11 Sept	28 Sept	87	B.
P/O J. W. Seddon	9 Sept	28 Sept	601	B.
P/O J. C. E. Robinson	7 Sept	28 Sept	1	B.
P/O G. A. F. Edmiston	10 Sept	28 Sept	151	B.
Sgt R. I. Laing	11 Sept	28 Sept	151	B.
Sgt I. A. C. Grant	11 Sept	28 Sept	151	B.
Sgt R. Holder	11 Sept	28 Sept	151	B.
Sgt D. O. Stanley	11 Sept	28 Sept	151	B.
P/O C. H. Headley	10 Sept	28 Sept	85	X.
P/O C. Savory	10 Sept	28 Sept	85	X.
P/O N. L. D. Kemp	10 Sept	28 Sept	85	B.
P/O A. R. F. Thompson	10 Sept	28 Sept	85	B.
P/O V. B. de la Perrelle	9 Sept	28 Sept	245	B.
P/O J. J. I. Beedham	9 Sept	28 Sept	245	X.
P/O W. T. Eiby	10 Sept	28 Sept	245	B.
P/O D. M. Whitney	10 Sept	28 Sept	245	B.
Sgt A. J. Hughes	7 Sept	28 Sept	245	B.
Sgt J. S. White	9 Sept	28 Sept	32	B.
Sgt A. H. Milnes	9 Sept	28 Sept	32	B.
Sgt R. J. Parrott	9 Sept	28 Sept	32	B.
Sgt J. Stenhouse	9 Sept	28 Sept	43	Battls.
Sgt H. E. Bennett	9 Sept	28 Sept	43	B.
Sgt G. Jefferson	7 Sept	28 Sept	43	B.
Sgt D. P. Stoodley	9 Sept	28 Sept	43	B.
Sgt J. B. Courtis	11 Sept	28 Sept	111	B.
Sgt K. Dawick	11 Sept	28 Sept	111	B.

Postings of Pilots from No. 6 OTU Sutton Bridge

Name	Date IN	Date OUT	To Sqn Number	Battles
Sgt A. H. Gregory	7 Sept	28 Sept	111	B.
Sgt C. W. MacDougal	9 Sept	28 Sept	111	B.
Sgt E. E. Croker	11 Sept	28 Sept	111	B.
Sgt J. Bayley	11 Sept	28 Sept	111	B.
Sgt R. L. Baker	11 Sept	28 Sept	?	X.
P/O T. R. Thomson	10 Sept	28 Sept	615	B.
P/O J. M. Storie	7 Sept	28 Sept	615	B.
P/O V. A. Carter	7 Sept	28 Sept	615	X.
Sgt N. M. Walker	9 Sept	28 Sept	615	B.
Sgt H. R. Mitchell	11 Sept	28 Sept	3	B.
Sgt G. C. R. Pannell	11 Sept	28 Sept	3	B.
Sgt G. S. Taylor	11 Sept	28 Sept	3	B.
LAC J. Murzyn	1 Sept	30 Sept	1 S of AC	X.
P/O J. Bryks	17 Sept	1 Oct	12 OTU	X.
P/O J. Postolka	17 Aug	2 Oct	311	X.
F/O B. (Billy) Drake	20 June	2 Oct	213	FB.
Sgt J. Kania	16 Sept	2 Oct	303	B.
S/L A. J. Biggar	18 Sept	3 Oct	111	B.
P/O W. C. Connell	21 Sept	5 Oct	32	B.
P/O R. C. Fumerton	21 Sept	5 Oct	32	B.
Sgt J. Pipa	21 Sept	5 Oct	43	B.
Sgt R. Ptacek	21 Sept	5 Oct	43	B.
Sgt O. Kucera	21 Sept	5 Oct	111	B.
Sgt M. J. Mansfeld	21 Sept	5 Oct	111	B.
Sgt J. Kurka	21 Sept	30 Sept	KOAS	X.
P/O H. H. Sprague	21 Sept	5 Oct	3	B.
P/O F. S. Watson	21 Sept	5 Oct	3	B.
P/O C. A. B. Wallace	21 Sept	5 Oct	3	B.
F/O R. C. Weston	21 Sept	5 Oct	3	X.
F/O G. F. McAvity	21 Sept	5 Oct	3	X.

Name	Date IN	Date OUT	To Sqn Number	Battles
P/O J. B. McColl	21 Sept	5 Oct	615	B.
P/O G. J. Elliott	21 Sept	5 Oct	615	B.
P/O R. Barrett	10 Sept	5 Oct	615	X.
F/O B. A. Hanbury	16 Sept	3 Oct	1	B.
P/O G. W. Varley	22 Sept	5 Oct	79	B.
Sgt A. H. Thom	22 Sept	5 Oct	79	B.
P/O J. M. Horrox	22 Sept	5 Oct	151	B.
P/O M. P. Wareham	22 Sept	5 Oct	1	B.
Sgt P. J. Richards	22 Sept	5 Oct	79	X.
Sgt R. T. G. Stirling	22 Sept	5 Oct	79	X.
Sgt H. H. Want	22 Sept	5 Oct	79	X.
P/O J. J. Robinson	22 Sept	5 Oct	85	X.
P/O C. Tarkowski	1 Sept	5 Oct	85	X.
P/O C. Gauze	1 Sept	5 Oct	85	X.
Sgt J. Plasil	21 Sept	8 Oct	1	X.
Sgt J. Prihoda	21 Sept	8 Oct	1	B.
Sgt J. Sika	21 Sept	4 Oct	43	B.
Sgt V. Brejcha	21 Sept	5 Oct	43	B.
Sgt K. Karber	21 Sept	9 Oct	32	B.
Sgt V. Foglar	21 Sept	9 Oct	245	B.
Sgt P. Brazda	21 Sept	9 Oct	313	X.
Sgt F. Brezovsky	21 Sept	9 Oct	310?	X.
Sgt J. Resnicek	21 Sept	9 Oct	313?	X.
Sgt O. Fiala	21 Sept	9 Oct	HQ Kemble	X.
Sgt A. Prougil	21 Sept	9 Oct	?	X.
Sgt F. S. Wood	22 Sept	9 Oct	?	X.
P/O G. E. Musgrove	1 Oct	14 Oct	79	X.
P/O F. G. Land	3 Oct	14 Oct	79	X.
P/O D. F. Knight	1 Oct	14 Oct	79	X.
Sgt J. T. Hitching	1 Oct	14 Oct	79	X.
Sgt F. J. Jessop	1 Oct	14 Oct	79	X.
Sgt L. D. May	30 Sept	14 Oct	601	X.
Sgt F. Mills-Smith	30 Sept	14 Oct	601	X.

Postings of Pilots from No. 6 OTU Sutton Bridge

Name	Date IN	Date OUT	To Sqn Number	Battles
Sgt F. J. Nicholls	30 Sept	14 Oct	601	X.
Capt C. J. M. P. de Scitivaux	29 Sept	14 Oct	245	B.
Sgt D. M. Beguin	30 Sept	14 Oct	245	X.
P/O V. Sikl	28 Sept	14 Oct	310	X.
P/O J. E. Hybler	28 Sept	14 Oct	310	B.
P/O J. Manak	28 Sept	14 Oct	310	X.
P/O F. Burda	28 Sept	14 Oct	310	B.
Sgt F. Vindis	28 Sept	14 Oct	310	B.
Sgt A. Dvorak	28 Sept	14 Oct	310	B.
Sgt J. Chalupa	28 Sept	14 Oct	310	X.
Sgt F. Sticka	28 Sept	14 Oct	312	X.
Sgt J. Sodek	28 Sept	14 Oct	312	X.
Sgt Otto Spacek	28 Sept	14 Oct	312	X.
P/O A. Velebnovsky	28 Sept	14 Oct	85	B.
P/O E. A. Foit	28 Sept	14 Oct	85	B.
Sgt J. Dygryn	28 Sept	14 Oct	85	B.
F/Sgt J. Strihavka	28 Sept	14 Oct	85	B.
P/O E. Cizek	28 Sept	14 Oct	1	B.
P/O F. Behal	28 Sept	14 Oct	1	X.
Sgt A. Zavoral	28 Sept	14 Oct	1	B.
Sgt J. Stefan	28 Sept	14 Oct	1	B.
P/O L. E. Allen	1 Oct	14 Oct	71	X.
P/O D. C. Brown	1 Oct	8 Oct	KOAS	X.
P/O A. Dawbarn	11 March	16 Oct	306	X.
Sgt V. Hruby	21 Sept	19 Oct	111	B.
Sgt O. Kestler	21 Sept	19 Oct	111	B.
P/O R. G. Lewis	28 May	20 Oct	1	FB.
Sgt E. Goy	8 Oct	28 Oct	1	X.
Sgt K. E. Markham	7 Oct	28 Oct	1	X.
Sgt A. S. Mackie	7 Oct	28 Oct	1	X.
Sgt M. Standera	28 Sept	28 Oct	312	X.
P/O S. Bachurek	7 Oct	28 Oct	312	X.

Name	Date IN	Date OUT	To Sqn Number	Battles
P/O J. Laska	7 Oct	28 Oct	312	X.
P/O B. Tonder	7 Oct	28 Oct	312	X.
Sgt Z. Karasek	7 Oct	28 Oct	312	X.
Sgt J. Mansik	7 Oct	28 Oct	312	X.
Sgt J. Vella	7 Oct	28 Oct	312	X.
Sgt F. Kruta	7 Oct	28 Oct	312	X.
Sgt Ondrej Spacek	7 Oct	28 Oct	312	X.
P/O R. Borovec	7 Oct	28 Oct?	312	X.
P/O J. Mackinder	7 Oct	28 Oct	245	X.
Sgt H. G. Todd	7 Oct	28 Oct	245	X.
Sgt L. G. Dawes	7 Oct	28 Oct	245	X.
Sgt G. H. Williams	7 Oct	28 Oct	245	X.
Sgt B. T. Vardy	5 Oct	28 Oct	245	X.
P/O D. C. Tufnell	7 Oct	28 Oct	43	X.
Sgt C. F. R. Mallett	7 Oct	28 Oct	43	X.
Sgt G. S. Sutcliffe	7 Oct	28 Oct	43	X.
Sgt J. R. Stoker	7 Oct	28 Oct	43	X.
Sgt G. M. Turnbull	7 Oct	28 Oct	32	X.
P/O P. D. White	7 Oct	28 Oct	601	X.
P/O R. G. Wyatt	7 Oct	28 Oct	601	X.
P/O D. S. F. Winsland	7 Oct	28 Oct	601	X.
P/O D. R. Stubbs	6 Oct	28 Oct	601	B.
Sgt G. L. Wincote	7 Oct	28 Oct	79	X.
Sgt J. W. Taylor-Duncan	7 Oct	28 Oct	79	X.
Sgt G. R. S. McKay	7 Oct	28 Oct	79	X.
P/O S. J. Thompson	7 Oct	13 Oct	KOAS	X.
Sgt A. D. Parr	7 Oct	28 Oct	?	X.
P/O J. A. Deschamps	7 Oct	28 Oct	?	X.
P/O T. D. Condy	7 Oct	28 Oct	?	X.
F/O F. V. Morello	10 Oct	29 Oct	501	X.

APPENDIX 3

Fatalities List

Fatalities associated with operations at RAF Sutton Bridge and Holbeach Range and other RAF burials in St Matthew's Cemetery, Sutton Bridge, between 1926 and 1946.

* denotes a burial in St Matthew's cemetery, Sutton Bridge.

Italics denotes an incident with personnel in a unit not operating from RAF Sutton Bridge.

Entries without * or *Italics* are fatalities involving individuals while operating from Sutton Bridge but with burials elsewhere.

Dates: yyyy mm dd.

e.g. (a) indicates same incident.

Date	Name	Accident Location	Unit
1927 07 20	Fg Off R. G. Pace	Holbeach range	32 Sqn.
1928 05 08	Fg Off G. Bradbury	Holbeach range	41 Sqn.
1928 08 02	Flt Lt L. H. Browning	Holbeach range	3 Sqn.
1929 08 14	Fg Off C. H. Jones	Sutton Bridge	23 Sqn.
1930 07 16	Fg Off P. B. Rogers	Gedney Dawsmere	23 Sqn.
1932 09 26	Lt H. M. King	Holbeach range	401 Flt FAA.
1934 05 18	Flt Sgt F. Baker	Holbeach range	41 Sqn.
1935 08 30	*AC1 B. S. Dunn**	*Motorcycle road accident.*	
1936 05 05	Plt Off J. W. H. Radice	River Nene, Guy's Head	111 Sqn.

Date	Name	Accident Location	Unit
1937 08 02	Plt Off A. Ferris	Holbeach range	6 FTS.
1937 08 04	Plt Off D. L. Bagot-Gray	near RAF Sutton Bridge	6 FTS (a).
1937 08 04	Plt Off P. H. Bailey	near RAF Sutton Bridge	6 FTS (a).
1938 09 14	Sgt T. F. D. Dewdney	Holbeach range	87 Sqn.
1939 01 24	Sgt J. T. Wyse	RAF Sutton Bridge	TT Flt.
1939 05 09	*AC1 J. Flannery**	*In sea off Mablethorpe*	*1 AAS.*
1940 06 25	Sgt C. F. Cotton	Upwell	6 OTU.
1940 07 29	Plt Off K. Olewinski* (Pol)	Walsoken	6 OTU.
1940 08 18	Sgt D. M. P. McGee*	Walpole Cross Keys (Collision)	6 OTU (b).
1940 08 18	Sqn Ldr K. Niedwiecki* (Cz)	Terrington St Clements (Collision)	6 OTU (b).
1940 09 03	Sgt F. J. Howarth	Saddlebow, King's Lynn (Collision)	6 OTU (c).
1940 09 03	Sgt K. Stibor* (Cz)	Saddlebow, King's Lynn (Collision)	6 OTU (c).
1940 09 30	Sgt J. Kurka* (Cz)	Walton, Peterborough	6 OTU.
1940 10 08	Plt Off D. C. Brown	Sutton Bridge airfield	6 OTU.
1940 10 13	AC1 J. R. L. Edwards	Wisbech	6 OTU (d).
1940 10 13	Plt Off S. J. Thompson*	Wisbech	6 OTU (d).
1940 11 01	Plt Off T. Patlejch*(Cz)	Tydd St Mary	6 OTU.
1941 01 04	Sgt K. A. Worthington	Hilgay Fen	56 OTU.
1941 01 17	Sgt E. M. Williams	near Sutton Bridge airfield	56 OTU.
1941 02 16	Plt Off D. F. Caird*	Hilgay station	56 OTU (e).
1941 02 16	Sgt A. J. Burley*	Hilgay station	56 OTU (e).
1941 02 18	Sgt J. C. Moores	Walpole St Andrew	56 OTU.
1941 02 25	Sgt J. M. Chambers*	Wiggenhall St Mary Magdelene	56 OTU.

Date	Name	Accident Location	Unit
1941 03 18	Plt Off W. L. Davis* (US)	Old Leake, Boston	56 OTU.
1941 04 11	*Sgt J. W. H. Bateman**	*Urris Hills, N Ireland*	*221 Sqn.*
1941 04 17	Sgt W. R. Rodger*	Gedney Drove End	56 OTU.
1941 05 23	*AC2 P. S. Story*.*		
1941 05 24	Sgt J. E. F. Dobbs*	Swaffham Common	56 OTU.
1941 06 06	Flt Sgt J. T. Craig DFM	Walpole St Peter (Collision)	56 OTU (f).
1941 06 06	Sgt I. Bidgood	Terrington St John (Collision)	56 OTU (f).
1941 06 11	Sgt A. M. Duthie	West Walton	56 OTU.
1941 06 14	*Uffz H. Schulz** *(German)*	*At mouth of River Nene*	*NJG2.*
1941 06 19	Plt Off K. Lancaster*	In sea off Donna Nook	56 OTU.
1941 07 25	*Plt Off C. E. B. Jones**	*Spalding*	*11 OTU (g).*
1941 07 25	*Plt Off C. H. Brown**	*Spalding*	*11 OTU (g).*
1941 07 25	*Plt Off R. M. Hill**	*Spalding*	*11 OTU (g).*
1941 07 25	Plt Off F. A. Grove* (US)	In The Wash off Hunstanton	56 OTU (h).
1941 07 25	Plt Off R. R. Wilber* (US)	In the Wash off Hunstanton	56 OTU (h).
1941 07 28	Sgt A. Innes	Salters Lode	56 OTU.
1941 08 16	Flt Sgt M. F. Mills*	2 miles S E Sutton Bridge	56 OTU.
1941 08 16	Sgt R. J. Henaux (Fr)	Harrington, Northants	56 OTU
1941 09 21	*Sgt G. K. Proctor**	*Holbeach*	*103 Sqn.*
1941 09 22	Sgt J. Schwartz* (Cz)	Wiggenhall St Peter	56 OTU.
1941 09 26	Sgt W. Booth	Suburbs of Cambridge	56 OTU.
1941 10 10	*LAC R. W. Seymour**	*RAF Llandwrog N. Wales*	*9 AGS.*
1941 10 20	Plt Off N. J. Choppen*	Reffley Wood, King's Lynn	56 OTU.

Date	Name	Accident Location	Unit
1941 11 07	Sgt D. L. Meisner* (Can)	Harpley, Norfolk	56 OTU.
1941 11 11	Plt Off J. R. Sale	Wayland, Norfolk	56 OTU (i).
1941 11 11	Sgt M. T. G. Willson* (Can)	Wayland, Norfolk	56 OTU (i).
1941 11 24	Sgt G. A. Johnstone*	Walpole St Andrew (Collision)	56 OTU.
1941 12 11	Plt Off T. R. Powell* (US)	Anmer, near Bircham Newton	56 OTU.
1941 12 13	Sgt N. C. Pow* (Can)	Friday Bridge, Wisbech	56 OTU.
1942 01 05	Sgt J. B. R. Lalonde* (Can)	Holbeach	56 OTU.
1942 01 07	Plt J. Zerovnicky* (Cz)	Walpole St Peter	56 OTU.
1942 01 17	Plt Off D. M. Browne	Earith, Cambs (Collision)	56 OTU.
1942 01 21	Sgt E. Eves* (US)	Clenchwarton	56 OTU.
1942 03 09	Sgt G. Brereton	Walpole St Andrew	56 OTU.
1942 03 09	Sgt H. E. Dolman (Aus)	Horsham St Faith	56 OTU.
1942 03 27	*Plt Off H. J. Appel* (Can)*	*Ouston, Northumberland*	*81 Sqn.*
1942 04 11	*Sgt W. A. McM Allen* (Aus)*	*Gedney Marsh*	*144 Sqn.*
1942 05 30	Plt Off D. Johnson	Holland, 1,000 Bomber raid	CGS (j).
1942 05 30	Flt Sgt J. Connor	Holland, 1,000 Bomber raid	CGS (j).
1942 05 30	Flt Sgt J. McLean	Holland, 1,000 Bomber raid	CGS (j).
1942 06 12	*Plt Off A. J. Majury**	*Churchill, Oxon*	*12 OTU.*
1942 07 01	Wg Cdr A. F. R. Bennett	near Sutton Bridge	RAE F'borough, attached CGS.
1942 07 02	Sgt C. I. Scott*	Cowbit, Spalding (Collision)	CGS.

Fatalities List

Date	Name	Accident Location	Unit
1942 08 17	Flt Sgt S. L. Vinten*	Wingland, Terrington St Clements	CGS.
1942 08 18	Sgt J. S. Jones*(NZ)	Moulton, Lincs	56 Sqn.
1942 09 07	Plt Off N. G. Bailey* (NZ)	Newton, Wisbech (Collision)	7 PAFU (k).
1942 09 07	Sgt D. D. Knott	Newton, Wisbech (Collision)	7 PAFU (k).
1942 09 07	Sgt F. N. Andrew* (Can)	Newton, Wisbech (Collision)	7 PAFU (k).
1942 09 07	Sgt K. Letch	Newton, Wisbech (Collision)	7 PAFU (k).
1943 02 13	Plt Off D. R. Reid*(Can)	Cowbit, Spalding	14 PAFU (l).
1943 02 13	AC2 K. R. H. Jones	Cowbit, Spalding	14 PAFU (l).
1943 03 22	Flt Sgt E. J. Davis	Terrington Marsh	CGS.
1943 04 09	Fg Off G. G. Thomas*	Tholomas Drove, Wisbech	CGS.
1943 04 10	Fg Off J. A. Town (Can)	Abbots Ripton (Collision)	CGS (m).
1943 04 10	Fg Off R. R. Hely (Aus)	Abbots Ripton (Collision)	CGS (m).
1943 04 10	Flt Lt T. C. Stanbury*	Abbots Ripton (Collision)	CGS (m).
1943 04 10	Flt Sgt C. Harrison	Abbots Ripton (Collision)	CGS (m).
1943 04 10	Flt Sgt E. Cooke	Abbots Ripton (Collision)	CGS (m).
1943 04 10	Sgt C. R. Archer	Abbots Ripton (Collision)	CGS (m).
1943 06 16	Fg Off R. E. G. Agassiz (Can)*	Clenchwarton	405 Sqn (n).
1943 06 16	Fg Off W. C. Davies*	Clenchwarton	405 Sqn (n).
1943 06 16	Flt Sgt C. L. Pudney GM (Can)*	Clenchwarton	405 Sqn (n).
1943 07 09	Flt Sgt K. W. Murphy*	Parson Drove	106 Sqn.

Date	Name	Accident Location	Unit
1943 08 27	*Flt Sgt W. T. Cheropita**	*In The Wash*	*410 Sqn (o).*
1943 08 27	WO N. M. Dalton*	*In The Wash*	*410 Sqn (o).*
1943 08 31	*Fg Off M. H. Davies**	Murrow, Gedney Hill	*78 Sqn.*
1944 05 16	LAC Z. Czaplicki (Pol)	Long Sutton	16 (P) SFTS.
1944 09 27	Plt Off H. A. M. McKell	Near East Lighthouse, Sutton Bridge	7 (P) AFU.
1944 12 15	*Sgt J. Nicholls**	*Holbeach Drove*	*12 Sqn (p).*
1944 12 21	*Unknown RAF Airman**	*Holbeach Drove*	*12 Sqn (p).*
1945 06 08	WO K. N. Doyle (Aus)	Spalding	7 SFTS (q).
1945 06 08	Cpl J. V. Fontinie (Fr)	Spalding	7 SFTS (q).
1945 08 13	Cpl C. G. Moitessier* (Fr)	Clenchwarton	7 SFTS (r).
1945 08 13	Cpl V. Maestracci (Fr)	Clenchwarton	7 SFTS (r).

Of the 106 fatalities listed, 77 relate to personnel directly involved with operations at RAF Sutton Bridge. Of these 77, 32 are buried in St Matthew's cemetery and 45 are buried elsewhere. 26 other fatalities not related directly to operations at RAF Sutton Bridge are also buried in St Matthew's cemetery. Three other fatalities, not related directly to operations at RAF Sutton Bridge but connected to a crew in St Matthew's cemetery, are buried elsewhere.

6 OTU Pilot Postings Out Matrix 1940

(March = 4)

Day	April	May	June	July	Aug	Sept	Oct
1		1		1	1		1
2							3
3				1	34	2	2
4				2			1
5			3			1	25
6			12	16	1		
7		1				2	
8			10		1		3
9		1	8			1	8
10		1			12		
11		7			35		
12		3				2	
13	1			1		2	1
14							29
15		20	8		1		
16		1		6	3		1
17		1	8	4	15	1	
18				4	2		
19							2
20				16	1	1	1

Day	April	May	June	July	Aug	Sept	Oct
21					1	35	
22				1			
23			6		1		
24		6	1		7		
25	2	13	1				
26	13				2	1	
27				1			
28						41	33
29				1			1
30			1			2	
31		1			18		
Totals	16	55	54	59	100	126	111

American Pilots

Listing of American pilots who, having sailed to England, trained at 56 OTU, RAF Sutton Bridge during 1940/41.
* = Did not fly with an RAF 'Eagle Squadron'.

No Boat recorded. To France August 1940; escaped to England, joined RAF October 1940.
Virgil Willis Olson

Boat 6, *Duchess of Atholl*, depart Canada 2 Nov 1940.
Morris W. Fessler

Boat 7, *Johan Van Oldenbarnevelt*, depart 6 Feb 1941.
Oscar H. Coen
William I. Hall
Hubert Layton Stewart
Rufus C. Ward

Boat 8, *Georgic*, depart 24 Feb 1941
William Lee Davis*
Joseph E. Durham
Hillard Sidney Fenlaw
J. M. Hill*
Loran Lee Laughlin
Carroll Warren McColpin
Thomas Paul McGerty
Edward T. Miluck
Collier C. Mize
Wendell Pendleton
Lawson F. Reed

Fred R. Scudday
Thomas C. Wallace

Boat 9, *Jean Jadot*, depart 25 March 1941
John A. Campbell
William R. Driver
Selden R. Edner
Donald Geffene
William D. Geiger
W. Hopkins*
Robert Louis Mannix
E. E. Pine*
Charles Wallace Tribken
Thaddeus H. Tucker
Vivian Eugene Watkins

Boat 10, *Alaunia/Royal Ulsterman*, depart 20 April 1941
Clarence L. Martin
Ross Orden Scarborough
John W. Warner
Jack W. Weir

Boat 11, *Unknown*, depart 30 April 1941
Fred E. Almos
Malta L. Stepp

Boat 12, *Unknown*, depart 23 May 1941
George Russell Bruce
Howard Macy Coffin*
Stephen H. Crowe
Hugh H. McCall
S. N. Muhart*
E. E. Steele*
Al W. Strauel*
Edwin E. Streets*
Don A. Tedford*
Lance C. Wade*

Boat 13, *Bayano*, depart 5 June 1941
Douglas E. Booth
G. L. Coats*
J. O. Daniels*
Forrest P. Dowling

W. A. Fawcett*
Fred Ambrose Grove*
Harry C. Hain
Marion E. Jackson
R. O. Jones*
Coburn C. King
Lyman S. Loomis
C. A. Marchbanks*
Cecil E. Meierhoff
James C. Nelson
William T. O'Regan
Vernon A. Parker
Robert L. Pewitt
Eugene M. Potter
Arthur F. Roscoe
Roy N. Stout
Walter G. Soares
George B. Sperry
Murray S. Vosburg
William J. White
R. E. Wilson*
Roland L. Wolfe

Boat 14, *Unknown*, depart 19 June 1941
E. C. Baldwin*
Lawrence A. Chatterton
W. R. Christine*
T. S. Chroniak*
Tony A. Gallo
R. E. Knowles*
R. A. McAnamy*
Richard E. McHan
Denver E. Miner
Robert S. Mueller
W. G. Owen*
E. F. Thacker*
R. A. Upsher*
Chester L. Van Etten*

Boat 15, *Olaf Fostenes*, depart 27 June 1941
John I. Brown
William J. Daley

Eric Doorley
Frederick A. Gamble
Leroy A. Skinner
Harold H. Strickland
Samuel F. Whedon
Robert Ruggles Wilber*

Boat 16, *Unknown*, depart 6 July 1941
Charles S. Barrell
L. M. Ray*

Boat 17, *Mosdale*, depart 10 July 1941
9 pilots to 52 OTU Debden. (4 Eagles; 5 No Eagles)

Boat 18, *Unknown*, depart 22 July 1941
9 pilots to 55 OTU Usworth. (8 Eagles; 1 No Eagle)

Boat 19, *Madura*, depart 4 August 1941
G. B. Alfke*
G. N. Arbuthnot*
Charles A. Cook
Wilson V. Edwards
W. B. Howell*
William R Wallace

Boat 20, *Unknown*, depart 15 August 1941
Robert V. Brossmer
William B. Rice*

Boat 21, *Fort Richepanse*, depart 25 August 1941
This ship was sunk by U-boat 567 on 3 September 1941.
William Mather Bishop* (Drowned)
John Richard Cox* (Drowned)
N. R. Echord*
T. M. Griffin*
Jack D. Gilliland
R. P. Grove*
Harry Hilts Hay* (Drowned)
J. P. Jordan*
Frank John Kruszynski* (Drowned)
Ben F. Mays

Robert Paroshian*

Boat 22, *Unknown*, depart 26 August 1941
G. M. Bains*
E. E. Edwards*
Walter J. Hollander
J. A. Lovelace*

Boat 23, *Manchester Division*, depart 26 August 1941
J. M. Bennett*
Edwin H. Bicksler
N. V. Crabtree*
R. W. Hooper*
Joseph M. Kelly
P. M. Lagette*
Leo S. Nomis
T. R. Powell*

Boat 24, *Bayano*, depart 27 September 1941
William H. Baker
J. W. Ball*
Carl O. Bodding
R. C. Colvin*
A. E. Crane*
Bruce C. Downs
Roy W. Evans
F. Gibbons*
James A. Gray
A. Horvath*
R. G. Hoyer*
William B. Inabinet
J. C. Joerns*
H. Kelly*
Jackson B. Mahon
Richard D. McMinn
Gilbert L. Omens
T. E. Tabb*
C. M. Waterbury*

Bibliography

Barclay, George, edited by Wynn, Humphrey, *Fighter Pilot, A Self-Portrait* (London: William Kimber, 1976).

Barker, Ralph, *The Thousand Plan, Story of the First Thousand Bomber Raid on Cologne* (London: Chatto & Windus, 1965).

Bennett, G. H., *The RAF's French Foreign Legion 1940–44* (London: Continuum International Publishing Group, 2011).

Beurling, George F & Roberts, Leslie, *Malta Spitfire* (London: Hutchinson 1943).

Blake, Hodgson and Taylor, *Airfields of Lincolnshire Since 1912* (Leicester: Midland Counties, 1984).

Bowman, Gerald, *Jump For It, Stories of the Caterpillar Club* (London: Evans Bros Ltd, 1955).

Bowyer, Chaz, *Fighter Command 1936–1968* (London: Dent, 1980).

Bowyer, Michael J.F., *Action Stations Vol 1* (Cambridge: PSL, 1979).

Brickhill, Paul, *Reach For The Sky, Douglas Bader his life story* (London: Collins, 1954).

Brown, Alan, *Flying for Freedom, The Allied Air Forces in the RAF 1939–45* (Stroud: History Press, 2000).

Caine, Philip D., *American Pilots in the RAF* (Washington: Brassey's, 1998).

Chorlton, Martyn, *The Thousand Bomber Raids* (Newbury: Countryside, 2017).

Cornwell, Peter D., *The Battle Of France Then & Now* (Old Harlow: Battle of Britain International Ltd, 2007).

Crook D. M., *Spitfire Pilot* (London: Faber & Faber, 1967).

Douglas, Sholto, *Years of Command* (London: Collins, 1966).

Finn, S., *Lincolnshire Air War, Books 1&2* (Lincoln: Aero Litho Co, 1973/1983).

Franks, Norman L. R., *Fighter Leader, The Story of W/C I R Gleed* (London: William Kimber, 1978).

Hall, Peter, *No.91 'Nigeria' Squadron* (Oxford: Osprey, 2001).

Bibliography

Halley, James J., *Squadrons of the RAF* (Tonbridge: Air Britain, 1980).

Halpenny, Bruce Barrymore, *Action Stations, Vol 2* (Cambridge: PSL, 1981).

Hancock, Terry, *Bomber County* (Hinckley: Midland, 2004).

Haugland, Vern, *The Eagle Squadrons* (Exeter: David and Charles, 1980).

Jackson, Robert, *Fighter Aces of World War 2* (London: Arthur Barker Ltd, 1976).

Johnson, AVM J.E., *The Story of Air Fighting* (London: Hutchinson, 1985).

Larsen, Tor Idar & Thorsager, Finn, *Viking Spitfire* (Stroud: Fonthill Media, 2012).

Major, Lt/Cdr F.S.W., *A century and a half of Skegness Lifeboats* (Skegness: B. S. Major).

Mason, Francis K., *Battle Over Britain* (London: McWhirter, 1969).

Middlebrook & Everitt, *The Bomber Command War Diaries* (London: Viking, 1985).

Neil, Tom, *Gun Button To Fire* (Stroud: Amberley, 2010).

Parry, Simon W., *Intruders Over Britain* (Surbiton: Air Research Publications, 1987).

Penrose, Harald, *British Aviation Vols 1–5* (London: Putnam and HMSO, 1969).

Pitchfork, A/Cdre G., *The Sowreys* (London: Grub Street, 2012).

Price, Alfred, *The Hardest Day* (London: Arms & Armour Press, 1988).

Pudney, John, *A Pride of Unicorns, David & Richard Atcherley of the RAF* (London: Oldbourne, 1960).

Ramsey, Winston editor, *The Battle of Britain Then and Now* (London: Battle of Britain Prints Ltd, 1980).

Rawlings, J. D. R., *Fighter Squadrons of the RAF and Their Aircraft* (London: Macdonald & Janes, 1976).

Richards, D. & Saunders, H. St G., *Royal Air Force 1939–1945, Vols 1–3* (London: HMSO, 1974).

Richey, Paul, *Fighter Pilot, A Personal Record of the Campaign in France* (London: Batsford, 1941).

Robertson, Bruce, *British Military Aircraft Serials 1878–1987* (Leicester: Midland Counties, 1987).

Scott, Desmond, *One More Hour* (London: Hutchinson, 1989).

Scott, Desmond, *Typhoon Pilot* (London: Secker and Warburg/Leo Cooper, 1982).

Shaw, Michael, *Number 1 Squadron* (London: Ian Allen Ltd, 1986).

Shores C. & Williams C., *Aces High* (London: Grub Street, 1994).

Shores C., *Those Other Eagles* (London: Grub Street, 2004).

Shores, C. Franks, N. & Guest, R., *Above The Trenches* (London: Grub Street, 1990).

Smith, D. J., *Spitfire Crash Logs Vols1 & 2* (Liverpool: Smith, 1978).

Stewart, Adrian, *Hurricane* (London: William Kimber, 1982).

Sturtivant, R., *RAF Flying Training & Support Units Since 1912* (Tonbridge: Air-Britain, 2007).

Taylor, Eric, *Operation Millennium* (London: Robert Hale, 1987).
Thetford, Owen, *Aircraft of the RAF Since 1918* (London: Putnam, 1957).
Thompson, D. & Sturtivant, R., *RAF Aircraft J1-J9999* (Tonbridge: Air-Britain, 1987).
Williams, Tom, *Gunnery Leader; WW2 Chronicle of Air Gunner W/C Ken Bastin* (Bognor Regis: Woodfield, 2007).
Wynn, Humphrey, *Desert Eagles* (Shrewsbury: Airlife, 1993).
Wynn, Kenneth, *Men of the Battle of Britain* (Norwich: Glidden Books, 1990).

National Archives documents consulted:
AIR27/1514, 254 Squadron Form 540.
AIR27/1553, 264 Squadron Form 540.
AIR27/1558, 266 Squadron Form 540.
AIR28/788, RAF Sutton Bridge Form 540.
AIR29/683, 6/56 OTU Form 540.
AIR29/860, RAF Sutton Bridge Station (TT) Flight Form 540.
AIR29/605, Central Gunnery School Form 540.

Web sites:
fcafa.com – Free Czech Air Force Association.
samilitaryhistory.org – South African Military History Society
ilot.edu.pl
lotniczyspacerpowarszawie.pl//en
en.museum.dk/museums-and-palaces/
   the-museum-of-danish-resistance-1940-1945/archives
www.afterthebattle.com
www.aircrewremembered.com
www.americanairmuseum.com
www.aviationheritagelincolnshire.com
www.bbm.org.uk – Friends of the Battle of Britain Memorial, London.
www.bcar.org.uk – Bomber County Aviation Resource.
www.bharat-rakshak.com – Indian pilots in the RAF.
www.charles-de-gaulle.org
www.danishww2pilots.dk
www.findagrave.com
www.4thfightergroupassociation.org
www.norwegianspitfire.com – Norwegian Spitfire Foundation.
www.ordredelaliberation.fr – Museum of the Order Of The Liberation, Paris.
www.paw.princeton.edu
www.polishsquadronsremembered.com
www.raf.mod.uk/display-teams/battle-of-britain-memorial-flight/
www.rafweb.org – Air Of Authority.
www.wingleader.co.uk – WW2 Images
www.yorkshireairmuseaum.co.uk – Yorkshire Air Museum

Index

AIRCRAFT

Henley, Hawker 53, 76–7, 88–9, 95, 181, 195
Hinaidi, Handley Page 52, 63
Hind, Hawker 71
Hs 126, Henschel 116, 121–22
Hudson, Lockheed 40, 193, 216
Hurricane, Hawker 37, 51, 74–7, 89–92, 94–5, 99, 101–02, 105–12, 114–16, 118, 126, 130, 132, 134–36, 139, 142–43, 147–48, 150–58, 160–189, 206–08, 235, 243
IIIF, Fairey 46, 53–4
Ju 88, Junkers 121–22, 170, 172
KC-135, Boeing 242
LA-5, Lavochkin 132
Lancaster, Avro 212, 215, 240
Long-range Monoplane, Fairey 38
Lysander, Westland 121, 158, 188, 195, 205, 208, 212, 216, 232, 236
Magister, Miles 28, , 81–2, 88, 181, 224, 236
Manchester, Avro 167
Master, Miles 94, 147, 150, 160–61, 163, 165, 167, 176–77, 181–82, 192, 214, 216, 218, 224, 232, 234–35
Mentor, Miles 89, 181
Meteor, Gloster 60, 241
Mosquito, De Havilland 49, 222
Moth, De Haviland 70
MS 406, Morane Saulnier 121–22
Nimrod, Hawker 58–59, 72
Overstrand, Boulton-Paul 72
Oxford, Airspeed 235, 236–38
P-11, PZL 116
P-38 Lightning, Lockheed 147, 214, 217
P-40 Kittyhawk, Curtiss 116, 147
P-47 Thunderbolt, Republic 218, 221
P-51 Mustang, North American 117, 193, 214
P-7, PZL 116
Prentice, Percival 241
Provost, Percival 241
Rapide, De Havilland 179
RE8, Royal Aircraft Factory 32–3
Sabre, Canadair 241–42
Scout, Bristol 32

Siskin, Armstrong Whitworth 11, 17, 28–30, 36–37, 48, 55
Snipe, Sopwith 30
Spitfire, Supermarine 52, 76–7, 84–6, 93–6, 106, 108, 116–17, 119, 125–26, 154–55, 158, 165, 169–70, 173, 190, 192–95, 202–03, 205–06, 208–09, 214–20, 222–26, 243
Stirling, Short 180–81
Tiger Moth, De Havilland 150, 156, 160, 177, 181, 236
Triplane, Sopwith 19
Tutor, Avro 174
Typhoon, Eurofighter 17, 242
V-22 Osprey, Bell-Boeing 242
Vampire, De Havilland 241
Venom, De Havilland 241
Wallace, Westland 53, 63, 72, 76–7
Walrus, Supermarine 154
Wapiti, Westland 49, 53, 63
Wellington, Vickers 69, 72–3, 96, 114, 176, 192, 194, 197–98, 201–04, 206, 208–10, 214, 218–20, 222, 236
Whitley, Armstrong Whitworth 214
Woodcock, Hawker 11, 17, 22, 30–1
Yak-1, Yakovlev 122
Yak-9, Yakovlev 122

PLACES

Acklington 89, 169, 184
Amman 46
Andover 22, 89–90
Aston Down 88, 93, 105, 106, 142, 146, 213
Bakersfield 142
Ballyhalbert 52
Bangalore 38
Bentwaters 242
Biggin Hill 110, 119, 124, 126, 213, 227
Bircham Newton 16, 17, 27, 51, 63, 72, 88, 268
Boscombe Down 40, 207
Brooklands 75, 186
Cambrai 28, 101
Cardington 78
Carlisle 127